The
Cultural Ecology
of
Chinese Civilization

The Cultural Ecology *of* Chinese Civilization

Peasants and Elites in
the Last of the Agrarian States

—◆—

Leon E. Stover

PICA PRESS

New York

Published in the United States of America in 1974 by
PICA PRESS
Distributed by Universe Books
381 Park Avenue South, New York, N.Y. 10016

Library of Congress Catalog Card Number: 72-92490
ISBN 0-87663-709-8

Printed in the United States of America

for Wutze

Contents

INTRODUCTION 1
OUTLINE OF IDEAS 5

PROLOGUE: COMMUNITY AND CIVILIZATION
Chapter 1. The Green Circle 13
Chapter 2. The Once and Always Bronze Age 24

PART I: FOLK CULTURE
Chapter 3. Hill Tribes and Peasants 65
Chapter 4. Sink of Death 79
Chapter 5. Subjects of the Realm 89
Chapter 6. Cult of Poverty 101
Chapter 7. Stars in Heaven 113
Chapter 8. The Kitchen God 122
Chapter 9. Sanctimonious Husbandry 133

PART II: HIGH CULTURE
Chapter 10. Rivers to Glory 143
Chapter 11. Lords of the Soil 167
Chapter 12. The Mighty Dragon and the Local Snakes 185
Chapter 13. Funerals and Ancestors 201
Chapter 14. Ladder to the Clouds 215
Chapter 15. Jack-o'-Both-Sides 226
Chapter 16. Games Chinese Play 242

EPILOGUE: END OF THE AGRARIAN STATE
Chapter 17. From Folk Society to Mass Society 267

BIBLIOGRAPHY AND NOTES 275
INDEX 299

Plates

(between pages 178 and 179)

I. Boat traffic on a canal in the lower Yangtze area near Nanking

II. Acrobat performing in the marketplace of Ling-fu-ssu, Kwangsi province

III. Portrait of a merchant-gentleman

IV. Conjugal family belonging to the peasantry

V. The Tartar Wall around Peking

VI. Joint family of three generations belonging to the gentry

VII. Brass brush case, brush holder, brushes, and ink pallet

VIII. Confucian temple at Peking

IX. A merchant's steelyard

X. A scholar's study

XI. Imperial troops marching over the Lion Bridge, Peking

XII. A scene within the walls of the Forbidden City

XIII. A Manchu princess

XIV. The patriarch Li Hung-chang

Plates I, II, V, XI, XII, and XIII, from photographs by Lucy Calhoun, are used with the kind permission of Henry S. Monroe. Plates III, IV, VI, and XIV are used courtesy of the Smithsonian Institution. Plates VII, VIII, and IX are used courtesy of the Chicago Museum of Natural History. Plate X, a photograph by Professor Michio Uchida, is used with the kind permission of Professor Uchida.

Drawings

by Mayumi Nathan

1. The Green Circle   14
2. A tribesman   66
3. Shen-nung, the Divine Husbandman   80
4. Peasant family at work   102
5. Gentlemen resolve a dispute from on high   114
6. Tsao-shen, the kitchen god   123
7. Driving piles in an embankment   147
8. A salt inspector   169
9. Bronze casting of a dragon   186
10. Confucius   227
11. Body ritual   243

Figures

1. The Chinese historical-developmental sequence 29
2. The Quatenary in China (Pleistocene and Recent) 33
3. Power and kinship in the age of Confucius 52
4. Cyclical Imperial Conquests 146
5. Transport canals 148
6. The Ten Kingdoms 160
7. Dynastic succession 161
8. Native classification of expenditures (1911) 171
9. Fictional flow chart of empire 194
10. Actual flow chart of empire 195
11. The sixty-six squares of the Promotion board 216
12. Insignia of bureaucratic rank 219
13. Provincial government 221
14. Imperial arcana 232

Maps

1. China Proper and Outer China   69
2. Key Economic Areas   145

Introduction

THE Agrarian State is a type of civilization whose political center and high culture proceeded out of prehistoric roots. It is the oldest political state in man's history and the most archaic form of civilization known to archaeology.

Archaic or primary civilizations are not derived from or affiliated with other high civilizations. They evolved out of their own primitive agricultural beginnings, out of the Neolithic village cultures that preceded the rise of high culture and urban power centers. As a result, the professional thinking men in these civilizations have always been preoccupied with the problem of origins—they never gave thought to the future or to the problems of change and development. The problem of high culture has been to rationalize the continuity between political power and its Neolithic origins—origins that are apparent in the survival of the Neolithic way of life as the economic base that sustains high culture.

The Chinese Agrarian State is one of seven primary civilizations. In the New World they are the Incan, Mayan, and Aztecan. In the Old World they are the Mesopotamian, the Egyptian, the Harappan, and, of course, the Chinese.

All are dead civilizations. The pattern of Inca culture died under Spanish colonialism. The native order in Egypt declined with Hellenization of royalty, and was decisively buried under the weight of Islamization. Although the fellah may be seen at his wellsweep as he was three thousand years ago, pharaonic Egypt was as dead at the time of the Arab conquest as it is today under Sadat. No one worships Osiris, no one can read hieroglyphics, no one mummifies their dead, no one is pharaoh. Confucian China alone among the primary civilizations survived into the twentieth century, after four millennia of continuous indigenous history. The monarchy lasted until the revolution of 1911. After that, there were no more emperors.

In China today people still eat steamed rice with chopsticks, a gastronomic pattern dating back to Neolithic times; Chinese people still read ideographs, a form of writing developed in Bronze Age times. Culture traits such as these persist from long ago, but the old configuration of the Agrarian State that once embraced them has indeed vanished. Under communism, the government reaches into village life to exercise unprecedented controls over production, values, and beliefs. The downward flow of directives and propaganda from the ruling authorities in Peking has created a participant society geared for change and mobilized to achieve developmental goals of some depth.

In the traditional society, only a tiny elite were politically active; the great masses of peasant-producers who fed them were politically passive. This book is about these two cultures of old China. The folk culture of the peasantry is treated in part I, and the *haute culture* of the elite is treated in part II. The treatment follows the same schedule for both parts:

	Folk Culture	*High Culture*	*Sphere of Life*
Chapter	3	10	Ecology
Chapter	4	11	Economy
Chapter	5	12	Politics
Chapter	6	13	Kinship
Chapter	7	14	Class
Chapter	8	15	Religion
Chapter	9	16	World View

These chapters are my lessons given to graduate students in cultural anthropology at Tokyo University from 1963 to 1965. I was invited by Professor Ishida Eiichiro, chairman of the department in his last year before retirement, to give a theoretical treatment of Chinese civilization. Professor Izumi Seiichi, the new chairman, kept me on for a second year. I declined appointment for a third year with reluctance.

Please do not imagine that I was invited to teach any new facts about China that my Far Eastern students did not already know. I was not asked to carry coals to Newcastle. I was asked to formulate ideas about traditional Chinese culture, not describe it. Specifically, I was asked to bring 'the ideas of my teacher at Columbia University, Julian H. Steward, to bear on a familiar body of knowledge. My job was to interpret the known facts about old China in terms of cultural ecology. By cultural ecology, Steward means the functional interrelationships between the basic spheres of life as this pattern is worked out in the course of man's cultural adaptation to the environment. (The environment includes the natural habitat as well as everything history has imposed on it.) From this viewpoint, the history of yesterday's imperial China is but one momentary pattern within a succession of changing Chinas. What is more, the whole sequence behind the Chinese Agrarian State is but one instance of like adaptations known from the history of all the other early civilizations.

Happy to say, my students took to Stewardian theory faster than I could articulate it. As Confucius said of his best pupils, they lifted three corners as fast as I lifted one. This was a fantastic experience for me, coming, as I did, from the intellectual climate in America, which is still fact crazy, theory shy.

One more point is worth serious attention—the use of the ethnographic present in this book.

The ethnographic present is the time at which a given event in this book took place, or takes place. Thus in our society it is 1970, the time of writing. In China, unless otherwise obvious or specified, it is sometime during the Ch'ing dynasty in the mid-nineteenth century for high culture, sometime during the Republican period in the first half of the twentieth century for folk culture. The use of the present tense is not a literal one. It is a convenience to anthropologists and first explained by Eliot Chapple and Carleton S. Coon in their *Principles of Anthropology*, published by Henry Holt and Company of New York in 1942.

This convention allows non-European peoples to be described as though they were available for our inspection as we would want to see them in their pristine condition, i.e., as a people discovered and observed by Europeans but before the people in question were radically changed by that contact.

Knowledge of China, however, has been complicated by the fact that high culture is self-recorded and folk culture is not. Sinologists began the study of the records of high culture some centuries ago, but it was not until the twentieth century that a new kind of student, the anthropologist, entered the villages to learn by means of observation and interviews what could not be learned about folk culture from documents.

The picture I have drawn here of the Chinese Agrarian State at its full maturity is taken from two historical periods.

With the revolution of 1911, the men of high culture borrowed European ideas about politics, economics, and literature. The backward-looking literati became a forward-looking intelligentsia, but they had not yet learned to apply these new ideas to action programs for the remaking of folk culture. Peasant life, for the time being, remained essentially unchanged. Western contact and the intrusion of cash cropping had made for new hardships, but how the peasantry coped with this new source of stress can be explained in the same terms by which it always coped with power differences between itself and the native ruling class.

Anthropologists have been at work in China for less than half a century, and the published output is little in volume. Yet this little has its place with the monumental volume of Sinological literature. Anthropologists did their fieldwork in the villages, the setting of the last sector to change in the dissolution of primary civilization in China. It was the elite sector that changed first, in its intellectual response to the West, and this sector only lately has begun to impress change on folk culture. In their study of folk society during the Republican period, anthropologists have been eyewitnesses to the last vestiges of community culture belonging to the Chinese peasantry.

My own fieldwork has taken me into the homes of an older generation of elite persons living abroad. I stayed so long in the home of my host that I was formally adopted. Interaction with my Chinese mother is the basis for Chapter 16. Her father was a high official under the Empire and one of the twelve founding fathers of the Republic. From her, a woman of traditional upbringing and modern education, I learned about Chinese interpersonal behavior. As long as she lives, our relationship embodies some of the old behavioral idioms of high culture belonging to the last of the Agrarian States.

LEON E. STOVER

Illinois Institute of Technology
Chicago, August 1970

Outline of Ideas

THE **Agrarian State** is an archaic form of civilization that in China lasted into the twentieth century.

PROLOGUE

1. *Community.* The energy resources on which this type of civilization is built are limited to cereal crops and the manpower of the peasant villagers who grow them. Peasants, by definition, are tribal farmers absorbed by civilization who are exploited by its ruling class for the support of high culture. A *tribal* folk is thereby transformed into a *peasant* folk. The folk community, or **Green Circle,** existed before the advent of civilization and was modified by civilization in such a way as to cause its inhabitants to look away from the life-style of the governing class and inward to their own local culture.

2. *Civilization.* The basic social feature of the Chinese Agrarian State emerged with its Bronze Age origins: a two-class system of privileged and nonprivileged persons. At bottom are the peasant folk, formed as a tribal folk in the preceding Neolithic Age; on top is a tiny elite that lives off the limited energy generated in the Green Circle. So limited is this energy that most of the productive efforts of the Green Circle go into sustaining its own human crop. The resulting civilization allows for a high culture that is shared across localities by the elite, but which restricts the folk culture of the peasantry to a parochial outlook. The qualities of this two-class system have persisted from the beginnings of the civilization until the twentieth century. Hence, **the once and always Bronze Age.**

This chapter includes a summary history from prehistoric times to the founding of empire.

PART I: FOLK CULTURE

3. *Ecology.* When Chinese civilization captured the Neolithic tribal village for its energy base, it fostered an emphasis on intensive plant cultivation at the expense of animal husbandry in China Proper. The animal husbandry half of the original mixed economy was selected as the basis for a steppe economy north of the Great Wall. The process of transformation by which the other half, crop cultivation, was selected by the Chinese south of the Wall may be understood from a comparison of **hill tribes and peasants.**

4. *Economy.* The absence of economic alternatives to farming on the part of the peasantry immobilizes it on the land. The capacity of the land to support human society is limited by the fact that the society specializes in only one type of economic landscape, that of cereal crops tended by villagers. This type of landscape, repeated in cellular units across China, can support only so many peasant-producers who in turn can support only so many elite-consumers. The surplus population is driven downward through the class system into the **Sink of Death,** there to die as expendable. Although there is some upward mobility, the overall consequences of the man-land relationship make for net downward mobility.

5. *Politics.* Much of high culture literature justifies the inequalities of the class system, with the view to admonishing peasants to keep their place. But **subjects of the realm** need no instruction in this matter; peasants are not responsive to ideology formulated outside their folk culture. They are forced to keep their place by an ecology that situates them on the narrow margin of the Sink of Death.

6. *Kinship.* The conjugal family of the peasant class is the productive unit that cooperates not only in doing the farm work but also in tightening its collective belt under hardship conditions. The joint family of the elite is geared to holding valuable resources in common across several generations. It serves a cult of ancestors that emphasizes the line of descent from father to son. The conjugal family of the peasant is small enough to cooperate in the business of doing without. It serves a **Cult of Poverty,** which points up the husband-wife team as the basis of acting out hardship, a

public display demanded by fellow villagers who view each other with suspicion as possible competitors.

7. *Class.* Peasants do not ordinarily covet elite status because they have little chance of reaching it in a society of net downward mobility. Thus they see themselves not as *under*privileged but as *non*privileged persons who are not motivated to aspire to stand among the rich and powerful. Gentlemen are as remote as the **stars in heaven.** Mobility aspirations are not part of an inward-looking folk culture that has no choice but to deny the existence of any other way of life.

8. *Religion.* The disadvantages of peasant life, which are acted out in the Cult of Poverty, include fear and suspicion that others in the village will gain advantage at the expense of self. This allows for no sense of community solidarity. The family stands isolated, as symbolized by worship of **the kitchen god,** a deity particular to each household. The existence of a household god at the expense of any community god gives moral backing to each family in looking after itself.

9. *World View.* Altogether, the disadvantages of peasant life shape an outlook in which pious contentment with one's lot is accepted as a necessity, but feelings about this are mixed. Attachment to the soil is thus not so much a case of sacral husbandry but rather a case of **sanctimonious husbandry.** Such ambivalent feelings about physical toil are conditioned by awareness that one cannot afford to pay attention to the comforts of high culture, and therefore one looks inward by default.

PART II: HIGH CULTURE

10. *Ecology.* The political organization of empire depends on the ability of the emperor to transport distant grain over inland waterways—the **Rivers to Glory**—and expend it on his court for the display of his superior majesty. The more cultural glamour he can finance, the more he can attract local power persons to curry favor with him and make them wish to enter the service of the crown and not seek to compete with it. The history of empire is summarized in this light.

11. *Economy.* In the Agrarian State, the ruling class finds nothing immoral in accumulating all economic alternatives to physical toil for its own self-aggrandizement. Even public office may be held for private gain without stigma. Because

all wealth may be traced back through taxation, rentals, and profits of office to the peasant landscape, the men who exploit this landscape—in or out of office—are all of them **Lords of the Soil.**

12. *Politics.* The emperor wages a constant struggle with members of the ruling class for the power to make their privileges dependent on the crown. The elite, on the other hand, attempt to trespass upon the royal prerogative of giving favors by claiming privilege as a right emanating from their knowledge of and their mastery over their home communities. This struggle between the autocratic principle of the emperor and the feudalistic tendencies of nonhereditary members of the ruling class to reduce him to a first among equals is phrased metaphorically as a struggle between **the Mighty Dragon and the Local Snakes.**

13. *Kinship.* Members of the ruling class organize power and property within large families, which act as corporations for the collective management of resources. Mortuary ceremonies and ancestor worship play an important role in focusing the attention of the membership on the center of the organization of which they are a part. The emperor encourages this filial concern for **funerals and ancestors** because it localizes the power ambitions of the ruling class to the winning of prestige in their home communities.

14. *Class.* In the Agrarian State, wealth tends to follow power, and not vice versa as in the industrial nation-states. Owning land is not as enriching as office holding, but land cannot be confiscated and it is a secure base from which to begin climbing the **Ladder to the Clouds,** i.e., the civil service examinations, by which the emperor distributes offices. The examination system makes for a wide range of internal stratification within the ruling class. The emperor is thus able to play the lower ranks against the higher in his divide-and-rule tactics, by way of preventing the whole body of officials from uniting against him.

15. *Religion.* Confucianism amounts to a state religion that affirms the power of the emperor on the one hand, and on the other affirms the right of bureaucrats to claim office by virtue of their merit, not as imperial favor. The result is a rather balanced contest between the principles of autocracy and feudalism. Significantly, Confucian ideology draws upon the literature of the feudal period in history, when imperial

ideas were foreshadowed but not yet applied. This makes Confucianism an appropriate instrument for both the Dragon and the Local Snakes, because it can give weight to either side, like a **jack-o'-both-sides,** depending on which way the struggle tilts. The outcome makes no difference for peasant culture.

16. *World View.* The outlook of the ruling class is self-consciously sociological, conditioned as it is by the need for highly formalized interpersonal relations. The interpersonal **games Chinese play** are all based on power differences between individuals that exist not only in the political world, but in family life—a life that brings relatives together not so much for the love of kinship as for the business requirement of holding corporate assets.

EPILOGUE

17. *Revolution.* In the traditional society, only the high culture of the ruling class had a common denominator in all parts of China. Folk culture was parochial in content, divided by its local manifestations. The rulers of Communist China, in projecting their ideological culture downward, have provided a common denominator for the peasantry as well, moving it **from folk society to mass society.** The peasantry, as such, has ceased to exist now that villagers are participants in a national culture.

Prologue

Community
and Civilization

CHAPTER 1

THE GREEN CIRCLE

THE basic unit of Chinese folk culture—its minimal community—is the peasant village and its surround of cultivated
plats within walking distance of the settlement at the center,
what its inhabitants call the *ch'ing chuan,* or Green Circle.
(Actually the term is a regional one used by the peasants of
North China. But we will borrow it as a generic tag for the
one million folk communities that compose the rural landscape of All-China.)

The Green Circle is at once the subject of its own community culture and an object of imperial control.

As its own subject, the individual village is not culturally
uniform throughout China. Walls of houses may be constructed of brick, pounded earth, woven laths of wood, or
bamboo plastered with mud; roofing may be tiled or thatched;
carts or wheelbarrows may be used instead of carrying poles;
women may wear skirts, not trousers, or skirts only at weddings. Rice is grown in the south, wheat in the north. Some
villages are organized along kinship lines as a single descent
group and others are not. Marriage preferences of the male
swing between his mother's sister's daughter or his father's
brother's daughter, and the range of feeling includes every
attitude from first choice, desirable, permissible, undesirable,
to outright taboo. A few of the great annual festivals associated
with high culture are everywhere observed. But aside from
three or four of these, other religious events celebrated are
strictly a matter of local culture, as are the languages spoken
by the peasantry, Sinitic and non-Sinitic.

But as the object of imperial control, the Green Circle is
everywhere caught in the same pattern. Everywhere the Green
Circle is an inward-looking, self-regulating folk society based
on intensive hoe-agriculture that presents imperial government with a target for taxation only, not for administration

A stylized village scene. After a Chinese print.

or political organization. Apart from levies, the outside world intrudes only so far as gentlemen of high culture make their appearance—in country estates or in marketing towns—as potent symbols reminding the peasantry of the unattainability of elite status.

Folk culture is insulated from high culture—from the politics, art, and literature pursued by gentlemen of the ruling class. Folk culture is divisive and parochial. High culture is cosmopolitan and is shared among its agents, wherever they may be. They find themselves in communication as members of a Great Connected Whole, the *ta t'ung,* or Great Society.

The Great Society is one of the backward-looking concepts of the literati that assume that the harmonious workings of civilization were laid down in the beginning. The Great Society is a Utopian society founded in the past. Mankind since then has been influenced by this ideal, conforming to it or deviating from it. In the *Li Chi,* Confucius is made to say:

I have yet to see the *ta tao,* the Great Way, flourish as it did under the eminent founders of the Hsia, Shang, and Chou dynasties, but I aim to restore it and make their way my way.

When the Great Way flourished, the public submitted to a common spirit, rulers were chosen by virtue of their wisdom and talents, and mutual confidence and harmony prevailed. . . . This was the period of the *ta t'ung,* the Great Society, the Great Connected Whole. [*Li Yun*: I:1–2]

We may therefore take the Great Society as an idealized picture of the ongoing civilization, as a tag for universal high culture and its exploitation of a passive and localized folk culture. In the Great Society, harmony so prevails that peasants keep collection costs cheap by not complaining about exploitation. Nothing indicates deviation from the ideal more than rebellion. Rebellion does occur in the Chinese Agrarian State, but the number of peasants involved in most uprisings is quite limited. It is possible to keep the ideal of the Great Society alive precisely because the peasantry *is not* in a constant state of revolt. In the case of large-scale revolts, the leadership invariably comes from some portion of the governing class. If the emperor is overthrown, the result is a new imperial regime given to exactly the same inequities as before, a cultured elite in the same position of domination over its Neolithic food base. The inevitability of this relationship can be explained by a theory of cultural ecology that sees folk culture and high culture as complementary parts of one dynamic, natural system of man, land, and society. That complementary relationship between the working parts of Chinese civilization, different as they are, is the focus of interest in this book and explains its title: *The Cultural Ecology of Chinese Civilization: Peasants and Elites in the Last of the Agrarian States.*

A real gulf sets the life of the ruling elite apart from the mass of villagers. The peasantry keeps its folk culture intact against the influence of high civilization. The folk preserve their precivilized heritage, which is a tribal heritage. For the Green Circle is a primitive horticultural village harnessed by the Great Society as its source of energy in the food plants grown there and in the manpower of the men who grow those plants. The Great Society acquired a working peasantry while the folk defend their precivilized community against the civilization that has incorporated them.

There are cities and towns in the Chinese Agrarian State, but no urbanization. Only in the nation-states are rural communities transformed under the influence of cities. National institutions, governmental and private, penetrate to the local level in the nation-states. The rural communities and small towns of America mirror national culture. The counterpart of the federal government is local government, and the political parties have their local affiliations. Organized religion has its community churches. The labor union movement is expressed in union locals. The system of formal education is rooted in a nationwide distribution of public schools and is upheld by federal guidelines for state laws requiring attendance up until the age of sixteen. Hospitals and physicians are guided by public health measures set by the federal government. People make their livings by exchanging goods and services in a market capitalized by a national web of banking services and protected by the legal defense of property rights. And the financial reward granted to the various occupations follows from widely shared beliefs about their value in a ranked order from most to least respected.

No such bridges as connect national and local culture in the United States exist to connect high culture and folk culture in the Chinese Agrarian State.

Local communities in the nation-states are so fully integrated within the body politic that they can afford to specialize, as those revolving around factory, mining, or dairy industries, not to speak of dormitory towns and suburbs from whence office workers commute to city jobs. Agriculture itself is but one specialty out of many. It takes only 1 million commercial farmers to feed a population of 200 million in the United States and provide an agricultural surplus for export.

The Chinese empire of 400 million can support only a limited number of nonfarmers, including 1.5 million gentlemen of leisure, business, and affairs, plus their dependents. Add another 1.5 million for the imperial aristocracy, and this minority comes to only 7.5 million persons, or not quite 2 percent of the total population. All the others are peasants, most of them living in rural folk communities. The remainder dwell in the slum neighborhoods of towns and cities where they find work as artisans, petty merchants, tradesmen, and laborers.

Because the peasantry normally renders up its quota of rents and taxes without expensive coercion, the men of high culture fancy that it is their moral suasion that accounts for compliance and low collection costs. The Green Circle is taken not so much as an object of substantive control as it is a target of moral guidance. The idea of the Great Society, as explained by its leaders, is a moral idea. There are those who render up and there are those who take. It is the responsibility of the elite to act out this paradigm by personal example. The model is well expressed in the *Lun Yu,* or *Analects of Confucius:*

> To rule is to be correct. If you lead along a correct way, who will not dare follow in correctness? [XII:17]

Ruling is the business of all gentlemen who hold legal title to elite status and who live off peasant production. Members of this consumption elite see themselves as managers of personal morality, and therefore of political order, which amounts to the proper ranking of status differences.

Elite persons think of themselves as educating the peasantry through their example. The example serves to display the cultural gap between peasant and gentry. The Confucian literati speak of leading in a correct way, so as to make correct the moral character of the common man; the common man is to stand corrected only insofar as he does not follow but actually avoids the life way of his betters.

To avoid the gentry model of life and behavior is to focus on the community culture of the Green Circle. To imitate the gentry model is to focus on the empire-wide connections of the Great Society. The exchange of one outlook for the other is not easy. Upward mobility in social status, from the bottom class to the top class, involves a difficult culture change. Unless motivated to unusual ambition, the peasant remains community oriented. Because looking inward to the village occurs by default, the peasant is uncertain about his identification with it. He will say to the anthropologist, "I can speak only for myself, my family, my village. If you want to know about other things, you must ask the landlord. He knows everything about us peasants." Asking a dignitary of high culture, the anthropologist will hear, "We Chinese do thus and so, we Chinese do this and that."

The reluctance of the peasant to generalize about folk culture is the other side of his deference to men of high culture, the literati, the men who know. The literati include the peasantry in their pronouncements starting with, "We Chinese do thus and so." Men of the Green Circle, however, acknowledge the potency of elite values not in adhering to them but only in deferring to the literati as the only arbiters of value.

In tribal culture each tribe sees itself as different from others like it in tribalism. With regard to the wider civilization, peasants do not assert their folk culture with any confidence whatsoever. The Hopi Indians, a tribal farming people, will tell the anthropologist: "This is the way we Hopi paint pottery, with the design close to the rim, not like our neighbors the Zuñi, who paint all over the pot." The Navajo will speak of the Navajo way in medicine, the Navajo way in dancing, or simply the Navajo way. Like many tribal self-names, Navajo simply means "The People." Chinese peasants do not speak of themselves as a people, and the folk inhabitants of the Green Circle do not speak of the Chinese peasant way. This reason is that, unlike genuine tribal culture, peasant culture is incomplete. It cedes judgment about itself to the elite. The elite are allowed to pronounce on all values and opinions about the nature of both folk and high culture.

Chinese peasant culture, however, is not an impoverished version of upper-class Chinese culture. It is a different culture. It is defined as legally different in the sumptuary laws of the empire. Peasants are forbidden to erect ancestral temples or to wear furs and silk. But these laws are simply descriptions of what peasants in fact avoid without being told to do so. It is to the men who control knowledge of law and literacy that the peasant reacts. Avoidance of high culture is what makes folk culture the different thing it is, neither a bargain basement version of the gentry way of life nor an independent tribal way of life. The peasant is what he is for what he rejects. In that way, folk culture is incomplete and therefore dependent on the civilization that absorbed it.

The peasant class embraces not only farmers of the Green

Circle but a coolie proletariat and other persons of marginal self-employment in the towns and cities. Urban commoners share the folk outlook of their brethren in rural community settings. Urban folk are city people but they are not urbanized; they are not any more acculturated to high civilization than are villagers.

All the same, agriculture is basic. The immobility of the peasant majority on the land is a convenience to the government that allows it to tax without delivering any administrative services in return. Commoners who achieve geographical mobility by entering urban life do not, however, achieve class mobility there on the basis of money income any more than they can as subsistence farmers in the village. The explanation is that in the Agrarian State economic power is weak apart from political power.

Folk culture is not high culture. Yet both cultures are equally representative of the civilization. The village is representative of the manner in which the civilization contains it, not as a shareholder in a stock of culture traits with other villages throughout the empire. What makes the folk communities of China part of Chinese civilization is not a shared inventory of traits, but a type of connection with the Great Society.

The folk community, as subject, varies in culture content with locality; as object, it is everywhere aligned with the Great Society as a dependent part, defending its broken tribal heritage by denying the wider civilization that rendered it incomplete by absorbing it.

From the viewpoint of elite persons, the Great Society is a universal cultural order—including moral sentiments, the hierarchy of court and domestic ritual, and the pageantry of office—which links them with the imperial Establishment. At the top, as a symbolic leader of all refinement, is the monarchy. The emperor opens his cultural umbrella over the nonhereditary elite of the realm. Officeholders are regional power persons who are thereby allowed to clothe their exploitation of the peasantry in the costume of a royal mission. Those not in office prepare for it by dint of a classical education with a view to passing the civil service examinations. This nearness to the imperial enterprise is sufficient to give their economic power in their home localities dignity as sharing in the collective goals of the Great Society. These goals include the exploitation of the peasantry in the name of a moral doctrine illuminated by the emperor. This doctrine holds that ruling is a liturgical exercise for the education of the exploited; that such education keeps the nonelite from reaching for a place in the Establishment; and that the resulting political passivity on the part of the ruled is what makes for imperial unity. The politics of liturgical leadership we designate as culturalism, in contrast with the more democratic politics of nationalism.

Only the ruling elite share any thoughts about the civilization as a whole, which for them is not a nation in our sense of the word, but a cultural system, which may contain a plurality of states, as during the period of Five Dynasties and Ten Kingdoms. The territorial reach of Sinitic civilization is not limited to the political borders of China, but may extend (say) into Annam and Korea, areas containing a large inventory of culture traits originating in China, such as monarchical government, ideographic writing, and boiled rice.

In the Chinese Agrarian State, the term *state* means the power arrangement between high culture and folk culture. Strictly speaking, the state is that sector of the formal governmental apparatus represented by the monarchy and the bureaucracy. The monarchy, with its nobility and imperial clansmen, is a hereditary domain; the bureaucracy is a nonhereditary domain, part of which (central government in Peking) is under greater control of the emperor than the rest of it (local government in the provinces). It is difficult, however, to identify the state exclusively with formal government and with formal government alone. Officials are drawn from a corporate elite who take the bureaucracy as but one resource among others in its monopoly on all economic alternatives to physical toil. Those upper-class persons not drawn into formal government office are still an elite of the realm because they dominate the peasant masses in their own home localities. Informal government partakes just as much as does formal government in the moral philosophy of culturalism. All men of high culture, in or out of formal government, are shareholders in the same theory of inequality, whose ideological fountainhead is the emperor.

The geopolitical basis of imperial unity rests with control by the throne of a large rice-producing area for the support of court life. If the emperor is to win the cultural loyalty of all nonhereditary power persons, he must win supremacy for his court in all the arts of high culture, from encyclopedic learning to gastronomic perfection. Should the cultural glory of the emperor not attract adherence throughout China, another region of high grain production, coupled with the means of transporting harvests to a capital city along natural or artificial waterways, may set up its own court in a bid for competitive influence.

The Great Society includes the high culture of the ruling elite as well as the folk culture of the ruled. But as it is a concept not shared by the peasantry, it gives emphasis to the elite who coined it. Members of each cultural tradition, however, are found in all the Chinese community types.

Peasant culture is populated by honorable commoners, the folk, subjects of the realm. The chief expression of this class is rural; it has its own community culture in the Green Circle. The farming peasant living there is equal with coolies, artisans, petty merchants, humble tradesmen, and other rural migrants to the lower-class neighborhoods of towns and cities. The peasant class is a corporate class of commoners who share in a tradition of nonprivilege vis-à-vis the privileges of the elite. The class is internally stratified by occupation and property, but the accession of property and wealth does not necessarily lead to genuine upward mobility across the power gap to the dominant class. In fact, the cultural policy of peasant life discourages mobility ambitions.

The de jure and de facto members of the ruling elite are the men of high culture. This class is internally stratified by power differences and is marked off from the peasantry whose members have no power. The de jure elite are men who hold titles of academic rank named after grades in the imperial civil service examinations and who may also hold office, or be retired from office. A de facto privilege attaches to a wide range of relatives of the titled and ranked elite. Big merchants may validate their wealth and gentry consumption habits through purchase of academic titles or of nominal posts. Perhaps one-third of the de jure elite owes its position to purchase. But elites of whatever status, rank, or provenance are identified with high culture, and their presence before a peasant audience as landlords or for other business reasons provides it with a model to avoid for the sake of defining the boundaries of folk culture.

If the Green Circle is the minimal locus of folk culture in community form the market area is the maximal locus of community culture at the folk level. The typical market area embraces about twenty villages, or about fifteen hundred peasant households, centered on a town in which markets convene periodically. Although the peasant lives in a relatively self-contained world, that world is not limited to the village but is given its biggest reach in the marketing area. A man may be suspicious and jealous of his neighbor in the village, but he is on a polite nodding acquaintance with every other male adult in the wider marketing community. The tea shops of the market town provide a cover of hospitality for all who go there. The members of the local elite take the marketing area as their typical arena of exploitation, based on their personal knowledge of all the peasant family heads within it. One way in which the gentry gains its knowledge of local persons is by holding court for the mediation of peasant disputes in the teahouses on market days.

Two other places important to understanding China are its walled cities and its non-Chinese enclaves. Walled cities are the seats of provincial governors and district magistrates. A city of this sort may coincide with the center of a marketing area, but it is unwalled if it is not also a seat of government. Non-Chinese enclaves are located in the hills of southern China, inhabited by culturally and sometimes racially distinctive peoples designated as "internal barbarians" by the Chinese. These barbarians live outside the Chinese ecology and therefore beyond the power of Chinese taxation, but not outside the pale of dependence on Chinese civilization.

The Green Circle is a natural community that was captured by Chinese civilization, in the course of its evolution, as its workhorse. From the viewpoint of the ruling elite, the passive response of peasant subjects to imperial control is an achievement of government policy. This is a conceit of high culture. Actually, the cultural policy of folk society is complementary to that of the ruling elite. The Green Circle first was the subject of its own self-regulating life before it was made into an object of imperial control. Its adjustment to a nonisolated con-

text has caused it to erect controls against further accultura-
tion to the Great Society that absorbed it. The political sway
of the emperor is a metaphor for boundary controls generated
by the target population.

CHAPTER 2

THE ONCE AND
ALWAYS BRONZE AGE

PEASANTS outnumber elite persons who live off them by fifty to one, persons who speak of these food producers as their "meat and fish." This is scarcely an image of embattled exploitation. One eats or one is eaten. The inequalities of this two-class system could not long endure for the benefit of the few if the target of exploitation, the Green Circle, was not self-policing. Such a stratified arrangement is made possible by the fact that, although the Green Circle is a captive of the Great Society, it is not assimilated to high culture. There is no middle class to mediate the power differences between top and bottom. This arrangement can be traced to the beginnings of the Agrarian State, and persisted until its dissolution in the twentieth century. By that time, of course, Chinese civilization had grown much more complex than it was at the time of its Bronze Age origin. But for all the internal development, the total society perpetuated a two-class system, even if the classes were separated only as a matter of social definition. But this definition is no less significant than power and wealth. The literati retained to the end the ability to impose their definition of social status, to judge who is elite and who is not elite.

In the Old World, all the primary civilizations were Bronze Age civilizations. They were founded on the technologies of the wheel, the sail, writing, and smelting. These civilized technologies, in turn, were founded on the Neolithic technologies of plant and animal domestication, carpentry, ceramics, and weaving. All the archaic civilizations, save China, were overwhelmed by Iron Age developments. These developments in their fullness included not only cheap iron for tools and weapons, but also the riding of horses, the alphabet, the use of money, the organization of craftsmen into guilds, and the organization of local kingdoms into empires tied together with a system of posts, as in the Persian and Roman empires. China utilized all these developments except the alphabet. Yet the Chinese Empire persisted as the only primary civilization to evolve its Bronze Age potential to the limit, undisturbed, using Iron Age culture traits in the process.

As examples, let us examine practices current during the ethnographic present. In this period the Chinese courier service does use mounted riders, but not to any great extent. Horse breeding, like the domestication of any barnyard animal except scavengers such as pigs and chickens, competes with horticulture. Consequently, pastureland is limited to a transitional ecological zone between the steppe and the sown. And this zone is contested by steppe nomads, at great cost to the Chinese military machine. Imperial dispatches often go by river and canalboat. The capital city of Peking is itself supplied with grain by the Grand Canal, not by horse-drawn carts. Inland waterways are still of supreme importance in China, even as the Nile was to ancient Egypt and the Tigris-Euphrates to Mesopotamia. Money exists, but metal currency is treated like Bronze Age bullion; coinage is still weighed in the steelyards of merchants, including the silver dollars of western import. Merchants, artisans, and craftsmen are organized in guilds; they may set their own price ceilings, unlike their counterparts who worked under royal overseers at Bronze Age courts. But even the biggest merchant can be defined as a member of the lower class by the arbiters of social status, the literati. It is the literati who define members of the upper class as those who live directly off the land—officials raising taxes, or gentlemen collecting rents, or both. The men of high culture, so defined as Lords of the Soil, are able to maintain their physiocratic doctrine and to depreciate the prestige of merchants even though their wealth and official connections place them among the consumption elite. Thus, peasant farmers are defined as the productive nonelite, and merchants—big and little—as mere appendages. The power to arbitrate a two-class system is closely associated, in the absence of a democratizing alphabet, with the restrictive literacy of ideographic writing. For literacy among the leisured men of high culture is what makes them cosmopolitan agents of the Great Society, and nonliteracy is what keeps folk culture parochial and divisive. Small wonder that literate merchants strive to acquire the official badge of literacy—through the purchase of academic degrees from the government, or by preparing their sons for the civil service examinations—by way of overcoming the scholastic snub of themselves. Absorbed in this struggle of definitions, merchants never emerge as an independent middle class as they did in the late Iron Age cultures of Europe.

The Chinese Empire is indeed a complex civilization based on Iron Age technology that makes iron available as a cheap metal for everyday tools and implements. But one overriding fact stands out. The elite share in a translocal cultural tradition, a common denominator that cuts across the Great Society, and peasants do not. The folk have no means, via a middle class, to align themselves with the wider civilization at large. They are reduced to and divided by their local cultural traditions. And this is the secret of control over so many by so few.

The dominance of a cosmopolitan elite over a parochial nonelite is reflected in the settlement pattern. The village is not integrated with the civilization that absorbed it. The village is small, isolated, nonliterate, composed of a few hundred persons who have been born and raised there and who will die there, persons who rarely, if ever, travel beyond the marketing town they share with about twenty other villages. They live there in a common effort to tend their gardens in husband-and-wife-teams, a community of rather self-sufficient families, each performing the same economic activities for itself. The few exceptions are the self-employed specialists in barbering, iron mongering, pawning, carpentry, bean curd making, tea making (or even hot water making where fuel is scarce), retailing of city notions, and the like. A village located within sight of the municipal walls of Peking is no less remote from the political activity of high culture than one a thousand miles away in a distant province.

No matter how much political organization has been built on Neolithic foundations, the village remains an economic resource for building civilization, never a participant. The Green Circle can survive without the rest of the Great Society, but the men of high culture cannot live without the peasantry.

Things might have been different had the coming of iron, sometime between the Ch'un-ch'iu and the Chan Kuo periods, precipitated a second agricultural revolution. But there was no second revolution. Farming in Western Asia, homeland of the first revolution, originated with the hoe-and-spade technology of Neolithic hand gardening, then went on to profit by the labor-saving benefits of plow cultivation. The sequence of events in the West was first intensive agriculture with the hoe, then extensive agriculture with the traction plow. In China, the original Neolithic technique of hand gardening had already committed the economic landscape to intensive methods before the animal-drawn plow arrived. Animal power can always be dispensed with if necessary, and in China the need is always pressing, given a landscape sown to food crops, at the expense of forage, to feed a dense human population. Thus the advent of iron, when it came to China in the sixth century B.C. (following its discovery by the Hittites of Asia Minor in the twelfth century), had little effect as a technological innovation with social and cultural consequences. The archaic pattern of Bronze Age civilization, erected on the Neolithic routines of the Green Circle, was shaken not a bit by the new metal or by its use in plowshares.

Bronze everywhere it appeared among the archaic civilizations was a luxury product, made into weapons and artwork for the rulers, never into farming tools for the common man. Farmers still used polished-stone hoes and flaked-stone sickles. Iron in China replaced these tools, shape for shape, and that was that. The Green Circle remained thereafter a Neolithic village with iron substituting for stone.

The Chinese developmental sequence shows the ultimate limits to which a primary civilization, erected on a Neolithic base, can evolve internally—an archaic civilization that never felt the full effects of the second agricultural revolution or the Iron Age technology of the West.

The Chinese Empire carries Bronze Age politics to the limit, organizing into one polity all the units of settlement and society that evolved in the preceding eras of Chinese cultural history. First came the Green Circle, which emerged in the Formative Era out of a food-gathering background.

The next level after the village is the county or district. It consists of a walled city, and several hundred taxable villages that extend for about thirty miles in every direction from the city. This scale of organization—city plus countryside within a day's cart ride out and back—came into being with the city-states of the Era of Regional Florescent States.

Districts, in turn, are organized into provinces, which are

the size of some of the territorial states that evolved during the Era of Fusion. These units are as big as European nations. Indeed, empire *is* the organization of states or kingdoms into a higher political order. The Chinese governors who head the provinces rule like kings, except that they are appointed for a fixed reign by the emperor, who sits on the Dragon Throne in the metropolitan center at Peking, capital of the empire.

The emperor's achievement, however, is not kingly despotism written large. The derivation of imperial influence over All-China out of kingly power at the regional level makes for something more rarified than control over men and materials in each district and province. Substantive power remained in the hands of regional and local power persons, be they kings and their fief holders, or be they governors, their appointees, and the local gentry.

Wealth created by immobilized Neolithic farmers can be exploited only in its immediate localities, unless it can be transported by water to some place of concentration. The emperor controls the biggest transport system in the empire, the Grand Canal, which connects his capital with an exceptionally productive source of grain revenue. With this ability to concentrate agricultural wealth, he is able to make his capital city a place of riches and culture on display. The political power generated by these means, however, is far more insubstantial. The emperor's influence is mainly cultural. He is able to so dazzle men's eyes with the glories of his court that others will reflect court ritual in their domestic ritual. Herein lies the politics of culturalism—the emperor's liturgical sway over the cultured men of the Great Society.

The Chinese developmental sequence, during which the various organizational levels of empire emerged, is summarized in Figure 1.

In the right-hand column are listed the conventional events of history and archaelogy. In the left-hand column are listed the culture eras as they have been worked out on a comparative basis by Julian Steward. The succession of cultures named here—from Preagricultural through Formative, Regional Florescent, and Fusion, to Cyclical Imperial Conquests—is the same for all the primary civilizations. These names refer to types of cultural pattern, not to specifics of cultural content.

All of the primary civilizations died sometime during their Era of Cyclical Conquests under the impact of Iron Age

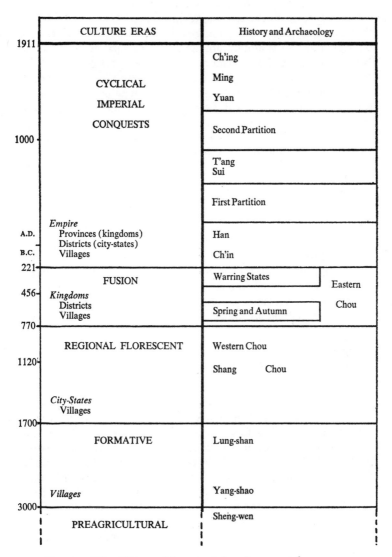

	CULTURE ERAS	History and Archaeology	
1911			
	CYCLICAL IMPERIAL CONQUESTS	Ch'ing Ming Yuan	
1000		Second Partition	
		T'ang Sui	
		First Partition	
A.D. B.C.	*Empire* Provinces (kingdoms) Districts (city-states) Villages	Han Ch'in	
221	FUSION	Warring States	Eastern Chou
456	*Kingdoms* Districts Villages	Spring and Autumn	
770			
	REGIONAL FLORESCENT	Western Chou	
1120		Shang Chou	
	City-States Villages		
1700			
	FORMATIVE	Lung-shan	
	Villages	Yang-shao	
3000			
	PREAGRICULTURAL	Sheng-wen	

FIG. 1   *The Chinese historical-developmental sequence*

cultures on them. All except China. In the Old World it was the influence from the derivative cultures of Greece and Rome that overwhelmed the founding order of archaic civilization in its Egyptian, Mesopotamian, and Indian birthplaces. In the New World, the Spanish conquest put an end to the native empires of Mexico and Mesoamerica. Northern and Central Europe began influencing China at a somewhat later date. It took the Industrial Revolution, with the combined influence of American and European nationalism, to put an end to culturalism in China. At that point, China evolved beyond her strictly native developmental sequence and entered upon the world *oikoumenê*, thereby extending the range of mankind's interrelated web of civilization. What makes China unique among the early civilizations is that her Era of Cyclical Imperial Conquests lasted the longest. As the subtitle of this book indicates, China is indeed the "last of the Agrarian States."

In addition to listing the culture eras in sequence, the left-hand column of Figure 1 also includes a summary of the basic organizational developments as reflected in the settlement patterns. Each newly emergent era has its newly enlarged political community named in italics, which subsumes the earlier ones under it.

PREAGRICULTURAL ERA (500,000–3000 B.C.)

This era includes the Paleolithic and Mesolithic periods, and begins with the appearance of the first humans in China. Paleolithic men led a nomadic life as hunters of big game, little bands of a few families who camped for a while in one place, then moved on to a new campsite, following the seasonal game trails. This way of life lasted for half a million years and covers two species of men. The Mesolithic is a transitional period between Paleolithic food collecting and Neolithic food producing, a transition set in motion by the disappearance of large game at the end of the Ice Age.

China had its own world of plants and animals long before man entered it. The prehuman ancestors of all mankind evolved first in Africa. These are the large-faced, small-brained creatures known as *Australopithecus,* the ape-men. Descended from tree-dwelling primates, they foraged in the open grasslands for plant foods, small animals, and carrion—the after-kill of the big cats. The ape-men were built like long-legged, short-armed chimpanzees, but they walked erect on their hind feet and manipulated objects with their forelimbs. They were not yet men, for their brains were scarcely larger than a chimpanzee's. Nonetheless, their way of life on the plains was so successful that they eventually spread out from Africa into similar landscapes in Arabia, India, Indonesia, and southern China.

The ape-men thus came to be scattered from Africa to the Far East. Here and there in that population the first men arose, a now extinct species named *Homo erectus*. The brains of *H. erectus* were slightly more than half the size of modern man's. But these half-brained men were able to make fire, strike off flint tools to a pattern, and evidently talk.

H. erectus was a hunter of big game, game animals larger than himself. Therefore he must have hunted in cooperative groups, more evidence of his budding humanity. He followed the game trails all over the Old World as far north as the January frost line. In Europe, the most famous *erectus* remains are the Heidelberg jaw. Java man is the most famous fossil example from Indonesia. And Peking man is the famed example from China.

H. erectus made his appearance in China during Middle Pleistocene times.

The original discovery of several skulls was made in limestone caves at Chou-k'ou-tien near Peking. The name given the fossils at the time was *Sinanthropus,* sometimes called Peking man. The basic similarity between Peking man and other fossil men from about the same time elsewhere in the world, such as Java man and Heidelberg man, has prompted anthropologists to classify them as one species, *H. erectus*. The Chinese subspecies is *H. erectus pekinensis*.

Fossil remains of the ape-man ancestor for Peking man have yet to be found. However, expectations for eventual discoveries are justified because of the high level of archaeological activity in China today. For the moment, one may use *Meganthropus,* the ape-man ancestor of Java man, to exemplify the type.

Be that as it may, the story of man in China, so far as it is known at this time, starts with Peking man, whose remains were first discovered in the caves of Chou-k'ou-tien in 1927. Other finds have since been made in South China as well.

The tools found in association with *H. erectus,* when they are found, are Lower Paleolithic butchering tools. In Europe, they are almond shaped; in China they are disc shaped and the stone is not completely worked. But despite such differences, the Paleolithic way of life and the technology supporting it were essentially the same everywhere.

From the viewpoint of technology, Paleolithic stone tools were shaped from lumps of glasslike material such as quartzite, chert, and flint. The tool was shaped by knocking flakes from a solid core. Toward the end of the Paleolithic period, man learned how to make tools out of the more delicate flakes as well. No doubt this refinement was made necessary as an economy move when raw material began to be scarce.

As a way of life, Paleolithic men everywhere lived by hunting big game. Apart from his own fossilized bones, *H. erectus* left behind few remains—his butchering tools, the bones of the animals he killed, and charcoal from the fires in which he cooked his kill. But this is enough to prove that he was a human hunter, not merely an animal predator. *H. erectus* had to make use of language, not only to teach his young how to make tools, but also to organize a team for the hunt. Teamwork is the only way to bring down game animals bigger than the hunters. No doubt Paleolithic hunters used spears and traps and snares, but only the tools for cutting up the meat were durable enough to survive. The use of fire indicates that family life was organzed around hearth and home. As among living hunting peoples, the males must have gone off in search of game while the females gathered plant foods, kept the fire going, and raised the children.

The Paleolithic way of life is nomadic—a constant treadmill of chasing after game animals, each in their seasonal migrations. There is no possibility of creating large, dense permanently settled populations. It is a hunting and food-gathering way of life that continued with only a few technological changes for half a million years until the end of the Pleistocene geological epoch.

By Middle Paleolithic times, flake tools were in common use. And by Upper Paleolithic times, when it was much colder, bone needles were used for making tailored clothing, close fitting skin garments designed to hold the body heat next to the skin. And for the first time, there is evidence for activities other than those necessary to maintain life. Orna-

GEOLOGICAL PERIOD		CLIMATE	MAN	CULTURE	YEARS AGO
RECENT		cool in the north, tropical in the south		Historic	
		mild and moist	Modern *Homo*	Neolithic	
		(post-glacial)	*sapiens*	Mesolithic	10,000
PLEISTOCENE	Upper	cool IV glacial		Upper Paleolithic	
		warm	Early *Homo*	Middle Paleolithic	
		cool III glacial	*sapiens*		200,000
	Middle	warm	*Homo erectus*	Lower Paleolithic	
		cool II glacial	*pekinensis*		500,000
	Lower	warm	(*Meganthropus?*)	Precultural	
		cool I glacial			2,000,000

(not to scale)

FIG. 2   *The Quaternary in China (Pleistocene and Recent)*

mental beads were made from perforated stone, and a form of religion can be assumed from the fact of burial of the dead.

The Paleolithic period came to an end with the end of the Pleistocene epoch. At this time, the climate changed, many of the familiar forms of animal life disappeared, and man had to adapt himself to new conditions.

The Pleistocene epoch is known as the Ice Age in Europe, where four times the great ice sheets advanced out of the mountains and down into the valleys. After the fourth advance, the ice retreated permanently, and a new geological epoch started, the Recent. The manifestations of the Ice Age were worldwide. In China, ice advanced from the highlands of Tibet, the Himalayas, and the mountainous regions of China, but did not actually enter the valley bottoms.

In China the effects of the Ice Age were reflected in four intervals of cold weather, alternating with warm and moist periods, the cold periods becoming progressively colder each time. When the sequence ended, and was replaced by a mild and moist climate, most of the cold weather animals, such as the woolly rhinoceros, were extinct. Others, such as the giant panda, found refuge in a suitable environment limited to southwest China along the Tibetan border.

With the advent of the Recent epoch, all the species of wildlife known to us today had made their appearance, including modern man. Man first appeared on the scene in Middle Pleistocene times as *H. erectus,* a half-brained species with heavy jaw and thick and heavy beetling brows. He was replaced by an early form of *H. sapiens,* known (for example) from the Ma-pa fragment, in the Upper Pleistocene period. The Ma-pa skull holds as many brains as modern man's, but the skull walls are still thick and the brow ridges are still heavy. Modern *H. sapiens,* with his thin-walled skull of egg-shell smoothness and his delicate jaw, makes his appearance at the very end of the Pleistocene.

Although an evolutionary change of species from *H. erectus* to *H. sapiens* took place, there was some continuity of physical features. For example, Peking man lacks the third lower molar and the back side of his incisor teeth are hollowed out. These same dental characteristics—the missing third molar and the shovel-shaped incisors—are common among Chinese and all other Mongoloid populations today.

Two species of men lived during the Pleistocene epoch, one after the other, but both lived a Paleolithic way of life. The use of tools by the first species stimulated the development of intelligence in the second species, which went on to improve Paleolithic technology, to open up the Mesolithic way of life, to domestic plants and animals, and finally to develop civilization.

The advent of the Recent geological epoch marks not only the establishment of modern animal life in China but also the arrival of the present-day physical landscape.

During the fourth and final cold interval of the Pleistocene epoch, winds off the Gobi Desert covered the highlands to the northwest with thousands of feet of fine dust known as loess. The erosion of the loess during the Recent epoch formed the river valleys of North China in which agriculture and civilization developed. The loess at first was covered with a heavy growth of trees and other vegetation made possible by the mild and moist climate with which the Recent epoch opened. Man started chopping down the trees in Neolithic times to make way for farming, and eventually the loessland was completely deforested, thereby encouraging more erosion. The Yellow River takes its name from the heavy load of silt it carries down out of the loess highlands, silt that is still deposited with every flood upon the river's plain, ever renewing its great fertility. These same floods also prevented urban development in the area.

By the end of Neolithic times, the climate again changed. The change this time was not accompanied by any vast geological events, as occurred with the ending of the Pleistocene epoch, but it had great significance for the development of culture in China during historic times. The change divided China into two main climatic zones, the North, which is cool and barren, and the South, which is tropical, its mountains covered with deciduous forests. The divide between the two zones runs along a line between the Yellow and Yangtze rivers. The division line for a third zone, the arid steppelands of Mongolia, runs along north of the Great Wall.

But during the opening millennia of the Recent epoch, all of China Proper except the flood plains of the Yellow River was covered with heavy vegetation, thanks to the mild and moist climate, and the Mongolian steppelands formed a great oasis belt inhabited by ostriches. The cold weather animals had disappeared with the Pleistocene landscape, and big game hunting ended. At this point, man in China turned to a new combination of hunting and fishing, taking fish by net from streams that ran through forests where small game animals were killed with bow and arrow.

This enriched food-gathering economy altered the Paleolithic nomadic pattern of constantly chasing after wild food, and prepared man to domesticate food. The Mesolithic way of life allowed for temporary settlement, not mere camping, along wooded streams where both meat and fish could be taken at leisure.

Toward the end of the Mesolithic period, the Chinese hunter-fishers began using pottery, perhaps for boiling wild grain. Pottery making is an unusual technology for a Mesolithic people to utilize and deserves some explanation.

Just as China was moving into the Neolithic, West Asia was moving into the Bronze Age. Mesopotamia is the homeland of mankind's first transition from food gathering, through the Mesolithic and Neolithic economies, to civilization. The basic technologies for this development spread from the West Asian center to other parts of the Old World. The making of watertight, fireproof ceramic containers is a West Asian invention associated with domesticated plants, also a West Asian invention, the former originating there about 5000 B.C. Knowledge of agriculture and pottery making then gradually spread outward in all directions to other peoples, reaching China around 3000 B.C.

Somehow, the Chinese Mesolithic hunter-fishers picked up the technique of making pottery before they adopted farming. The kind of pottery they started making for themselves was a coarse, gray, hand-coiled ware finished by beating with a wooden paddle wrapped with cord. This gray, cord-marked pottery represents the oldest tradition of pottery making in China—the Sheng-wen tradition—and it persists throughout the Formative Era.

Appearance of the Neolithic way of life in China is complicated by the fact that its technological components—plant growing, animal domestication, pottery making, stone polishing, weaving, woodworking, house construction—filtered into the area out of a source somewhere else through a process of cumulative diffusion. Wheat and millet clearly are West Asian cultigens, and sheep and cattle are domesticated animals from the same area.

Where a unified Neolithic complex first assembled in China is not known. Most likely the pattern first manifested itself in a region where the Fen and Wei rivers flow into the Yellow River, where the boundaries of present-day Honan, Shansi, and Shensi provinces meet. On the basis of Neolithic village life organized there, Chinese Bronze Age civilization was erected.

It seems that pottery making was the first element of Neolithic technology to arrive. The people who received this technique into their life evidently were Mesolithic food-gatherers who combined hunting and fishing. Fishing remained important during early Neolithic or Yang-shao times, and may have provided enough food for seasonal village settlement in Mesolithic times. Pottery must have been adopted to expedite cooking of wild vegetable foods. The result was the use of pottery before farming, the reverse of the original situation in West Asia, where farming evolved before the use of pottery. But this peculiarity is to be expected when elements of the Neolithic complex, once formed in its original pattern, were then diffused as independent elements for anybody to borrow.

Sheng-wen or Gray Pottery is the domestic ware of the entire Neolithic period, the utilitarian vessels of that time, not its fancy pottery. Gray Pottery, made with a finer temper and in new shapes, persisted up until the Shang dynasty, when it is known by art historians as White Pottery. Indeed, many of the bronze containers of Shang manufacture follow Gray Pottery shapes dating back to Lung-shan times. Lung-shan pottery supplies the prototype for a cast bronze ritual vessel, the *li* tripod, which traditional-minded Chinese to this day take as emblematic of their civilization. Gray Pottery thus represents the mainstream of the prehistoric industry, being produced through the Neolithic period, from early to late, as its workaday containers, a tradition starting in Preagricultural times and lasting to influence the design of White Pottery and the bronze shapes of Shang times.

FORMATIVE ERA OF BASIC TECHNOLOGIES
AND FOLK CULTURE (3000–1700 B.C.)

The Formative Era is so named because the Neolithic technologies of folk culture—plant and animal domestication, pottery making, basketry, weaving, house building—appeared at this time.

According to art historians, the era is known in China from two types of mortuary furniture, Gray Pottery being ignored because it is ugly and utilitarian. The two are Painted Pottery, named Yang-shao from its type site in Honan, and Black Pottery, named Lung-shan from its type site in Shantung. Painted Pottery is a hand-coiled, black-on-red ware fired in an oxidizing atmosphere. Black Pottery is a wheel-turned ware made from naturally black paste, unpainted but burnished. The two types may be taken to indicate two stages of Neolithic culture, Painted Pottery for early Neolithic, Black Pottery for late. Both stages share a common inventory of grains (millet, barley, sorghum, wheat), barnyard animals (cattle, sheep, pigs, horses, dogs), and polished stone tools (adzes, hoes, sickles, mealing stones).

Yang-shao, the Painted Pottery culture, represents the end of food gathering and the beginning of food production in China. The area where Yang-shao sites occur is the loessial uplands of North China. Loess is a fine, porous, yellowish dust blown off the Gobi Desert during the fourth glacial interval of the Pleistocene epoch. It covers the plateau region of the northwestern provinces up to several hundred feet deep. Although this area has scant rainfall, the capillary action of loess returns its meager ground moisture to the surface. Redeposited loess, washed down from the highlands, is a valley-filling alluvium, but does not obstruct natural drainage in the lowlands of the central Yellow River region. Flooding and meandering occur farther east on the delta plain. Thus loessial soils supported Neolithic agriculture without the need for man-made irrigation or drainage systems.

Arnold Toynbee holds the view that only the "challenge" of a watery chaos of overgrown swamps could have elicited the "response" of civilization in China. But a reconstruction of the terrain of early civilization in China will not support his argument. Archaic civilizations evolving out of their Neolithic heritage need easy conditions of rainfall agriculture within the capacity of self-sufficient farming communities to cope rather than a Toynbeean scourge, "The Stimulus of Hard Environments." These conditions the belt of loessial soils in North China, both high and low, provide.

An area too wet and flooded for hunters and food-gatherers would have been just as uninviting to the first food producers. No Mesolithic sites have been found in the Yellow Delta. An important Mesolithic assemblage at the Sha-yuan site in the Wei River valley, near its confluence with the Yellow River, points to an ecological succession in this area from food gathering to food production. South China is rich in Mesolithic finds, but this part of the continent remained underdeveloped, marked by Paleolithic survivals and dependence on changes emanating out of North China.

The loessial plateau must have been as congenial to the first Yang-shao farmers as to their ancestors, the Mesolithic hunter-fishers. The latter found game in the woods and in the nearby running waters; the former found that the woods covered the only land they could cultivate with simple gardening tools. Today the loessial highlands are denuded, and have been since before recorded history. The Neolithic axman is responsible, with his celt of compact stone, ground and polished into shape as a wood-cutting tool.

The Yang-shao stage of culture reflects its food-gathering heritage. Yang-shao sites contain a full inventory of Mesolithic hunting and fishing equipment: arrowheads, spearheads, skin-scraping knives, harpoons, fish hooks and net sinkers. The Sheng-wen horizon, as yet poorly documented, may be taken for a terminal food-gathering stage founded on both woodland and water resources rich enough to support a semisedentary way of life. Yang-shao habitations presumably follow the precedent of streamside settlement set by Mesolithic hunter-fishers. Painted Pottery is often figured in fish motifs.

Yang-shao farming, however, is not merely supplementary to food collecting. Food production is basic. Yang-shao technology shows a decisive commitment to the Neolithic way of life: hoes, spades, digging sticks, weeding knives, mealing stones, kilns and pottery molds, spindle whorls, sewing needles, stone polishers, and woodworking tools such as adzes and chisels. And, of course, the ax. Yang-shao people cultivated millet and kaoliang, and they kept dogs, pigs, cattle, sheep, and goats, starting with pigs and dogs. But the space for these gardens and stockyards was cleared by the ax.

The omnipresence of the stone ax in Yang-shao ruins indicates that the first farmers of North China practiced swidden agriculture. Swidden means that trees are cut down or killed by deep incision, the fallen timber or dead wood razed by fire, and the clearing put to seed. Then after a few plantings, the old clearing is abandoned for a new site.

Few Yang-shao sites have been excavated more thoroughly than the one at Pan-p'o-ts'un, located on a river terrace along the Ch'an tributary of the Wei River. The accumulated debris, ten feet deep from possibly four successive occupations, contains the remnants of more than forty single-family dwellings, most of them pit houses. The typical Yang-shao pit house was raised over a circular or squared plaster floor, ten to sixteen feet in diameter, walled in by wattle-and-daub construction and covered by a thatched roof supported on wooden posts. Each successive occupational level has been inhabited by about a dozen families: true folk communities.

A later occupation contains, in the midst of the single-hearth pit houses, a multiple-family dwelling whose floor plan measures 41 by 65.5 feet and is marked by several hearth areas. Its outside roof supports and frame structure rested on a low foundation wall of pounded earth, and two wooden columns set in deep holes within were erected to give additional support to the roofing. The pit houses surround this longhouse, their doorways facing the center. A cemetery is attached. Other sites in the upper levels of excavation that have a longhouse share a cemetery with one or more other villages.

The Yang-shao longhouse, with its planned location within a circle of humble pit houses, points to an emerging class structure. Perhaps the longhouse was occupied by a line of families who held their prominence in the community because they headed a ceremonial leadership, perhaps by presiding over burial rites at the cemeteries. And perhaps the villages agreed to bury their dead in common ancestral grounds to symbolize their relatedness as daughter villages. After all, the Neolithic way of life supports a denser population than will food gathering, and the Neolithic revolution increased the capacity of the land to sustain human life. Thus as the first Neolithic villages became crowded, the expanding population would cause families to migrate from them to found new villages, but ties of kinship would remain. Perhaps the religious leadership centered in the longhouse evolved to celebrate these ties at the graveyard in a Neolithic cult of ancestors. The image of the elevated person serving this cult may be represented in a painted bowl from Pan-p'o-ts'un, which pictures a shaman's head tattooed in the face and decked with fancy headdress. The headdress is fitted with fish emblems and other fishlike ornaments, shades of Mesolithic times! Fish symbolism has continued to hold importance in the sacred carp associated with Confucius.

With the successful purchase of a Neolithic foothold in North China, Yang-shao settlers slashed and burned their way in two directions, east and west. To the west they cut a swath up the Ch'an River, from the center of development, then down the T'ao River and into the Kansu corridor. There the movement stopped. The Kansu epicenter remained thereafter an area marginal to Chinese civilization. The march toward civilization took place in the east. In reclaiming the bottomland of the central Yellow River valley, the Yang-shao axmen cleared the way for the sudden Lungshanoid expansion of the Black Pottery people, who in turn laid the foundations of the civilization that followed.

The Lung-shan explosion spread the agricultural revolution down the Yellow River to the sea, down the Hwai River, down the middle and lower Yangtze, and all along the Pacific seaboard. In the subtropical jungle valleys of South China, the Lung-shan farmers, a fully fledged Neolithic people, experimented with aquatic plants and brought forth domesticated rice. Soon cultivation of rice spread into North China, even into some of the late Painted Pottery villages on the eastern margin of the Yang-shao area.

Yang-shao and Lung-shan are sequential cultures. The latter established permanent agriculture practices on the swidden foundations laid down by the former. The best evidence for the full sequence in the Yellow River valley is the stratigraphy at Hou-kang in northern Honan province, which shows Lung-shan over Yang-shao and Shang over both. This sequence first revealed archaeologically at Hou-kang is doubtlessly applicable elsewhere in North China. Not only that, Hou-kang may be central to the area where Shang culture—and Chinese civilization—first emerged.

For all the regional diversity of the Lunshanoid horizon,

it was everywhere geared to the same developmental level: full-time farming and permanent settlement. The famed and lustrous Black Pottery of the Lung-shan type is by no means universal, but the decline of painting is everywhere evident. More important, the art of pottery making had by this time become the object of industrial specialization, with elaboration of ritual and mortuary forms. Yet the basic house type continued to be the Yang-shao pit house, and the longhouse still occurs. Agricultural productivity had increased enough to allow the husbanding of grain reserves in large storage pits. And in the cemeteries, some men were buried with more grave goods than others, indicating a growing stratification of wealth and power among the living. The material basis for this growing social complexity was new agricultural techniques, such as fertilization with river silt and well irrigation, which made possible the change from the swidden method of slash-and-burn cultivation. Farming had become efficient enough to support permanently settled village life. And at this point, units of settlement became units of fortification as well. Walls of pounded-earth construction indicate that an era of peaceful propagation of the Neolithic complex had come to an end and that intercommunity raiding had started.

ERA OF REGIONAL DEVELOPMENT AND FLORESCENT STATES (1700–770 B.C.)

This era is marked by the flourishing of regionally distinctive cultures, and, among them, the rise of Bronze Age civilization. The city-states of this time began as theocratic ones and ended as militaristic ones. But from the beginning interstate competition entailed prestige for warriors in heroic combat. The priesthood cultivated record keeping, a specialty passed on to their bureaucratic successors when military action resulted in the capture of satellite territories calling for secular administration.

Archaic civilization everywhere it evolved did so not by altering the Neolithic way of life but by taking it into the body politic. The rise of city-states in Shang times created two ways of life, rural and urban, where before there had been only one.

All the barnyard animals and cultigens of the Formative Era were retained. The only new domesticated animal was the water buffalo. No new plant life was brought under control, and farming methods changed not at all.

The new technologies were bronze casting, wheel making, and writing—all belonging to a newly risen class of overlords.

Bronze metallurgy began in Mesopotamia around 3000 B.C., was known in India around 2000 B.C., and arrived in China about 1500 B.C. The whole style of West Asian warfare—bronze armor and weapons, horse and chariot, compound bow, square-walled encampment—is embodied in the equipment and residences of the Shang kings as revealed in their tombs and settlement patterns. Writing is part of the package together with chariotry and metallurgy. The new techniques were probably brought by chariot-driving warriors originating in the Iranian plateau who, after oasis hopping across Chinese Turkestan for generations—marrying locally and sending their sons ever eastward—finally arrived in the densely settled area of North China and there conquered the native Neolithic population, the Lung-shan people.

The conquest may be understood as part of the Chinese development sequence, stimulating the local potential for civilization to flower in terms of its own cultural background. The Chinese evolved their own unique style of civilization in isolation from the other archaic centers, notwithstanding stimulation from the outside. They imposed a Neolithic technology on a Mesolithic base and, later, a Bronze Age technology on a fully developed Neolithic base.

The point of contact between the warrior overlords and the native populace must have been the shaman of the longhouse who served the Lung-shan cult of the dead. The purpose of the contact must have been to win domination over Neolithic agricultural resources, for the booty-seeking marauders, who had initiated their eastward thrust some two hundred years earlier, found no booty but only productive land with people living on it and working it.

It is possible that the Chinese shamans mediated between the invading overlords and the Lung-shan people in the founding of a royal house—perhaps they even arranged intermarriage with the local women—thereby acting as priests in the service of the first Shang kings. Shamans practiced scapulimancy without the aid of writing in Neolithic times. They took the shoulder blades of oxen, or sometimes the plastrons of tortoises, gouged out the underside of the material, then touched scorching heat to it, which resulted in T-shaped cracks on the upper surface. Now, as priests of the Shang government, they inscribed their questions on the surface, dated them, added the answer as interpreted from the cracks, and filed the entire oracular message with others like it, often in bundles tied together like a primitive book. The names of the kings written on these oracle bones, which were discovered at Hsiao-t'un in storage pits evidently serving as state archives, correspond with those listed in the *Shu Ching*, thus verifying the historicity of the Shang dynasty.

It is interesting to note that the cracking process can be controlled by a skilled diviner, depending on how he prepares the undersurface and how he applies the heat, probably with the tip of a red-hot bronze knife. No doubt this manipulation was used by the Shang priests to feed proper advice to the king in the only way he could accept it—through indirect means. The authoritarian character of the Shang kings can have been no less fierce than is that of the emperors, who find direct reply to their orders treasonable. Divination, like omen reading, is the ideal way to complete the feedback without insulting the ruler to his face. On the other hand, if the skills of literacy belonging to the priesthood were not shared by the king, his participation in court life was to that extent incomplete, his control over affairs that much curtailed. This imbalance reached critical proportions in the time of Confucius, when literate administrators manipulated property records to their own advantage at the expense of their nonliterate rulers.

Judging from the written content of the oracle bones, Shang scapulimancy was addressed to the ancestors of the king, including Shang Ti. Its purpose was to find out from them what spirits should be sacrificed to and with what offerings, what were the prospects of bagging a tiger on the royal hunt, what were the chances of capturing sacrificial victims in the next military campaign, what would the weather be like, how were the crops growing, was a recovery from illness possible, and would each coming week of ten days be lucky or unlucky.

Shang Ti is the ultimate ancestor appealed to in these questions, an eponymous ancestor who goes back far enough in time to have fathered the royal line as well as the *chung-jen,* the "multitude of people." If the uninscribed scapulimantic remains from Neolithic times also served a cult of ancestors, then the old shaman in his new priestly function brought to the royal house a workable relationship between king and people, causing the latter to render up obligations to the former in terms of familiar religious practices. Given the idea of Shang Ti as everybody's common ancestor, the *chung-jen* of any Shang city-state could be considered to be members of an extensive clan whose highest-ranking members were represented at court and there topped by the king. The position of the king would be understood as the head of all family lines radiating from the nobility to the *chung-jen* at large. Perhaps each village at that time stood as a single kinship unit, operating communally owned lands. It may be that these village units owed food supplies and labor to the king on the basis of real or imputed kinship ties. It is possible that these exactions were phrased in terms of ceremonial obligations and were discharged at times on the royal calendar when villagers gathered on the palace grounds to participate in (not merely view) rituals connected with the king's worship of his ancestors—and by extension, ancestors of all the people.

Perhaps the royal tombs at An-yang were constructed under a similar set of obligations. These tombs, located at Hsi-pei-kang, are part of a single urban complex incorporating a number of community buildings. The entire An-yang complex, a site straddling the Huan River near An-yang in Honan province, covers about 2.3 square miles and embraces the palace center at Hsiao-t'un, the royal cemetery, and a number of industrial centers for making pottery, bronze, and other luxury products. The city-state was completed in its surround of Neolithic villages, such as the one at Hou-kang, all within sight of the palace at the center. The palace buildings were nothing more than Neolithic longhouses sitting on pounded-earth platforms embedded with stone plinths. A typical platform measures 65.5 by 33 feet and is 6.5 feet thick. The largest one is 98.5 feet long. These platforms are the foundations of the various houses, temples, and ceremonial quarters required by the royal house. The technique of pounded-earth construction was a Lung-shan invention. Loose earth is piled into a frame and pounded down in layers about 2 inches thick, the frame is then raised to the next level, and so on to the top.

The Shang tombs, larger and more difficult to construct than houses of the living, are underground. The largest is at Hsi-pei-kang, one of eleven installed there to accommodate the twelve kings that tradition says reigned at An-yang (the twelfth perished in the palace ruins at the time of the Chou conquest). A huge burial pit, 43 feet deep and 65 feet square was excavated, with four lengthy sloping passages leading out from the bottom of the pit in a cross-shaped arrangement. The burial chamber itself was sunk and timbered 10 feet beneath the flooring of the pit to receive the body of the king. The king's mortuary goods, including war chariots, horses, slain retainers, and war captives, were laid out on the wider floor above him. The entire excavation then was filled with earth and pounded every inch of the way to the top. The estimated labor involved is a minimum of seven thousand working days.

The men who worked on these constructions were not slaves and were not treated as slaves, but as participants in the royal cause. The fact that the *chung-jen* participated in the actual burial ceremonies indicates that commoners did indeed relate their labor under royal command to some interest said to be their own.

The Shang king held his realm by virtue of his headship of a royal lineage reckoned superior in a ranking clanship of lines that included all his subjects. But this embraced only a population that remained in sight of the palace grounds. The Shang king was not, after all, far removed in time from the shamanistic leadership of the Neolithic longhouse, which was elevated to the urban dignity of a ceremonial community complete in itself in the temples and altars of the royal pre-cincts at Hsiao-t'un. The graveyards that Neolithic villages used to share, and over which the shaman presided, were elevated to the royal tombs at Hsi-pei-kang, which commoners were invited to build and rejoice in as the final resting place of their kings.

The Shang king called himself the Son of Heaven, a title adopted by the emperors. Heaven, or *T'ien,* is another name for the high god of the Shang theocracy, Shang Ti. *Ti* means "deity," and *Shang* in this usage means "high" or "above." It is a different word from the name of the ruling house. That *Shang* means "to give advice, to consult, to deliberate." No-body knows why this is the name for the ruling dynasty, but here is a guess. If the Lung-shan shamans made themselves useful to the conquering warlords as mediators with the con-quered people, and if they monopolized literacy under this regime, they would be in a position to name it for history. And they would have named it for their own role in mediating between ruler and ruled. The ideograph for Shang is quite revealing in this light. It is made up of two parts fused in a peculiar way. One-half is a unit called "speech" 言, which in itself is made up of two elements, "mouth" 口 with "sounds" 𡆧 of speech issuing forth. The other half of the ideograph is a unit called "inside" 冂. The two parts are fused in this way: the "mouth" is inside the "inside," with the "sounds" emanating from out of it 啇. Is this the ideographic representation of a Lung-shan shaman, brought in as a priestly voice within the palace council, from which vantage he can speak to or for the outside world of the *chung-jen?*

Be that as it may, Shang Ti may be taken for the ultimate ancestor of the Shang population, who fathered kings, royal line, nobility, and common people alike. The Heaven that the Shang kings worshipped was anthropomorphic. That of the emperor is not. Also the manner and meaning of Heaven worship is different. When the Shang king sacrificed to his ancestors, he chopped off heads in a public show by way of rallying his subjects to pay their dues to the royal house. But the emperor worships in private as the only person in the realm privileged to communicate with Heaven by way of validating, in the eyes of his officials, his sovereignty over a vast empire. Heaven worship on the part of the emperor clearly derives from the ancestral cult practiced by the Shang kings, but it has become amputated from any suggestion of real or fictive consanguinity between the ruler and his subjects.

The emperor retains the old Shang title, Son of Heaven, but Heaven worship has come to serve a much different political order. Chinese historians, however, do not see it this way. They read empire back into the plurality of kings and city-states of like political culture. The Chinese historiographical tradition views Shang civilization as the political expression of a centralized empire embracing the entire Shang culture area throughout the lower Yellow valley, with a powerful emperor seated in his capital city at An-yang. This is in keeping with Confucian tradition. Mencius quotes Confucius to the effect that,

> Just as there are not two suns in the sky, so there can not be two kings on earth. [*Meng Tzu,* V:ii:4]

An-yang is seen as the seat of a dynasty whose line was over-thrown and replaced by barbarians on the model of the con-quering dynasties such as the Yuan, which overthrew the Sung. But the Shang and Chou cultures are two versions of the same Bronze Age civilization of North China, the one situated in the Yellow River valley to the east and the other in the Wei River valley to the west.

An-yang, the star city-state of the Shang domain, was over-run by allied Chou forces, arriving from their chief center at Hao, near present-day Sian. The conquest took an unknown length of time, but the destruction of the Shang capital oc-curred about 1120 b.c. Then, about 770 b.c., a number of other states still farther to the west set upon the Chou. But they failed to conquer, only routed, the Chou court, which withdrew from Hao to an eastern situation at Loyang. This event marks the cultural divide between Western and Eastern Chou.

This divide between Western and Eastern Chou is conspicu-ous for its discontinuity in city building. The Bronze Age city, beginning in Shang times, consisted of a walled enclosure in which the palace buildings and homes of the nobility were located; the industrial workshops were placed outside the wall in special settlements of their own, like the farming villages. The enclosure, the *ch'ang,* is a square or rectangular wall of earth reminiscent of the Indo-European charioteer's fortified encampment, a form that in the West persisted in the quadri-lateral campsites of the Roman army. From the time of West-ern Chou, the *ch'ang* came to be surrounded by an outer wall, the city wall proper, which brought within it the workshops formerly located in the countryside. The Chinese word in use today for city is *ch'ang,* originally the wall enclosing the aristo-cratic center of the Bronze Age warlords, and which has sur-vived in Peking as the inner wall around the Forbidden City, the home of the emperor and his court.

Shang and Western Chou, however, are sequential phases of the same cultural era. The Chou princes systematized and geographically extended the pattern of Shang authority. Par-ties of warrior-noblemen and artisans spread out through and beyond the Shang domain, taking over city-states where they found them and installing new ones in the midst of unex-ploited Neolithic farmers elsewhere.

The Chou king who initiated the conquest took the title

wang, from the Shang kings at An-yang. One may use the vocabulary of European feudalism and speak of a royal house and of princely or ducal houses. The standing of the members of the nobility in relationship to the king of the royal house of Chou depended on their closeness to or remove from the king and the king's ancestors, as calculated in terms of descent in the male line. Whole branches were thus ranked in relationship to each other by way of ranking themselves relative to the king's line.

Some fifty-three of the feudal lords who set out to conquer and colonize were royal kinsmen. The political unity they founded they called the "older and younger brother states." Another group of eighteen were linked to the royal family by marriage. The states they founded they called the "sororal nephew and uncle states."

Each of the feudal states of Western Chou was built around a single urban center, walled and garrisoned, which contained as its chief structures the ancestral temples and palace buildings of the ruling feudatories. The city itself was a sacrificial community, militarily defended. Peasant vassals supplied their masters with food, clothing, and labor service. Attached artisans produced specialized goods and weapons. Merchant-clients brought luxuries and raw materials from beyond state boundaries. Each state was the private family business of its lineage head, whose ceremonies of state were those of ancestor worship. The rank of the nobleman, as duke, marquis, earl, or whatnot, followed from his genealogical or affinal standing with the king, and it determined his protocol in dealing with other feudatories. The heads of state usually called themselves dukes, but eventually almost all of them usurped the kingly title, *wang.*

Kinship ties among the warlords of the Chou domain were no bar to interstate conflict. The militarism of this time, however, remained at the level of raiding by self-equipped warrior-heroes as in Shang times. Warfare organized for the purposes of territorial annexation did not come into style until the Era of Cultural Fusion.

ERA OF CULTURAL FUSION (770–221 B.C.)

From this time onward, the desultory raiding and individual heroics of early Bronze Age warfare gave way to serious business, the capture of satellite states by stronger ones. The outcome was the conquest of empire by the one state that won victory over all the others, the state of Ch'in.

The period of expanding militarism began with the feudal states heavily armed against each other. War campaigns were not yet conducted under professional generalship, however, and the action usually lasted no more than a day. Still, the engagements were no mere tourneys to be rewarded with booty. A defeated army on the field meant a defeated state, the murder of its ruling house, and the absorption of its territory.

The social changes of the Ch'un-ch'iu period destroyed feudalism and fused the local cultures of the various Bronze Age states into the universal culture of All-China.

The Ch'un-ch'iu period, which is the first division of historical time within the Era of Cultural Fusion, is named after one of the five Classics, *Ch'un Ch'iu* or *Spring and Autumn Annals*. It is a spare chronicle of events covering 722–481 B.C. in the state of Lu. In the sixteenth year of Duke Ai (480 B.C.), it reports the death of Lu's most famous native son.

> In summer, in the fourth month, on chi ch'ou, K'ung Ch'iu died. [XII:xvi:3]

K'ung Ch'iu is Confucius.

Entries such as these are so dry that little can be learned about the times without appeal to the more expansive set of annals, covering a number of states during approximately the same period, known as the *Tso Chuan* or *The Commentaries of Tso,* one of the Thirteen classics. Together, these two sets of annals show that the rulers of China had attained to some shared cultural assumptions. This does not mean there was no warfare. The states fought each other, but they called themselves "The Multitude of States." Construed as singular in Chinese, *Chung Kuo* or "Central State" is still the key word in identifying China as a political entity on the world map.

The results of warfare in Ch'un-ch'iu times were the capture of territory to the enlargement of the conquering state. But what is significant is not the fighting but the self-identification of participants in the conflicts as members of the same order of mankind. The explanation for warfare stressed punishment for deviation from a shared norm of civilized conduct, a

rationalization that exactly represents the sense of cultural
unity responsible for the rise of the Era of Cultural Fusion.
This is what the duke of Sung had to say in 545 B.C. about
the function of war:

> It is by the force of arms that Tsin and Ch'u keep the smaller
> states in awe. Being intimidated, the small states are com-
> pliant, and the major powers are beneficent. With compliance
> on the one hand and beneficence on the other, all states big
> and small can live in peace and harmony. We in Sung survive
> by virtue of that very compliance. If we were not kept in awe
> by the big powers, we should become haughty. With haughti-
> ness would come disorder, and being disordered we would be
> put down. We as a minor power could never survive being
> suppressed. Wood, metal, water, fire and earth—the five ele-
> ments are given by Heaven to all people to use for their needs.
> Nobody can do without any one of these elements. Likewise,
> who can do without the instruments of warfare? Arms are a
> commodity necessary to a state's standing. Arms are a means
> of terrorizing the lawless and of illuminating the virtues of
> civilization. Men of wisdom are elevated by them, men of
> confusion are cast down by them. Weapons exist precisely in
> order to cast down evil and raise up good, to preserve decent
> states and destroy bad states. They separate enlightenment
> from disorder. That is why arms exist. [*Tso Chuan,* IX:xxvii:2]

One of the strongest intellectual currents of the era was the
belief that some kind of stratagem—military, political, or
ethical—could unite the embattled states under a leadership
acceptable to all. The strength of the idea led to its realization
in empire. In fact, the men of imperial high culture came to
look back on the *haute culture* of the Spring and Autumn
period as the source of their intellectual heritage. It was,
after all, the age of Confucius.

The social and political trends of the Era of Cultural Fusion
may be seen by looking into the history of Lu, the best documented of the central states owing to the association of Confucius with it.

Lu was founded 450 years before the birth of Confucius by
Po Ch'in, oldest son of the duke of Chou, who was the brother
of King Wu, the leader of the forces that overcame the Shang
city-states. It was, in fact, the duke of Chou who founded the
eastern capital of the Chou domain at Loyang, to which the
royal court repaired at the start of Eastern Chou. It is the
same duke of Chou whom Confucius held up as the model of

feudal rectitude when he commented that the state of affairs
in his own lifetime had departed from that model. ·

The old feudal order, inevitably, had to change. And the
greatest of changes was the rise of great families other than
those of the ruling houses of the Chou feudatories. Continued
branching among the founding nobility contributed to this.
Power struggles within the states, on top of interstate conflict,
eventually ended feudalism.

In the end, the politics of power seeking grew too complex
to be contained as a family business. Territorial states emerged,
administered by private persons whose claims to power and
office were not hereditary.

During the Ch'un-ch'iu period, the kinship organization of
a ruling house could be diagramed this way:

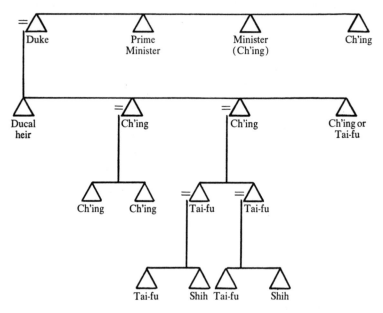

FIG. 3   *Power and kinship in the age of Confucius*

This diagram shows how offices of state ideally were
distributed according to one's inherited place in the kinship
system. Brothers of the ruler were close advisers. Sons of the
ruler, excepting the eldest one, the ducal successor, were min-

isters. Younger grandsons of the ruler were *tai-fu* or great officers, acting as advisers to the ministers or *ch'ing,* whose sons in turn were *shih* or knights, except for the eldest who was a *tai-fu* of one grade or another. The knights were the lowest-ranking members of the ruling class who could attend court, which was held in the duke's ancestral hall. All who could attend court were members of the political state. They were *chun-tze,* descendants of the ruler. Of course, not all who happened to be descendants of the ruler were *chun-tze.* Those who traced their descent beyond a certain point belonged to the nobility no longer, but to the *hsiao-jen,* or little people. All *chun-tze* were landed, with the exception of some *shih.*

The Kung-yang commentary on the *Ch'un Ch'iu* says:

> The ruler regards the State as his body, and one ruler comes after another. Hence the ruler and the State form one body. [III:iv:4]

But the Ch'un-ch'iu ruler soon found his body rent to pieces. Offices that once he had distributed to his male relatives in accordance with their genealogical remove from him, now found their way into the hands of those too remote for decent calculation.

Ministerial families enfeoffed their own ministers, and got away with it because their services had become vital to the enlargement of state power. It was the ministers who were in charge of interstate relations, diplomatic and martial. The ruler enfeoffed them, for their victories, with districts of the vanquished states. Success like this bred further need for their services. The sons of the ruler no longer enjoyed official position by reason of birth. Indeed, the ducal rulers themselves often became mere figureheads. Some were assassinated, some driven into exile; others were kept in nominal charge and were spoken for by a prime minister chosen by the oligarchy of great families who, by their own mutual struggles, had reduced their ruler to impotency.

Confucius, in his thirty-sixth year, took note with alarm of such a situation in his native state. At that time the ruler was Duke Chao, supposedly the twenty-fourth duke of Lu. But the real power was in the hands of three families who traced their descent from the sixteenth duke of Lu, Duke Huan, from about 170 years previously. This family oligarchy was known as the "Three Huan." Normally the nobility of its members would have decayed over a period of from five to six generations, had the rules of descent been followed. Somewhere along the line the families of the Three Huan must have been rewarded with fiefs substantial enough to found their own powerful branches. Or at least such must have been the case among the dominant family of the three, headed by Chi P'ing-tze.

To indicate how far things had moved away from Western Chou feudalism of Confucius's admiration, each of the Three Huan had their own walled town. They contested as rivals with the duke and with each other. While they claimed certain offices by hereditary right, at the expense of the duke's immediate family, their mutual struggles for domination over the duke's weakened state caused them to strike a balance in the choice of prime minister. They agreed to select for life whoever was the oldest family head of the three. Normally, the prime minister would have been a brother of the duke. The de facto ruler of Lu, however, was P'ing-tze of the dominant Chi family, who held the throne as regent.

Confucius, always a strict legitimist, voiced his alarm in the following observation:

> The Chi allow themselves eight rows by eight of Pantomimi in their ancestral hall! If they dare usurp the duke's very own temple ritual, what *can't* they get away with? [*Lun Yu,* III:1]

The use of eight rows of sixty-four dancers in the forecourt of the Chi family temple was the outward sign that Chi P'ing-tze had "gotten away with" usurpation of the throne, for eight rows were the ritual prerogative of dukes and of the Chou king. Indeed, shortly after this episode, Duke Chao was driven out of Lu into the state of Ch'i and Confucius followed after.

But while Confucius upheld ducal succession, he also helped promote another idea, the results of whose later adoption would have surprised him. It was the idea that officers of state should be trained, not born, to serve their prince. He even founded a school for this purpose in Ch'i. Ironically, the rise of the professional administrator, so appealing to a state ruler for his neutral ethics and loyalty to the task, helped end the ducal power he was educated to serve.

While ministerial and official families unrelated to the ducal courts had taken effective control of many states, members of the lower stratum of the feudal hierarchy, the *shih*, were also breaking away from court ties. The character *shih* in Chinese is read as samurai in Japanese. Anybody who has seen Japanese historical movies about masterless samurai roving from one castle to another, looking to hire out their swords, will be able to visualize Chinese knights of the Spring and Autumn period. Not only masterless knights roamed the countryside but also masterless scholars, statesmen, artisans, and merchants, all seeking employment and enrichment for their services under one ruler or another. In fact, by hiring such men from the outside, a ruler was able to acquire talent for his cause and bypass the local parvenu nobility. But this method of defending the ducal cause ended the cause. It reinforced the trend toward divorcing political office, with its focus on the tutelary spirits of the duke's ancestors, from state religion.

Peasants wandered about, too, looking for an improved situation. They no longer belonged to a noble family as its poor-relative vassals. They rather attached to the great families as tenants. But instead of owing their overlords unrestricted labor service, the peasants paid a fixed amount of rent in kind for use of the land. To this extent they gained a measure of freedom, as reflected in their geographical mobility. One factor giving them mobility was the opening up and cultivating of "wasteland," i.e., land not belonging to fief holdings.

Confucius himself became a masterless *shih* after the flight of his duke. Being a legitimist, he certainly never would have considered working for the Three Huan. The skills he withheld from them, however, were not those of the self-equipped knight. By his time, the class of *shih* came to include not only knights, but also stewards and clerks to the houses of the nobility and great families. His father had been a *shih* of the knightly type, famed for his feats of battle, but impoverished. Chariot-riding knights skilled in shooting and hacking were increasingly going out of demand. Heroic Bronze Age warriors of the Western Chou period, who would fight only their social equals in single combat, were gradually replaced by infantry. It was not long after the death of Confucius, at the start of the Chan Kuo period, that chariot warfare was replaced with massed divisions of foot soldiers drafted from a free peasantry and led by professional generals. The nobility, before its disappearance with the end of feudalism, had gradually withdrawn from the sport of warfare, which had been growing more unsportsmanlike in any case, and gave themselves to the more studied pursuits of administration and diplomacy. Hence the impoverished condition of Confucius's father, who had dropped to the bottom of the social scale within the ranks of the *chun-tze*. The saving grace for the *shih*, it turns out, was a noncombative talent for literacy. The rulers, nobility, and great families typically did not know how to read and write, for they considered literacy as too servile for their exalted status.

Confucius met the growing need for literate officers of state. In his school he taught that administrators ought to be as upright and princely as the best of the nobility they served. His idealized princely man he designated as a *chun-tze,* and, as the real nobility was in fact disappearing as a class, he was able to make his redefinition of the term stick: a cultivated, not a hereditary, gentleman. And naturally, a school for gentlemen would not give itself over to a curriculum of nothing but business and management. The new *chun-tze* schooled by Confucius were versatile worthies of generalized moral superiority. As the *Lun Yu* says, "*chun-tze* are not tools" (II:12). In fact, it was their morality, generalized to the point of complete detachment from clan politics and court religion, that made them attractive to the ruling authorities of the time. Quite a few of the master's students won positions of high trust.

The market for the new *chun-tze* was conditioned by the threat to nonliterate rulers posed by their literate servants. The technology of writing extended the administrative reach of the ruler to include conquered territories he could never have absorbed solely by means of oral communication with his kinsmen. But territorial authority was still extended at the cost of dilution of that authority, more and more of it passing into the hands of nonrelated managerial experts who controlled information that could be kept secret from the ruler. This meant the managers could control landed resources for their own enrichment at the ruler's expense. But the *chun-tze* of Confucian persuasion were not to use literacy as a means of keeping secrets:

> The first thing is loyalty and keeping one's word. [*Lun Yu*, I:8]

Being loyal, the *chun-tze* does not aspire to win some of the ducal real estate for himself:

> The *chun-tze* thinks of virtue; the small man sets his heart on getting land. [*Lun Yu*, IV:11]

The Confucian administrator disallows innovation; he prevents what has previously been done from going out of fashion:

> I am a transmitter of the old and do not make new things. [*Lun Yu*, VII:1]

> I am one who is fond of antiquity and seek my knowledge there. [*Lun Yu*, VII:19]

In promising that the *chun-tze* is no mere tool, Confucius also promises that he is not just a medium. He is also a message about the *use* of that medium. And the message is: the *chun-tze* guarantees to use writing only as a means to contain the old, traditional word-of-mouth loyalties.

But in the end, the stress on voluntary loyalty to the ducal cause was not sufficient to uphold it. The *shih* rose to become the scholar-bureaucrats of imperial times, when the sovereign himself granted them their autonomy from hereditary concerns of the throne in the state cult of Confucius.

The rise of the *shih* in preimperial times owed to the advantages won from the initial development of militarism in Ch'un-ch'iu China. The *shih* came to serve the old nobility and the new family oligarchies in much the same way as ministers used to serve the ruler. Enfeoffed with conquered satellite territory, ministerial families won power independent of the ducal court. The ducal court was a place where services of ancestor worship were conducted, in keeping with the fact that under Chinese feudalism the business of statecraft was not separable from the business of running a corporate lineage or clan. Ancestor worship functioned to rally clan members to the business of government, which was vested in them as inseparable shareholders related and ranked by blood ties.

Chi P'ing-tze, in usurping the duke's temple ritual, did not in fact, as Confucius lamented, usurp ducal power. Actually, the Chi family emerged under a new pattern of power that had not yet acquired its own symbolism. The symbols of the ducal order that Chi P'ing-tze took into his family's ancestral hall did not serve as a means to rally his clan in the business of governing. Under the regime of the Three Huan, the office of prime minister, originating as the office for the duke's favored brother, had become a political football between three contending families. The office was freed from the influence of any sanctions the Chi family could exercise by means of worship in their ancestral hall. Though P'ing-tze was the de facto ruler of Lu, he was not the substitute monarch of Lu. He was something else. The stewards, accountants, scribes, and property managers that worked for him did not come and sit at his court as did the *shih* of old in the duke's.

Confucius disallowed himself employment with family oligarchies such as the Three Huan. He observed the internal contradictions of feudalism and had no intention of accepting them. On the one hand, states were being enlarged with the capture of satellites; on the other, these states were being divided up among contending families. He looked for a good ruler to serve, one who would employ his philosophy of service in defense of feudalism. But under good rulers or bad, his philosophy helped destroy feudalism by undermining its religious support. Confucius advocated the separation of temple and court, or, as we would say, the separation of church and state. By removing the conduct of office from the procedures of ancestor worship, Confucius promoted a new brand of political loyalty to the ruler's cause at the expense of old political forms.

Below are summarized the factors, noted in Lu, which combined to undo feudalism. In the left-hand column is a list of traits characteristic of Western Chou feudalism, and in the right-hand column are the changes during the Era of Cultural Fusion.

Western Chou Feudalism	*Changes in the Era of Cultural Fusion*
Division of the population into noblemen, warriors, and a regulated peasantry, the latter normally excluded from military service.	Demotion of warriors to the lowest ranks of court attendants. Military careers opened to peasants.

Western Chou Feudalism	Changes in the Era of Cultural Fusion
Relative unimportance of classes other than nobles and peasants.	Merchants freed of retainer status to choose their clients for mutual profit. Writing transforms a kinship hierarchy among the nobility into a hierarchy of civil, not military, offices.
Individual authority of nobles over peasants.	Direct authority over peasants weakened as a result of their promotion from vassals to payers of tribute (rent), thus preparing them to meet the claims of taxation by imperial government.
The custom of rewarding military and administrative services by grants of land.	Enfeoffment for services meant branching and the rise of great families competitive with the ruling house.
Combination of such tenure of land with jurisdiction over a regulated peasantry.	No longer owing unrestricted labor service, the peasantry paid only a fixed amount of rent in kind for use of land.
Administrative positions form a simple hierarchy, with no division of function as among military, fiscal, judicial, and general administrative authorities.	Cadet branches of the nobility and career officers make for divided allegiance and the possibility of abstract job morality.
Dispersion of power, up to the point of complete independence, by local feudatories.	Vanquished states, after the liquidation of their ruling families, become administrative satellites of the victors on a bureaucratic model.

The growing seriousness and importance of warfare is obvious in the emergence of standing armies, officered by professional generals. Armies no longer were raised from the household resources of the nobility, but were a coordinated force, trained, armored, provisioned, supplied, and disciplined under the authority of a centralized general staff. Armies required the support of engineers, intelligence, and camp fortifications in the field. The previously undrilled foot soldiers levied by the nobles from their properties for a day or so of undirected assault were not even fed, and would have starved if kept long in the field. The troops of the Chan Kuo or Warring States period were conscripts who trained and fought for years. When not fighting, they worked on the construction of walled fortifications along strategic state boundaries or irrigation facilities and monumental palace buildings.

The effect of heightened militarism was to consolidate small political units into larger units. In *Sun Tsu*, the classic of war of the time, it is said:

> Generally in war the best policy is to take a state intact. [III:1]

Victorious state rulers, designating themselves as kings after the exclusive title of the Chou regent, installed professional officers in the place of the nobility and the family oligarchies they liquidated in the process of conquest. The upshot of this increasing consolidation was the emergence of territorial kingdoms. The basic political unit expanded from the city-state to the regional state.

The one state that conquered all the others in its quest for empire was the state of Ch'in in northwest China.

Ch'in prepared well for its ambition. In 246 B.C. it opened up one thousand square miles of wasteland in the alkaline valley of the Wei in central Shensi by means of an irrigation canal, one hundred miles long, between the Ch'ing and Lo tributaries of the Wei. That canal, the Chengkuo Canal, fixed the economic potential of Shensi for centuries. By opening up this newly fertile land to immigrants, Ch'in bypassed the nobility and acquired a free peasantry. After that, Ch'in stopped granting fiefs. The surviving nobility came flocking to the capital city of Hsien-yang, attracted by its new glories, where the king of Ch'in bought them with gifts from a store of overpowering wealth no feudal locality could raise.

Earlier, in 300 B.C., Ch'in had infiltrated the Bronze Age cultures of Shu and Pa in Szechwan. Shu and Pa seem to have been on the verge of state organization under the indirect influence from the Shang and Chou cultures of North China on the one hand, and from the state of Ch'u in southeast China on the other. Under direct Ch'in influence, a mighty pocket of civilization was built there on a compact plain of about seventeen hundred square miles. Ch'in governors irrigated the plain by diverting and subdividing the Min River to all parts of the alluvial fan simultaneously. Szechwan has remained one of the most fertile, productive, and densely populated garden spots in all of China.

With huge grain supplies stored as far west as Kaifeng, Ch'in launched its massive armies from there in 247 B.C., and subdued every rival except Ch'u in the southeast. Ch'u based its very considerable strength on the naturally fertile plain of the lower Yangtze. Ch'in gathered its forces in Szechwan and the upper Yangtze. Ch'in struck from there in 223 B.C. and finished Ch'u. In 221, the king of Ch'in designated himself as a new kind of ruler, Ch'in Shih Hwang Ti, the First August Sovereign of the Ch'in Empery.

Tradition records that the First Emperor read 120 pounds of documents every day. The significance is not the weight of the reports he read daily, but that he read at all. The first man to rule over All-China was a literate ruler, unlike the non-literate kings of the local states that preceded him. He was able to process all, or nearly all, the important papers of state by himself and thus keep in direct touch with his appointed officers in all parts of the empire. He also traveled, visiting his appointees personally. By such means he hoped to establish a tradition of centralized government at the imperial level that would last a thousand years. It lasted for fifteen. But the tradition that learning to read should be part of the emperor's training lasted for all time.

ERA OF CYCLICAL IMPERIAL CONQUESTS
(221 B.C.–A.D. 1911)

After the failure of Ch'in Shih Hwang Ti to play superking, the emperors gradually struck a rough balance between the feudalism of old and the autocracy of a strong kingdom writ large. On the one hand, the emperor aimed to control appointments to his bureaus (autocracy), and the men of merit who vied for these jobs aimed to make the emperor a captive of their own interests (feudalism). Because Confucianism gave voice to the strivings of empire in the language of feudalism, it was the perfect ideological weapon for both sides. But no matter how the struggle between the emperor and his local officials turned out, it made no difference to the peasantry, no more than did military struggles for conquest of the throne. The Green Circle went on as ever, under native or alien emperors, or under no emperors at all.

Part One

Folk Culture

CHAPTER 3

HILL TRIBES AND PEASANTS

THE peasant heritage is a tribal heritage. Folk culture and high culture parted ways in their Neolithic beginnings. The pit house went its way and the longhouse went its way. High culture emerged out of the longhouse and installed itself in a new community setting, the city. Folk culture remained behind in its old tribal setting, the Neolithic village. But tribal culture, contained in the Green Circle, came to be something different when absorbed by civilization than it was *before* the rise of civilization.

As civilization spread outward from its center of origin in North China, and as it evolved new levels of organization out of its Bronze Age beginnings, it captured more and more tribal cultures along its expanding frontiers for its working peasantry. But the Neolithic villages along this frontier were touched by civilization before they were absorbed by it. Peasants are not recruited directly out of a tribal state of culture.

Tribal culture can exist only in isolation. This is not to say that tribal peoples are not in contact with each other. All human communities exist in a cultural environment that includes other human communities, alike or different. Tribal communities exist only in an environment of like communities. Yang-shao and Lung-shan villages were tribal villages in their day. But civilization makes for differing types of communities, rural and urban, within the same cultural environment. The inhabitants of an isolated tribal community are converted into a peasantry when absorbed into archaic civilization, or their community is changed to a semitribal one if it exists on the *edge* of such a civilization. Peasants then are recruited from the semitribal people.

The type of semitribal people who can be captured by Chinese civilization for its working peasantry is known as Nan Man or the Southern Barbarians. The most famous example is the group of so-called hill tribes named Miao.

A Miao-Lolo tribesman. After G. Devéria, La Frontière Sino-Annamite, *Paris, 1886.*

The Miao number almost three million people, most of whom occupy the mountains of southeastern Kweichow province, the last big pocket of undigested semitribal people in imperial China.

The Miao land is located about three thousand feet above sea level, and the people cultivate millet, maze, barley, and kaoliang by the swidden method of itinerant agriculture. They keep some combination of sheep, goats, cattle, pigs, and chickens. Hunting and fishing are important. The Miao culture evolved from a Yang-shao tribal culture based on a Neolithic mixed economy of plant cultivation and animal domestication, plus Mesolithic food gathering. The forest clearings of their swidden farms are opened with metal axes forged by local smiths from Chinese iron. The Miao do not use stone axes as did their Yang-shao ancestors. To obtain metal, the Miao trade with the Chinese, selling them such mountain products as tea, tung oil, tobacco, sugar cane, and indigo. This trade is not large because the Miao have little to offer that the Chinese want. But what little the Miao get from it—metal and selected luxury goods—is crucial to their way of life as a semitribal people.

The use of metal allows for an occupational specialist in the person of the smith, and luxury goods uphold a petty nobility within the native system of status ranking. Without trade with the Chinese, the social complexity of Miao culture would collapse and the people would revert to a primitive condition of tribal simplicity and isolation. The Miao are so dependent on plains goods that their nobility organizes armed raids against Chinese settlements to steal what they cannot get by trade. It is this dependent relationship with plains civilization that elevates the Miao beyond a purely tribal state of culture and predigests them, as it were, for capture as a peasantry.

The Ch'ing government, however, has no power to command the assimilation of the Miao. As the frontiers of Chinese civilization spread southward, filling the bottomland and valleys, the local barbarians simply move out of range by installing themselves on higher ground. The result is that the Miao can raid Chinese settlements, but the Chinese cannot exploit the Miao habitat. Indeed, individual barbarians come down from the hills and live among the Chinese for a time, and then return home. The Miao are well versed in the details of Chinese life. These are subjects for singing and talking about. Miao knowledge of Chinese culture is geared to imitating it as much as possible. They have the mobility to learn about another culture. This they lose, of course, when they learn too much about Chinese culture, enough to be captured and immobilized by its ecological system.

The ecological basis of the Chinese Agrarian State is highly specialized in one direction only, and is not diversified in any significant way. This is the primitive condition of archaic civilization. Given a population of four hundred million, the average density is one hundred persons per square mile. But people do not distribute themselves across the land with statistical regularity. Less than 4 percent of the total population lives in the huge areas of Outer China. Everybody else lives in China Proper. See Map 1 for these areas.

That means that 96 percent of the total population is located in a small eastern segment that makes up less than one-quarter of the imperium. Land useful for farming in China, Chinese style, amounts to only some 233 million acres. Almost all of this is located in China Proper. Calculating the population for this restricted acreage, the average density is about eleven hundred persons per square mile in places where the Chinese actually live. But even here, people do not live in terms of average distribution. There are high points of up to twenty-four hundred or even thirty-six hundred persons per square mile.

Chinese farmland is located in the valley bottoms of three great river systems. They are the Hwang Ho (Yellow), the Yangtze, and the Hsi (West). A map of the population distribution shows that it follows the drainage of these rivers, from the wide deltas where they empty into the Pacific, on up through each trunk and its tributaries in a branching, dendritic pattern. It is on this limited type of land that population density and nutritional density nearly coincide.

The specialized landscape on which the Chinese peasantry is located reflects a speciality of agricultural method. The method is horticulture—hand gardening—and the basic implement is the hoe. The method sacrifices the productivity of labor for the productivity of the land. The effect is the reverse of extensive agriculture, which is to produce high yields per man hour at the expense of low yields per unit of land. In the industrialized nation-states, the farm is a capitalized food factory that produces for regional, national, and international markets. The American food factory, which feeds two hundred million persons with one million commercial farmers, is but one of many interlocking economic landscapes, all based on different land forms. By contrast, the Agrarian State exploits a single landscape. The bulk of the population lives on the immediate scene where the energy source for building civilization is produced. The principal crop in China, so to speak, is the farm population itself. The men of high culture, using vivid Mesolithic imagery, say that the human crop is their "meat and fish."

The rural population is distributed primarily on arable land

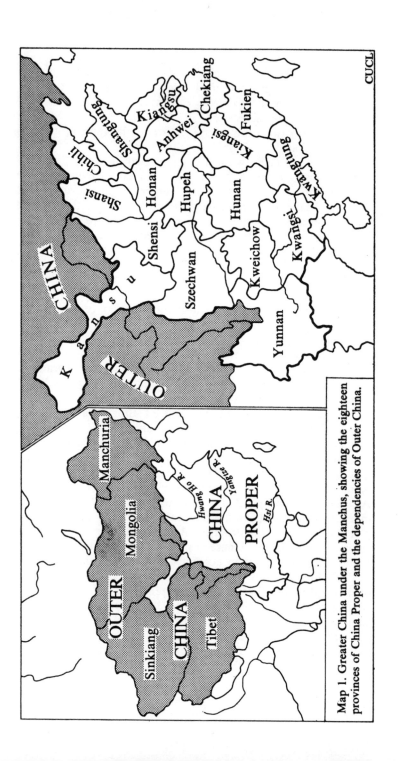

Map 1. Greater China under the Manchus, showing the eighteen provinces of China Proper and the dependencies of Outer China.

of premium fertility. It takes just as much hand labor to cultivate garden plots of mediocre as of highly fertile soil. The Chinese peasantry therefore presses on bottomlands that best will repay intensive labor.

The urban population groupings follow the rural groupings. And more than half of the urban population, a small fraction of the whole to begin with, is concentrated in just a few large and medium-sized cities. It is not distributed downward among an increasing number of smaller centers as in the industrial nations. The perfect rank-size order of cities in the United States, where rank times size is a constant, is related to the initial role of cities there in focusing economic redistribution between a variety of specialized landscapes. The preindustrial cities of the Chinese Agrarian State are political centers for the exploitation of a single landscape in the immediate countryside.

Hand gardening is both a cause and an effect of high population density, a condition that follows wherever colonists penetrate the frontier and open up new alluvial valley floors. The rural population tends to concentrate on the only land that will accommodate horticulture. There, the peasant is rendered as immobile as the plants he cultivates because horticulture is incompatible with livestock raising.

A Neolithic farmer of precivilized times was a mixed farmer: he planted crops and kept animals. The Neolithic farmer working for civilization is specialized: crops are basic. The most numerous barnyard animals in China are chickens and pigs, both scavengers. Others such as cattle eat too much plant food for the meat and dairy products they produce. An acre of hand-planted wheat will provide five times as many calories as the milk that cattle pastured on the same plat left to grass will produce. As high as 98 percent of the caloric intake of the Chinese is supplied by carbohydrate plant foods. It is the elite who account for the meat that is eaten.

The Chinese claim they eschew milk and cheese as a point of national honor; that to take food relished by their sometime conquerors from north of the Great Wall would only serve to commemorate defeat at the hands of pastoral barbarians. This patriotic, but fanciful, tale nonetheless validates hard ecological fact. Chinese concentrate on vegetable foodstuffs to the exclusion of livestock, while pastoral nomads of the northern steppelands practice animal husbandry to the exclusion of plant domestication. The steppe and the sown land divide between them the animal and plant components of Neolithic mixed farming. Both are equally specialized landscapes.

This ecological divide between steppe and sown land is marked by the Great Wall. A Chinese farm family of four, removed from a two-acre plat of alluvial soil on the Yellow River plain to fifty acres of soil north of the Wall, would starve to death if it were required to continue work at hand gardening. The growing season would be over before even a fraction of the field were fitted. Migrants who cross this ecological divide must either adopt mixed farming in the transitional zone, or, farther north, rely wholly on stock breeding. The result is that Chinese, who retain the plant-cultivating half of the formative Neolithic complex, turn themselves into non-Chinese pastoral barbarians possessing the other half if they migrate far enough north. The Wall was constructed from the northernmost state walls of the Chan Kuo period by the First Emperor to keep the Chinese in, subject to taxation, as much as to keep pastoral nomads out.

The Chinese are limited by geography in extending their landscape north of the Great Wall. Expansion has to take place to the south. Chinese colonists gradually clear the tropical valleys south of the Yangtze, and there install their rice paddies, terraces, and irrigation ditches. The newly extended Chinese landscape fills in with dense population. And the power of the Chinese state soon follows with branch offices to exploit it.

The Great Wall marks a natural frontier. To migrate north of it means crossing into another land and becoming a different kind of people. No such natural frontier marks off South China from North China. To the south, the frontier is wherever the vanguard of Chinese colonization is. The native peoples who live beyond that moving frontier, or above it, in the hills, are not ecologically specialized. Their land does not receive Chinese into it and remake them into a different kind of people as does the steppeland. The natives are made into Chinese.

The Nan Man are convertible into Chinese because their swidden agriculture, livestock breeding, and hunting and fishing make for a generalized Neolithic state of culture capable of moving in a specialized direction. The reverse is not true. The Chinese cannot unspecialize and revert to an early Neolithic state of tribal culture.

But the Nan Man are not strictly a tribal relic of Yang-shao swidden days. The effect on the Nan Man of indirect contact with civilized developments to the north of their native forest land has always been to prepare them for absorption into civilization when it eventually advanced directly upon them. The most spectacular example is the barbarian kingdom of Nan Chao on the Ta Li plain, located in present-day Yunnan province. Nan Chao built up a small-scale state in imitation of the T'ang dynasty and came to power about A.D. 740. This kingdom was powerful enough to defeat Chinese armies sent against it (sixty thousand T'ang troops were wiped out in 751, for example) and it did not fall until the coming of the Mongols, who conquered Nan Chao for the Yuan dynasty in 1253. With decapitation of the Nan Chao leadership, the Chinese state found for itself a ready-made peasantry. The Min Chia, integrated with Chinese migrants in the region, have remained a working peasantry for the Chinese empire to the end. They still speak Min Chia, a T'ai language, wear Min Chia costumes, celebrate Min Chia holidays, and worship Min Chia gods. The peasantry of China Proper differs greatly in community culture from region to region precisely because it is recruited from a variety of precivilized peoples. The Agrarian State does not have to account for differences of local peasant culture because it never administers its work force. It merely exploits it.

However, the advancing southern frontiers of Chinese civilization do not always encounter a ready-made peasantry as with the one belonging to the barbarian kingdom of Nan Chao. Sometimes recruitment follows as a by-product of military reprisal against those Nan Man who try to get their share of civilization by raiding Chinese settlements. In defense, the best the Chinese can do is disperse the enemy, never exterminate it. But such engagements always involve the loss of barbarian territory to the Chinese, despite great losses to the Chinese soldiery. Further, while some of the enemy may lose ground and retreat, others stay to be acculturated on the ground won by the Chinese. Such was the outcome of the historic battles on the Miao frontier in Hunan province during the Han dynasty. Here is a sample chronology of events.

A.D. 2 A census of this date establishes the presence of 717,499 Chinese migrants spread out from the area of Lake Tung-t'ing through thirty districts of *hsien,* covering about half of the present-day province of Hunan.

A.D. 47 By this time the plundering of Chinese border settlements by the Miao has expanded to the proportions of a full uprising. The imperial government sends ten thousand troops up the Yuan River against the enemy. But once it penetrates into the hilly, jungle stronghold of the Miao, the army is surrounded and annihilated.

A.D. 49 A bigger army of forty thousand men is sent to rout the Miao, who by this time have retaken their homeland all the way to the shores of Lake Tung-t'ing. Again the enemy is driven up the Yuan River. After a long siege, during which half the Chinese army is wiped out, the Miao, too, are sufficiently weakened to agree to a truce. The enemy is dispersed.

A.D. 137 A Miao force of twenty thousand men strikes at Chinese cities along the Li River. The revolt is quashed with the help, significantly, of several thousand "loyal natives" who have complemented government troops.

A.D. 140 According to a census of this date, Chinese colonists in Hunan number 2,813,266 in thirty-four departments. The military frontier of A.D. 49 has been breeched, and Chinese settlements now extend up the Tzu and Li rivers.

A.D. 157 The Miao take the city of I-yang near the mouth of the Tzu River.

A.D. 160 The Miao resurgence reaches north of Lake Tung-t'ing into what today is part of Hupeh province. Simultaneously the city of Ch'ang-sha on the Hsiang River is attacked and Chinese officials there are killed.

A.D. 162 Ch'ang-sha is again threatened by the Miao and again rewon by the Chinese.

In the course of these seesaw battles, the Miao eventually were beaten back into the hills from valley areas subject to Chinese landscaping.

For those Miao who were transformed into Chinese peasants, the result was quite unintentional. Chinese colonists entered into the Miao habitat, deforested the bottomland, and installed rice fields, irrigation ditches, and terraces. The Miao counterattacked by overrunning these facilities and driving the Chinese out. But the landscape regained by the Miao is altogether different from the one they lost in the first place. Like Humpty-Dumpty, the jungle wilderness cannot be put together again. So the Miao lived like Chinese on what they got back from the Chinese. When Chinese power returned to the scene and attempted to lift taxes from the resident Miao, some fled, some stayed. Those who stayed were Sinicized to the extent that they were made captives of the Chinese landscape, but their semitribal heritage remained part of their local community culture.

Those Miao not absorbed by Chinese civilization as newly recruited peasants continued to raid and maraud Chinese settlements. As late as the Ming dynasty the struggle with the Miao still was so unrelenting that the government attempted to stabilize the frontier in Honan province At the upper reaches of the Yuan River a wall was started in 1615, modeled in conception after the Great Wall, to contain Chinese and prevent their migration into barbarian territory. But this little wall was misconceived because it was artificial, marking no natural frontier. The Chinese inevitably projected themselves into the wilderness beyond, the wall crumbled, and it was never rebuilt. The Chinese could not be stopped from occupying new places in which to be Chinese.

By Ming times, however, the Chinese government learned that it could not crush the barbarian nuisance. Nor could it keep colonists out of trouble. One thing that did work fairly well, however, was to award Nan Man chieftains with Chinese titles recognizing them as sultans or *t'u-ssu*. The system provided a chieftain with an official claim to his domain against neighboring rivals and fixed a line of hereditary succession against internal rivalry. A tribal chieftain was assured his feudatory in the maps and genealogical registers kept by officials of high civilization, an attractive offer. Indeed, the heir to a chieftain's rank was given a stamped warranty of his legitimacy. In return for this emblem of imperial grandeur, the Nan Man were to pay tribute. But this was of less satisfaction to the Chinese government than its delight in the exercise of the slogan, "Control barbarians through barbarians," which summarized a hope that the *t'u-ssu* system made for self-regulating frontier affairs.

Ironically, the registration of rank and title among the Nan Man helped them organize more formidable attacks against the Chinese. A native aristocracy was strengthened, in its greater power of leadership for war, by its official connections with Chinese civilization. The barbarians came to be more like the Chinese in their local class structure. And political dealings with the Chinese could only increase their knowledge about the Chinese.

But the Nan Man barbarians have always been in contact with Chinese civilization, with or without the *t'u-ssu* system. Their dependence on Chinese goods for metal axes, necessary to efficient slash-and-burn agriculture, and luxury goods necessary to uphold a leadership group, is matched only by their curiosity to know everything possible about the Chinese. Their dependency on the Chinese leads them to raid for what they cannot get by trade, and their knowledge about the Chinese heightens the odds of their success in raiding.

An account of a Miao sortie against the prefectural yamen at Chenyuan in Kweichow province is given in the eighteenth-century novel, *The Scholars,* by Wu Ching-tzu. Prior to the assault, Brigade General Tang, with troops garrisoned at the yamen for the purpose of defending against the Southern Barbarians, had launched an inconclusive campaign. The tribal chieftain, Pieh Chuang-yen, and his rebel leader in charge of guerrilla forces, Feng Chun-jui, escaped the onslaught. The Miao warriors dispersed and prepared to regroup for a counterattack.

To insure success, the two Miao noblemen planned first to lead a raiding party into the yamen to assassinate General Tang. Because the general's intelligence was good, however, he learned of the Miao plans from an informant, who says:

> "On the eighteenth of the first month, they say, the spirit of Iron Stream comes out, and everybody in Chenyuan stays indoors. They mean to dress up as ghosts that day and break into your yamen, sir, to take their revenge."

The narrator explains:

> This was, in fact, the tradition in Chenyuan Prefecture. On the eighteenth of the first month, the local people said, the dragon king of Iron Stream gave his younger sister in marriage. But because she was so ugly that she wanted no one to see her, he sent an escort of shrimp soldiers and crab generals

to conduct her to the wedding. All households had to close their doors, and it was forbidden to go out and watch. If the dragon king's sister caught anyone spying, she would send such violent wind and rain that water would lie three feet deep on the level ground, and many people would be drowned. This was an old belief here.

On the seventeenth, the general summoned his bodyguard. That night the raiding party went into action.

Disguised as country folk going to the fair, but each with a hidden dagger, Pieh Chuang-yen and Feng Chun-jui came to the North Gate at midnight. When they found the city gate open, they rushed to the stable wall of the brigade general's yamen. A dozen of them, with weapons in their hands, climbed the wall and dropped into the courtyard.

At that moment, the general's men, who had been lying in wait, rushed out with iron prongs and spears and captured the enemy.

Not one was allowed to escape. They marched them to second hall, where the brigade general counted them, and the next day they were taken to the prefect's yamen. Prefect Lei was delighted to see that the rebel chief and Feng Chun-jui had been captured. After saluting the emperor, he brought out the imperial decree and imperial sword, had the rebels' heads cut off to display to the public and the other tribesmen killed. This done, he sent a report to the capital.

Here is a picture of the Miao showing them to be knowledgeable enough about Chinese folkways to take advantage of them for military purposes. The Miao are capable of dual cultural participation, in their own hill culture and in Chinese civilization. The mobility of the Miao reflects their dependency on the plains civilization, but this marginal involvement with Chinese civilization is the first step toward capture by it. Once the Miao are absorbed as peasants, they, too, will lose their mobility along with the rest of Chinese village folk. It is this very immobility that defines the peasantry.

One factor keeping the peasant on the land is the specialization of his commitment to it. The other side of the coin is the dependence of high culture on a peasantry that can be exploited without the trouble of coercion or the cost of providing administrative services in return. The Green Circle is *the* strategic resource as far as the state is concerned. For the individual peasant, of course, any given holding is more important to him than it is to the state. His dependence on the Green Circle is the more extreme. And the only claim the peasant has to his stake in the Green Circle is in delivering his quota of taxes, rent, and labor. This is all the individual peasant has to offer to high culture in order to keep his place on the land. But as such, it is much more than hill tribes have to offer to pay for *their* dependency on Chinese civilization. What they have to trade for goods strategic to them is not regarded as worth much by the Chinese; and the Chinese state accordingly is not interested in exploiting them. Besides, the Agrarian State does not have the technology to equip itself for the conquest of more than one economic landscape. Hence its strategic dependence on the Green Circle.

The bargain won by the peasantry may appear to be an unequal one, but within the system of rewards of the Agrarian State, it is not. The peasantry is exploited, i.e., used as a resource, but it is given a place in the Green Circle, the only option open to it in an archaic civilization. So long as the peasant pays his dues to the state, he is allowed to retain his place in the state. The peasant thus lacks any power of self-determination beyond the freedom to pursue a modified Neolithic way of life in the absence of supervision. The price of this freedom and this way of life is defensive ignorance of the outside world. The peasant must act *as if* he were living inside an isolated tribal community, even though his community is located inside a civilization. His political status is defined by nonparticipation in imperial politics. His cultural status is defined by nonprivilege in high culture. The collective need of village society is noninvolvement in the Great Society. This is a convenience to the state as well. The boundary controls of the Green Circle complement the state's reliance on these controls for cheap collection costs.

It is instructive to compare the ecological setting of peasants with those semitribal hill peoples, such as the Miao, whose destiny it is to be absorbed into the Agrarian State. A comparison highlights the peasant situation.

Hill Tribes	*Peasants*
The resource base is of marginal utility to plains civilization.	The resource base is vital to the support of the political state.
Hill tribes need civilization more than it needs them, making a one-sided dependence on the plains for the support of hill culture.	Civilization and its peasantry are mutually dependent, but folk life may survive without the state and the opposite is not true. Peasant culture is sustained by its denial of high culture.
Dependence on civilization is open and the hill tribes are receptive. Tribesmen learn to seek knowledge about the civilization they need.	Peasants hold ambivalent feelings about the wider civilization that needs them more than they need it, and take the defensive position of learning not to learn about it.

The southern frontier zone actually represents a continuation of the Chinese landscape, because the Nan Man who live there are an emergent peasantry. The Miao thus stand as an evolutionary type midway between an isolated state of tribal culture and a digested state of folk culture. But civilization does not change the culture content of the peoples it digests. The Green Circle is therefore dissimilar in all its localities as a subject of its own community culture; it has a varied tribal background. However, the Green Circle is everywhere similar as an object of imperial control because digestion brings about a uniform attitude of defensive ignorance.

CHAPTER 4

SINK OF DEATH

THE memory of the Agrarian State is long. In its mythology and legendary history it preserves memories of its prehistoric roots. High culture, ever striving to be complementary with its folk base, draws on its precivilized folk origins for cultural materials to rationalize and embroider.

The myth of Hwang-ti, the Yellow Emperor—the giver of metallurgy, writing, and palace architecture—embodies in the personality of a single culture hero the memory of the emergence of royal government in Shang times. If Hwang-ti recollects the transition from Neolithic society to civilization, the myth of an earlier sovereign, Shen-nung, recalls the transition from Mesolithic hunter-fishers to a Neolithic folk. Shen-nung is the giver of agriculture and pottery making.

But the combined gifts of Shen-nung and Hwang-ti opened up a Sink of Death. Shen-nung gave agriculture. Hwang-ti put it in the context of civilization. But using Neolithic agricultural methods to support a class system means that the few who live off the many are going to breed more than can be kept in a privileged position. Upward mobility always brings some new blood to the ruling class, but net downward mobility is the condition when the Sink of Death swallows up at least 10 percent of the population.

Bandits, petty criminals, village bullies, urban beggars, landless laborers, homeless, and underemployed—these are familiar types scorned by decent people as wicked, lazy, or improvident because they are forced to live by charity or theft. But they are no mere social deviants, cast out of society, man by man, for bad character. They form a *class* of expendable persons, a class marked for disease, starvation, childlessness, and early death. With no effective means of birth control in force, and with employment potentials predetermined by the agricultural economy, the Agrarian State produces more people than it can keep at, or above, the subsistence level. The sons of small landowners who inherit handkerchief-sized

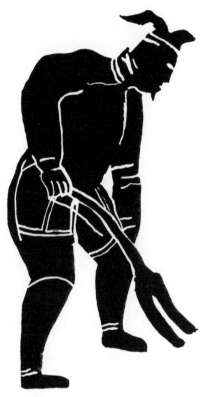

The Divine Husbandman and legendary emperor, Shen-nung. After a Han dynasty representation.

plots, the sons of tenant farmers or landless laborers or poor artisans who inherit nothing but the clothes on their back and a parental blessing—these men often seek work as porters or rickshaw men, in fatal competition with animals that carry or pull loads, and the daughters may find equally short lives as prostitutes serving slum dwellers too poor to get married.

In the industrialized nations of the world, wealth generates more wealth out of the dynamic interaction between specialized economic interests. The ecological base is broader, the capacity to support human life larger, than is the case with the Agrarian State. The Agrarian State is built on one, all-purpose landscape, that of the Green Circle. And as the Chinese say, "Land breeds no land." Land is a facility of fixed productivity that passes from one owner to another. Riches are somebody's disproportionate, but perfectly legitimate, share of a fixed supply. Poverty is the loss of one's share to somebody else. But strictly speaking, the distinction is not between richness and poverty, but between privilege and nonprivilege. Without expansive productive facilities made possible by capitalized enterprise and industry, the net result for the human population dependent on the fruits of the Green Circle must be downward mobility for both classes. The population dynamics of the Agrarian State require it. In a single landscape economy, the human crop increases faster than the food crop. There must always be a shortage of high status positions for the elite; the overspill is reduced to a peasantry. There must always be too many hands for available jobs; the remainder is pressed into extinction.

Two limited possibilities exist for the Agrarian State to relieve its surplus population without pouring it down the Sink of Death. They are opening up new geographic frontiers or new economic frontiers. The former opportunity was given with colonization of southern China; the latter was given around A.D. 1000, when a manorial elite moved to the cities and opened up a field for supply and service industries operated by merchants. In time, these possibilities were exhausted.

A third possibility was made available with factory industrialism and international marketing after contact with the West deepened. But the advantage of these new sources of wealth went to the elite at an increased disadvantage to the peasantry.

Industry in China, initiated by western enterprise, was from the start geared to export. That finished goods were shipped abroad was preordained in the use of "cheap labor," that is, native producers excluded from the native consumer market. Neither the profits nor the products were returned to China on a large enough scale to enlarge sources of capital or to raise the standard of living.

The effect of western investment in factory installations on Chinese soil was to invite Chinese investment capital. But Chinese capital came mainly from land rents; and because investment depended on outside markets, the economic result was a net loss to the Green Circle that produced that capital. Village culture can support a native Chinese elite, and has been doing so for centuries; but peasants cannot afford to give away any more of their substance to that elite when it makes common cause with foreign businessmen engaged in world trade. The added burden of supporting world trade was too much to bear and it ruined the peasantry.

The basic bipolar social structure of Chinese civilization did not change with the fall of the monarchy in 1911. It remained closed by toil and exploitation at the bottom, and open at the top with power and privilege. Under the Republic, peasants no longer were legally designated as subjects, but still they had need to seek their security within the closed boundaries of the Green Circle. The elite sector no longer was validated by government issued titles, but still it secured its privileges by means of its ancient monopoly over all economic alternatives to manual labor and productive work.

It naturally fell to the Republican gentry, then, to win all the advantages of industry and international trade. They simply added to their historic privileges the exploitation of economic opportunity originating from outside Chinese society. The power differences between China and the West thus enhanced the traditional power differences between peasant and gentry. The added burden crushed the life out of the old peasant morality and tended to make the Green Circle receptive to political messages redefining villagers as an impoverished, underprivileged people.

A broadening of the economic alternatives at the top of the class system weakened the ties of folk culture to its narrow resource base at the bottom. The multiplication of capital wealth in the elite sector hurt the peasantry insofar as it was reinvested in land. Increased purchase of land bid up the price for everybody, to the cost of abnormal rates of tenancy and landless labor.

Just as the Republican gentry found new sources of investment for their land revenues in western enterprise, so a coolie proletariat recruited from dislocated peasants found an outlet in the same nexus of foreign-dominated business by seeking employment in the cities as factory laborers, dock workers, stockers, rickshaw boys, and street cleaners in the fastidious international settlements. But this rural-urban migration was occasioned more by the push of rural overcrowding than by the pull of urban opportunity. While the cities offered new employment opportunities, they conferred no economic advantage on relocated peasants. Rather, migrants moved from one disadvantaged position in the country to perhaps an even more vulnerable one in the cities. The move, in short, is from low-productive agricultural work to marginal self-employment. Lao She, China's greatest modern writer, hits on this point in literary image when he describes the rickshaw vehicle owned by Happy Boy as a platform of ersatz land on wheels:

> Happy Boy seemed to have forgotten that he had been a farmer; he did not think of how fighting ruins the farmlands, and paid no attention to whether the spring rains had come or not. He thought only of his rickshaw. It could produce hot rolls and steaming rice and all his other foods for him. It was a plot of soil in which everything could be grown, and which very conveniently followed him around; a piece of precious, living farmland.

Economic alternatives to farming, however, only create a surfeit of cheap labor diverted from the soil; the rewards cannot exceed those gained from the make-work operations of hand gardening. In fact, the liabilities of wage earning are greater, and lead easily to beggardom and into the Sink of Death. The rickshaw boy or the factory worker cannot command any higher price than a hired farmhand working during the busy season for a landed peasant. All are thrown on the mercy of depressed money incomes.

If the postrevolutionary gentry, deprived of its imperial political tradition, find new sources of power and protection in money investments tied to foreign enterprise, peasants also come more and more to depend on money income. The Chinese peasant traditionally supplemented his edible farm products with a cash income from some cottage industry such as basket making, weaving, silk reeling, or the manufacture of paper and pottery. The slack season in the agricultural cycle only exaggerates the need of the peasantry to find constant new uses for manual labor. But the traditional balance between the handicraft industry and agriculture is thrown off by foreign competition.

Countrywomen can no longer sell their homespun in competition with machine-woven yard goods because they sell for less and present uniform quality. Gentry purchase of foreign goods squeezes native products out of the home market.

To replace income lost from decline of the handicraft industry, the peasantry must take up the cultivation of agricultural raw materials, such as cotton and tobacco, for sale to foreign markets. But this form of dependence on cash involves the peasant in a money relationship with a world market. He has no protection against its fluctuating prices nor does he have any bargaining power with the native middlemen. The penetration of a western purchasing market for raw materials poses a contradiction that peasant society by its very nature cannot resolve. Cash crops cannot replace food crops. The Green Circle cannot contain both a money economy and a subsistence economy. It will break down first.

For the gentry, however, commercial agriculture can bring nothing but profit. The same businessman can be landlord, moneylender, and manager. As landlord, rents are higher because cash crops bring more on the market than food crops. As money lender, interest is up because cash crops require investment, as in bean-cake fertilizer for tobacco plants and charcoal for drying the leaf. And as business manager of a string of middlemen, he holds the advantage of collecting from numerous petty producers and centralizing for the ultimate purchaser or manufacturer. Cash crops add one more resource to the traditional economic base controlled by the elite, one that enables them to capture money from the outside world. The elite sector can afford to lose its cultural isolation but the peasant producer cannot.

Isolation of the Green Circle from outside economic transactions will keep it from adopting a money economy, but the *loss* of isolation brings with it a train of difficulties, economic at first, but which soon alter the social fabric of the whole community. The peasant community, restricted to one economic setting, cannot help suffering a disturbance by the invasion of industrial enterprise, whose fingers stretch around the world in search of raw materials, markets, and manpower. The fingers poke into local systems without offering a sure source of income to pay the penalties of lost self-sufficiency.

This is what is meant by "semicolonialism." Peasant loss of isolation to cash cropping for a world market is the symptom of a "dual economy." A dual economy is any systematic contact of an international capitalist economy with a localized subsistence economy.

Under a dual economy, the peasant is the same person who supplies the labor for both cash crops and food crops; his part-specialization in commercial agriculture thus entails a more expensive, more roundabout way, of earning the same old subsistence. Money earnings take the peasant further away from self-sufficiency without enlarging his productive base. Though he traffics in money, money belongs to an exotic economic system. Not that the use of money is unfamiliar in the traditional folk economy. But the peasant economy is a penny economy; it uses cash only for consumption purposes and for the payment of debts, rents, and taxes. Commercial agriculture brings the peasant into market relations and monetary exchange through channels that reach far beyond his immediate locality, making the gap between the western firm and the precapitalistic household costly to bridge.

Although the income from cash crops is attractive, in a capital-scarce economy the peasant requires money advances in order to undertake the more expensive cultivation. For example, he must buy tobacco seed and bean-cake fertilizer on credit. But he must also buy his food on credit while the tobacco matures because a portion of his land is given over to a nonedible crop and his food stores will run short before harvest. To pay these money debts, at a high rate of interest, the peasant loses a large part of his return from sale of the product; the cash reward for the cash crop has little purchasing power because most or all of it goes for the payment of debts.

His returns are subject finally to the buying policy of the tobacco-collecting station. If the price of cigarettes drops, or if the quality of the leaf does not meet the standards of (say) the British-American Tobacco Company, or if blight hits the growing plants, the loss, whatever its cause, is debited to the weaker party, the peasant producer of the raw materials. Yet the chance to earn cash is so rare and the need so pressing, that the peasant grows a marketable crop so long as he can obtain even the smallest fraction of its final price. Any increased demand for tobacco will never reach the producer in the form of a higher price because it will be divided among the number of buyers who will instantly multiply, while the output of the peasant remains fixed. He dare not wholly replace his food crops with cash crops or his rice bowl will be completely in the hands of dealers and the market.

Perhaps the vulnerability of peasant labor under the dual economy is nowhere better expressed than in the fiction of Mao Tun, one of the best modern Chinese writers. Mao Tun is presently minister of culture in the People's Republic. The story reported here, "Spring Silkworms," was written in 1932. It is an early example of the effort of the modern Chinese intelligentsia to redefine peasant dislocation under the dual economy as a social ill in need of treatment.

When Old Tung Pao in the story discovered the doors of the local silk houses shut, he exclaimed:

> "Nobody ever heard of selling cocoons until the foreign devils' companies started the thing!"

Tung Pao's exasperation is founded on more than his prospective loss of supplemental income. He also stands to lose his heavy investment in mulberry leaves. It takes about two thousand pounds of leaves to feed the worms that will grow from one ounce of eggs, the amount the average family in the Lake Tai area starts with. Overcommitting himself to the silk industry on the grounds that in the past he had prospered from the expansion of the foreign market, Tung Pao borrowed money to buy twice again as many mulberry leaves as his own trees produced to feed the added trays of worms. In fact, his stand of trees he put up as collateral for the loan, an expensive proposition. It probably cost him three dollars to pay for every picul of mulberry leaves he bought when the price five months earlier may have been only seventy cents. The interest would come to 65 percent per month.

> Last year at this time buyers of cocoons were streaming in and out of the village. This year there wasn't a sign of even half a one. In their place came dunning creditors and government tax collectors who promptly froze up if you asked them to take cocoons in payment.

Learning that a silk house below the city of Wusih was still open, Tung Pao conferred with his elder son Ah Sze about going down the Yangtze and disposing of the cocoons there.

> Ah Sze agreed. They borrowed a small boat and bought a few yards of matting to cover the cargo. It was decided that Ah To should go along. Taking advantage of the good weather, the cocoon-selling "expeditionary force" set out.
>
> Five days later, the men returned—but not with an empty hold. They still had one basket of cocoons. The silk filature, which they reached after a 270-li journey by water, offered

extremely harsh terms—only thirty-five dollars a load for foreign breed, twenty for local; thin cocoons not wanted at any price. Although their cocoons were all first class, the people at the silk house picked and chose only enough to fill one basket; the rest were rejected. Old Tung Pao and his sons received a hundred and ten dollars for the sale, ten of which had to be spent as travel expenses. The hundred dollars remaining was not even enough to pay back what they had borrowed for that last thirty loads of mulberry leaves! On the return trip, Old Tung Pao became ill with rage. His sons carried him into the house.

Ah Sze's wife had no choice but to take the ninety odd catties they had brought back and reel the silk from the cocoons herself. She borrowed a few reels from Sixth Treasure's family and worked for six days. All their rice was gone now. Ah Sze took the silk into town, but no one would buy it. Even the pawnshop didn't want it. Only after much pleading was he able to persuade the pawnbroker to take it in exchange for a load of rice they had pawned before Clear and Bright.

That's the way it happened. Because they raised a crop of Spring silkworms, the people in Old Tun Pao's village got deeper into debt. Old Tung Pao's family raised five trays and gathered a splendid harvest of cocoons. Yet they ended up owing another thirty silver dollars and losing their mortgaged mulberry trees—to say nothing of suffering a month of hunger and sleepless nights in vain!

Subject to the buying policy of the filatures, and pressed for cash, Tung Pao is like putty in the hands of the silk agents. His position of helplessness, however, is not dictated by the power of foreign capitalists over the Chinese social structure—a manifest impossibility; rather, that position preexisted in the old order to be exploited, from either inside or outside the society. The dual economy is weighted irreversibly in favor of the western side in any of its transactions with Chinese labor, in field or factory, because folk culture never possessed any channels of redress in the face of domestic inequities. But the native elite helps bleed the Green Circle, not just the foreigner.

Economic decisions affecting the Green Circle always have been made from the outside, in the tax registers of the district magistrate, in the arbitrary whims of the tax collector who earns his pay by exacting what he can collect over the amount owed the magistrate, and in the rental and interest rates fixed by the landlord.

In the language of anthropology, a peasant is not the same thing as a farmer, and the two words, strictly speaking, are not interchangeable. A peasant is a farmer who belongs to a civilization that holds control over his labor. Actually, a peasant need not farm at all to meet the definition. A coolie proletariat amounts to the same reduction of economic alternatives. Farmers, in the strict sense, are enabled by their greater productive and purchasing power to exercise a measure of control over their own economic destiny, typically as members of rural pressure groups organized to adjust the price and market regime. The position of the peasant, on the other hand, is passive and supplicating. He can only pray he will not slip into the Sink of Death.

CHAPTER 5

SUBJECTS OF THE REALM

THE village as an object of imperial control does not exist on the books as an administrative or even as a fiscal unit. Only the names of the heads of households appear in the tax registers of local government. The village is taken into the empire as a self-regulating subject of its own folk culture.

From the viewpoint of the ruling elite, however, the passivity of the Green Circle is taken for an effect of policy dictated by government, when actually government takes advantage of that passivity. This conceit of high culture is nowhere better expressed than in the *Sheng Yu* or *Sacred Edict,* a document originating in a series of sixteen maxims pronounced by the K'ang-hsi emperor in 1670, and later treated to exposition by his son and heir, Yung Cheng. Officials are supposed to make regular public readings of the edict, but this is not done. There is no need for it.

Folk culture is not responsive to political messages issued by high culture. The message of the *Sacred Edict* is: keep your place, respect authority, obey the laws, pay your taxes. Peasants scarcely need to be told this.

But the edict is nonetheless valuable as a guide to the rationalizations of high culture, and as an indication of its continuity with folk culture.

In theory, the empire is a great family or *kuo chia.* Political obedience to the emperor, the family head or *kuo chang,* is phrased in terms of filial piety. The *Sacred Edict* says:

> To be perfectly loyal to the Emperor, and to fulfill your filial duties to the utmost, is the whole duty of man. [VII:15]

Loyalty to the emperor is synonymous with family loyalty:

> If you are dutiful to your parents and are respectful of your elder brothers, then as subjects you will be well conducted. [I:9]

In equating political duty with domestic duty, the edict shows a correct appreciation of the fact that the regulation of life in the Green Circle is subadministrative. Government nonetheless takes credit for the political order that obtains there by claiming that it has persuaded villagers to follow a certain brand of morality, the one set forth in the *Sacred Edict*.

The *Sacred Edict* aims its message at peasant subjects, yet it admits that they are unreflective and ignorant of high culture, especially of the gentleman's ritual code of conduct.

> The rituals of *li* are exceedingly numerous. If we were to mention them, you people would necessarily be unable to learn them. As to the root of the matter in the practice of *li,* everybody has it. For example, honor to parents, respect for superiors, love among brethren, regard for relatives—these are in you by nature. What need is there to seek outside yourself for principles? [IX:3]

For their ignorance of high culture, peasants are elsewhere called foolish people (VII:6), great imbeciles (VII:14), stupid ones (XIV:5), dull and empty-headed (VIII:5), doltish, unacquainted with the law (XVI:12), and naturally perverse, not understanding of reason (VII:6).

Yet there is some equation in what the *Sacred Edict* expects of people and what they do. It says to them: politics and *li* are too complicated for you; just obey your parents and harmony will prevail. Harmony prevails. But that is not because the edict instructs in the particulars of loyalty to the emperor; it describes what people do and defines *that* as loyalty to the emperor. In the Agrarian State, learning, laws, and all forms of rationalized culture are complementary with its folk base.

The vocabulary of familism and filial piety in the language of duty to the state is a rationalization of the fact that government expects to exploit its subjects, not provide them with administrative services. Confucian doctrine is emphatic about that.

> Without the elite there would be no one to control the rural folk. Without rural folk, there would be no one to feed the elite. [*Meng Tzu,* III:i:3]

For the *Sacred Edict* to say that the empire is a magnified family is a way of saying that subjects of the realm must look to the self-help of home and kinsmen.

To be accurate, government does more than collect taxes. The district magistrate on certain days of the week will hold a court of law and sit as judge, jury, and prosecutor to try any disputes brought before it. But the *Sacred Edict* assures everybody that litigation is itself an offense against harmony.

> You people who live together in country places are well known to each other. Your fields adjoin, your houses touch, you meet as you go in and out, you hear each others' fowls and dogs, you intermarry—which of you is not intimate with your neighbor? Now, since you are all either friends or relatives, if certain among you are bent on falsely accusing others, all of you search out the cause and get to the bottom of it. Do not become a frequenter of the law courts; it is a line of things in which whether you are a plaintiff or defendant you are sure to suffer loss. [III:1; XII:8,9]

The message is: stay away from court or you will get hurt. This is good publicity for the magistrate. The more cases that come before him the more likely he is to get fired, on the grounds of not sufficiently awing his subjects into self-helpful harmony by the force of his moral example. But this is Confucian double-talk for the terror of the law, which needs no advertisement.

For all litigants, innocent or guilty, engagement with the law means personal disaster.

> Underlings of the mandarin will shame the litigants and the mandarin himself will not hesitate to extract confessions under torture even from the innocent party. [XVI:3]

For the object of law is not to distribute justice or to right wrongs or to prove that crime does not pay, but to redress harmony: to bring the litigation to rest. To this end the magistrate decides the case entirely by himself, without the complication of lawyers and advocates working on behalf of the parties before him.

On receipt of a complaint, clerks at court will issue subpoenas to all persons likely to be implicated, neighbors or relatives, and then demand a fee—as a cut of the fee collected by the police—to prevent arrest. In theory, relatives and neighbors of a culprit are subject to no-limit joint responsibility, duty bound to what the *Sacred Edict* calls "mutual espionage" (XV:4). But this judicial theory of mutual responsibility rests with the venality of the underlings, not with a strategy of government. The underlings seek money and goods in bribery and blackmail, their only source of pay, not oppression or political control as agents of government. No one who can buy off his arrest would think of submitting to it for a term in jail, there to wait, perhaps years, for an appeal, all the while making payments for the delivery of food. Although imprisonment is not a statutory form of punishment, a term of it waiting for sentence is often worse than the sentence, not only in the effects of the dark, the damp, the filth, the chains, but in the ruin of family life, the loss of farm labor, the cost of food that can incur debt and force the sale of property. As the underlings say, "Even if chaff is squeezed hard enough it will give up oil."

The yamen of the district magistrate—a combination courthouse, office, and official residence—swarms with unpaid underlings waiting about for assignments into the surrounding countryside, which measures perhaps a thousand square miles in area, and is dotted with market towns and hundreds of villages for an average population of 250,000 subjects. Yamens in the largest districts harbor up to one thousand underlings, the smallest ones from one hundred to two hundred. These are in addition to the magistrate's salaried retinue, paid out of his own pocket, of about eight clerks and copyists, some ten degree-holding scholars brought with him from his home district to serve as private secretaries and business experts, and from ten to twenty trusted personal servants.

The underlings go by a variety of titles according to assignment, as lictor, jailer, gatekeeper, runner, policeman, tax collector, but they all are essentially the same person, usually a soldier from the local garrison. Underlings, of course, have no official status and therefore are not bureaucratically ranked. With other commoners they share power at the zero point. Only officials are ranked by grades of power, which are emblematized in the color and type of precious button set atop the official headdress. Runners wear an official hat without a button indicating rank.

But every runner in effect becomes an official the moment he leaves the yamen walls behind and steps into the Green Circle. He can report nonpayment of taxes and turn the delinquent over to the magistrate for punishment. He will, of course, accept a bribe for allowing delay, an exaction the delinquent is more than willing to pay rather than face imprisonment while awaiting sentence. And the runner will not hesitate to blackmail those who pay on time for the tax receipt owed them. The word for this type of blackmail payment is *kan-hsieh* (the Amoy pronunciation gives our word "cumshaw"), which means "many thanks." Thanks are given on both sides of the exchange of cumshaw, not the least by the giver, who is spared the terror of entering the magistrate's yamen to prove his case, not to say the cost of bribing the clerks with even more cumshaw to pull out his records and admit the case to the magistrate. But the runner himself, in the end, is just as vulnerable to his master, who for punishment can just as easily confiscate his minion's accumulated cumshaw, dismiss him, beat him, or all three.

The venality of yamen runners in exacting cumshaw from peasant subjects is the outcome of village politics. No leadership within the Green Circle interposes itself between the authority of the magistrate and his rural subjects. Some villages own to a headman, but the headman is a runner for the local gentry.

The headman provides information to the magistrate about the village. But he is not appointed by the magistrate, nor is he voted into office by the villagers. He holds his post at the pleasure of the rural gentry, which the *Sacred Edict* designates as the real "heads of the common people." But gentry are not going to fill the post themselves because they often outrank the magistrate, and they would be uncomfortable in bowing to a lesser man. Contact between the magistrate and the local gentry takes place in the yamen at the elevated level of gift exchange and informal consultation.

Backed up by gentry nomination, the headman is entitled to report directly to the magistrate. This channel of communication links him with the seat of local power, whose advantage he serves at the expense of the Green Circle because other villagers have no means of redressing his authority. The local elite sanction the headman's monopoly of communication with the district magistrate.

The magistrate, or *chih-hsien* ("knower of a district") needs information about the villages because, like all local officials, he is appointed to a place far removed from his home district.

What is more, his post is the bottom one in the bureaucratic hierarchy, the one that holds court and collects taxes among four hundred million subjects in only about fifteen hundred districts. If the runners are his "claws and teeth," the gentry are his "eyes and ears." And serving the gentry is the headman, with his personal knowledge of the ownership of all the numerous and scattered small plats of land held by the villagers.

The headman, then, is not a community leader. He is rather the agent by which the local gentry does business with the magistrate. There simply are no village-wide organizations, no communal activities. Group action of a sort does exist, however, in the crop-watching associations, for example. These associations collect dues for the payment of guards to watch over ripening grain against expendables, the "grass and ashes" peasantry for whom stealing is necessarily a way of life. But any given village will have more than one of these groups, organized along factional lines, and they are rivals. By no means may these or any other similar groups, such as loan societies or pilgrimage societies, all organized to meet a temporary local need, be taken as an organizational link between village interests and the outside world. They rather concentrate the focus of self-help. The village is not a political sodality even to its folk inhabitants.

The absence of village solidarity follows from the fact that the Green Circle defaults its organizational potential to the local elite, to the "men who know." If, for example, peasants depend on a village-wide system of irrigation, they look to the gentry to organize their own labor, directed by the headman, in excavating or clearing the ditches and canals. For this service gentry section supervisors are paid in the produce of some allotted plats of irrigated land. Lin Yu-tang tells a humorous story about the gentry in their managerial role:

> There was once a gentry scholar who made a living by undertaking repairs of bridges, roads and temples. On such pretexts, he could always solicit contributions and pocket large sums for himself. When he died, Yenlo, the King of Hell, looked into his life record and sent him into a dark cell in hell in common with other souls. One day the gentry ghost got up and harangued his fellow ghosts in hell as follows: "This is a place of darkness and iniquity. We must change it into a better world to live in. You contribute a dollar each to me, and I will have a window put in our cell."

With similar initiative, local gentry order the headmen to mobilize village labor at the magistrate's call for the repair of city walls, bridges, roads of the imperial post, and river dikes. At one time the magistrate could draft unpaid labor for these tasks. But after the sixteenth century the magistrate paid for it via the headman. A land tax and a separate labor draft formerly were exacted from the peasantry, but later the two obligations were consolidated into one uniform levy, the so-called single-whip method of taxation based on property. In time, this combined land-and-labor tax could be paid in cash, because of the large influx of silver from foreign trade with the West. Local government then simply spent its bullion on hired labor for the jobs it needed done or for the purchase (say) of millet stalks used to reinforce dike walls in time of flooding. The headman's authority is thus backed up with the opportunity to earn a salary from squeeze on these public monies.

Villages exist without their resident gentry, but they are without headmen as well. These blanks are filled in by the headman and his aides under the control of gentry from another village. A rather complicated network of such agents covers the countryside, which is viewed by central government as an extension of its own organization, rationalized as a uniform, precise *pao chia* system of pyramiding tens: ten households to a *pao* and ten *pao* to a *chia*.

This rationalization is a credit to the gentry, the real power in the countryside, whose equation of interests with government is thereby acknowledged.

Local gentry by their control of headmen ensure the magistrate his fiscal control over the countryside; the magistrate in return extends political protection over economic interests in the countryside. These interests should coincide with peasant interests under normal conditions. For example, the peasant may have his land recorded in the magistrate's tax register as the holdings of some local gentleman, who has the power over the yamen clerks to enter it as unproductive land. The peasant pays the full tax on productive land to the gentleman, who transmits the lesser tax on inferior land and pockets the difference. The magistrate gets his taxes in promptly. And the peasant earns protection from the venality of the magistrate's underlings. Of course, those peasant households not under gentry protection will have to be taxed harder to make up for the amount of productive land redefined as inferior. But that only goes to illustrate how competitive the peasant situation is at bottom, and how easily he can be crowded off his narrow resource base.

Members of the gentry are defined in terms of privileges in accordance with their official rank, academic title, or both. Those holding a post in the imperial bureaucracy are *shen*, officials, and they necessarily hold an academic degree as well. Those who hold an academic degree only, acquired by passage through the government-sponsored examination system, are *shih*, scholars or literati. About one million degree holders join with about twenty-five thousand civil officers to form the *shen-shih*, the jural body of scholars and officials. But there is naturally a halo effect on the de facto status of kinsmen of men who have status de jure. All are addressed as *lao-yeh*, "My Lord," by commoners. As the *Sacred Edict* notes:

> When people see scholars, they all treat them with respect. [VI:2]

The elite of the realm are easy to recognize by their style of life. Of course, while holding a post away from home, they wear official costume. Yet they are conspicuous enough as retired officials or as nonbureaucratic gentlemen in their cultivation of leisure and detachment from manual toil. Some live in cities, some in market towns, and some in the Green Circle. Those living in the countryside are often branch families of powerful families living in district or provincial capitals, where their great wealth is protected behind city walls. Given the constant effect of downward mobility in a birth elite that cannot provide high status for all its members, some of these rural branch families are settled on the properties of the parent family to work in the manner of peasant farmers. But most of the rural gentry are at least the social equals of the local magistrate.

Not every village has its local gentry. But peasant folk never lack for the experience of meeting men of high culture. At the very least tenants meet with their landlord at his office in the nearby market town. Gentry influence in the countryside is not simply a by-product of its powers of economic control. In a very real sense, power and privilege does not exist unless acted out before two audiences, that of peers and that of inferiors. On the one hand, members of the gentry record their charities, scholastic achievements, and other notable doings in gazetteer form, perhaps to be noticed at the imperial level of recognition by government compilers of the dynastic history. And of course their participation in high culture requires inter-local communication by means of letters, travel, the handing around of manuscript compositions, the display of artwork, or the publication of poetry, essays, stories, or critical editions of the classics.

On the other hand, gentry status may be acted out in the Green Circle, by way of exhibiting cultivated manners differ-ent from the ways of the peasant, yet related. The *Sacred Edict* notes the fact this way:

> How is it that scholars stand at the head of society? Because they study the books of the Sages, know the right of things, and are examples to the people in word and deed. If in every deed all scholars were to conduct themselves aright, the neigh-bors, country people and villagers would all love them, and respect them; and following their example learn to be good. Can it be that manners would not without exception change for the better? [VI:2]

Privilege thus is rationalized by high culture as a service to the nonprivileged. Speaking of the literatus in the first person, the *Sacred Edict* explains:

> When I became a *hsiu-ts'ai* or took my higher degrees, no sooner had the announcement arrived in my home community than everybody came and offered me their congratulations. How came this about? It was simply that because they ex-pected me to look to their welfare. But if I presume on my literary status to treat the people of the place as meat and fish to eat, they will not consider it fortunate to own a man of rank. Hence I must not rely on my having a degree to oppress the man who has none. [III:4]

The rationalization is not hypocritical in the context of the native civilization. Cultivated manners are indeed different from those of the folk. But they are related to the folk only insofar as they provide a model for avoidance. The peasant of course resents his inability to become one of those who exploit him. That's exactly what the cultivated manners of the gentry tell him: He is what he is because of what he is not.

But to China's intellectuals, the role of the gentry came to be viewed as oppressive to the aspirations for human dignity

and freedom on the part of humble folk. A good example is
Lu Hsun's story, "The Divorce," published in 1925. Lu Hsun
was the first of China's modern writers of fiction to write about
common people and their problems. The problem invariably is
the exploitation of the little people (pictured as good and
decent) by power persons (always fatuous, immoral, and
dominating).

In "The Divorce," Lu Hsun draws a savage portrait of
gentry high-handedness. The peasant heroine of the story is
Ai-ku, who has just left her husband because he and his family
cruelly mistreated her. After returning to her parents' home she
decides realistically that, after all, the public shame of a divorce
to a woman is a worse fate than the personal unhappiness of a
hopelessly bad marriage. But she is denied even this shred of
human dignity by the forces of feudalistic evil.

Ai-ku's father takes her before Mr. Wei, head of a gentry
family in the next village, in the hopes of negotiating a settlement with the husband's family, also present. The reader
knows Ai-ku expects to place her confidence in Mr. Wei's
seventh son, the most learned one in the family. Standing there
in the reception room she thinks to herself:

> "Just because he exchanges cards with the magistrate doesn't
> mean he can't talk our language, does it? These scholars who
> know the truth will always stick up for justice. I must tell
> Seventh Master the whole story, beginning from the time I
> married at the age of fifteen. . . ."

But the first sight of seventh master establishes his disinterest in problems of the people. He stands there, face glisten-
ing from the lard rubbed into the skin, discussing something
with his brothers who listen to him in awe.

> "This is an anus-stopper, which the ancients used in burials."
> Seventh Master was holding something which looked like
> corroded stone, and he rubbed his nose twice with this object
> as he spoke. "Unfortunately, it comes from a recent digging.
> Still, it's worth having; it can't be later than Han."

Ai-ku's father stands there trembling in fear, but Ai-ku
herself is not frightened and is ready to stand up for her rights.
She addresses Mr. Wei.

> "Seventh Master is a man of wisdom and learning, very dif-
> ferent from us villagers, with a knowledge of what is right.

I have been wronged, and I wish to appeal, therefore, for justice."

She then tells her story of abuse by her in-laws and by her husband who chased after harlots.

"Seventh Master knows all this," said Mr. Wei, interrupting her. "Unless you change your attitude, Ai-ku, you will accomplish nothing. You are still the same, I see. Look how sensible your father is! It's a pity you and your brother aren't like him. Suppose you do take this matter to the magistrate, won't he consult Seventh Master? But then the case will be dealt with publicly, and nobody's feelings will be spared. . . . That being so. . . ."

"I'll stake my life if need be, even if it ruins both families!"

"There's no need for such desperate measures," put in Seventh Master at last. "You're still young. We should all seek harmony. 'Harmony breeds wealth.' Isn't that true? I've had your husband add a whole ten dollars to the settlement. This is already a kind of justice higher than heaven. For if your father-in-law and mother-in-law say 'Go!,' then go you must. This is true not only locally but also in Shanghai, Peking or even in foreign countries. If you don't believe me, here's a young man who has just returned from Peking." He turned towards a sharp-chinned son of the house. "Isn't that so?" he asked.

"Ab-so-lutely," replied sharp-chin, making his body stiff and his voice low and respectful.

The affair is settled in favor of the other family. Divorce it will be. The wedding certificates are exchanged back. Ai-ku is then given to say that she accepts Mr. Wei's hurtful decision. She says, "For scholars who know the classics and truth know everything." Irony is intended in these words that in earlier times would have been a perfectly apt observation for a peasant to make.

But Lu Hsun is writing as a revolutionary, and his sympathetic characters are young peasants who struggle nobly against rotten tradition. In Lu Hsun's first story, "A Madman's Diary," written in 1918, he describes the elders of the elite establishment as man-eaters, cannibals. The concluding line, "Save the children," moved a whole generation of young intellectuals to redefine the rationalizations of high culture as hypocritical, false, and destructive. And the accusation came to be true. The contact with the West that had brought new ideas about interclass relations also brought, with the dual economy, new disadvantages to the peasantry that were insupportable under the traditional class structure. The men who read Lu Hsun in their youth stand among the leaders of Communist China today.

CHAPTER 6

CULT OF POVERTY

BOTH peasants and gentlemen of high culture are equally family centered. They have to be. The family is the key institution of self-help in a society lacking other helping institutions.

But family life in the two cultures of peasant and gentry differs greatly in organization and purpose. Among gentlemen of the Great Society, the family is a big family of several generations; it is a miniature state, given to the corporate management of its property holdings, business dealings, and political connections. And it has its ceremonies of state, as it were, in the cult of ancestor worship. The little people of the Green Circle have no such resources around which to organize; they cope with their absence of privilege in a small family, whose ritual expression is the Cult of Poverty.

The two cultures of Chinese familism could not be more different. Yet the men of high culture insist that the big family is normal for all Chinese—it's just a matter of the peasantry being too poor or too stupid to achieve that norm. High culture is everybody's culture, but not everybody can attain to it. In reality, peasant family life is caught up in the life of the Green Circle, which has its own folk culture and is not merely an inadequate version of high culture. The aim of the literati, however, is not to explain the facts in the manner of modern social science, but to perpetuate the power difference between high culture and folk culture. Otherwise, these spokesmen for high culture could not arbitrate cultural values for all men of the imperial *kuo chia* by way of acting as moral exemplars. The business of the literati in the Agrarian State is to rationalize the continuity of folk culture and high culture in consideration of the fact that the latter grew out of the former. If they say that the peasant lives a poor-culture version of their own culture, very well; they are just doing their job by saying that. It is true for them, but not for us.

For example, the dynastic code prescribes unilateral inherit-

The conjugal family at work. After a Chinese print.

ance in the male line among all sons equally, the rule of
homoiogeniture. As the *Ta Ch'ing Luli,* or *General Code of
Laws of the Ch'ing Empire,* puts it:

> All family property moveable and immoveable must be divided
> equally between all male children whether born of the prin-
> cipal wife or of a concubine or domestic slave. [Li 88]

If the rule of homoiogeniture is followed, that is, if property
is divided equally between all legitimate heirs, the family will

be a conjugal family of husband, wife, and unmarried children. This rule holds for peasants—law follows custom here —but not for the gentry.

The code, however, must account for elite custom as well. Indeed, this must have prior concern. Only the men of high culture are in a position to rationalize behavior of any kind; they are the exclusive arbiters of value. Law, then, must reflect their values. The code specifies homoiogeniture, yes. But only *if* property is to be divided in the first place. And this is disallowed, under threat of punishment, unless permitted by the family elders.

> During the lifetime of grandparents or parents, the sons or grandsons are not allowed to set up separate establishments and register them as such, nor to divide the family property, under penalty of one hundred blows, but the parents or grandparents must be the complainants. [Lu 87]

In the end, the code sets out conditions that favor the joint family, the customary form among the elite, and then rationalizes this as a form belonging to everybody. The elite class accumulates to itself all sources of income other than physical toil, be it land renting, moneylending, labor supervision, business management, or office holding. No conflict of interest obtains among these different activities, and one family may take on all of them. Indeed, the joint family is a business corporation made up of two or three generations of conjugal families, with a chairman of the board recognized in the oldest male of the oldest generation. All economic returns and political connections are held in common. Power and property are magnetic, attracting the individual share-holding families to a common enterprise against the threat of downward mobility, which is certain if the family divides into its small-family components.

If the big family breaks up, the punishment is one hundred blows to the sons who move out—*if* their elders bring the case before the magistrate. The law does not punish unless a wronged party brings a complaint.

> The full penalty of the above law is incurred if the sons separate and divide the property, though they do not register themselves. If, however, the parents permit the division, there is no objection to its being done. [Li 87]

But of course, peasants never bring complaints. The conjugal family, under its own roof and situated on its own property, is customary among them. The conjugal family serves the peasant as a production unit based on husband and wife cooperation in physical toil and in economizing practices.

Peasant culture and gentry culture each has its own type of family organization. The conjugal family of the peasant is supported by peasant needs and values, but these repose in no body of literature. The peasant defers value making to the "men who know." The rationalized culture of the elite, as instituted in civil law, speaks not only for the joint family, with its need for corporate management of complex economic and political resources, but also claims to speak, in umpiring the value of values, for inarticulate folk culture by legislating the joint family as a universal model. The joint family is not, in fact, universal. Nonetheless, the model is relevant to the peasant condition: violations of the gentry norm are acknowledged as such. After all, as the *Sacred Edict* endlessly repeats, the little people of the villages are empty-headed ignoramuses. That being the case, the literati may intellectually accommodate the conjugal family of the peasant to a universal model by viewing deviation as a product of ignorance, just as peasants are understood to be ignorant of *li,* the gentlemanly code of conduct. The literati take the fact that the folk are unreflective as evidence that the peasantry lacks any cultural norm of its own. That is why the literati may pose as moral exemplars.

It is true that some rich peasants have big families and some poor gentlemen have small families. But this continuum in family size betweeen peasant and gentry does not bridge the two life-styles. Folk culture includes both poor peasants and rich peasants; the latter may own enough land to encourage the married sons to stay and work it. Some men of high culture are so poor that their consumption habits are as restricted as those of the majority of peasants; and their family size may be as small as that of a poor peasant and reduced to a conjugal type. But these facts nonetheless do not allow a "typical" Chinese family to be created out of statistics. Reducing everything to a common denominator will yield an average family size of five persons. This is useless information. It does nothing to highlight the more important fact that a legal distinction exists between an elite population and a mass-depressed nonelite population. The elite, rich or poor, are incumbents of a political privilege that allows them the luxury to orient themselves intellectually to the matters of high culture that are empire-wide in their distribution. And the families of these men tend to be large in number and organized as multigenerational joint families. The nonelite, excluded from political power, are captives of the Green Circle; their outlook is not reflective and it is localized in the village and the marketing area. The families of these men, for the most part, are small and organized as conjugal families. No idea of a typical Chinese family can be made to prevail over the fundamental distinction in life ways as between folk culture and high culture.

The peasant way of life is community oriented by definition. But the village community is merely a setting for the residence of families. The round of folk life reduces to family life, family members, family property, family reputations, and family gods.

People know everything about the personal and family circumstances of their neighbors, or at least everybody strives to know these things. The villager cannot easily lie about himself. There is no hiding from others. But this is not to say that personal relations are valued as such. They are not. The content of these relations amounts to smothered hostility and secret distrust. Mutual suspicion is far from impersonal.

If folk culture is family centered, it is because kinship is the only defense against mutual suspicion. Each family is necessarily thrown into competition with every other owing to the fixed availability of land within the Green Circle. Beyond the fields of one village lie those of another. The agricultural landscape is filled in. Landed wealth cannot be expanded. It can only be divided, redistributed, exchanged, bought, and sold. Villagers are acutely aware that any gain in property by one family is another's loss. It could be *anybody's* loss. So everybody else feels that it is *his* loss.

What is more, there is nothing any family can do to increase wealth through harder work on the land it does own. The intensive methods of Chinese agriculture automatically raise the productivity of the land to its limit. Labor is not cost-accounted but is freely expended in pushing the yield to that limit. No amount of hard work can surpass it. Not only that. Through time the population increases. Given intensive agriculture as both a cause and an effect of high population density, and given the unavoidable custom of homoiogeniture, the result must be smaller and smaller shares of land inherited by sons from their fathers. And the risk of falling into the Sink of Death increases.

Such factors cannot help but make for mutual suspicion between families. The disadvantages of peasant life do not induce a communal spirit of sharing in hard times. There is rather a sense of rivalry. A face-to-face vigilance of envy and distrust, based on a realistic appreciation of liability to loss, acts to police all property transactions. If this mutual suspiciousness does not actually tend to equalize holdings, it does enforce an overdesigned industriousness and thriftiness.

In defending himself against the suspicion, the gossip, and the envy of others, the peasant strives to present himself to others as one who overly exploits himself in hard work, who underconsumes to the point of starving himself, who is sanctimonious in his thrift, and never throws anything away. Deprivation is real enough in peasant life, but peasant morality demands that it be dramatized in a Cult of Poverty. Habits of underconsumption, together with concealment of material gain, are a way of signaling to neighbors that one is not trying to get the better of them. A Cult of Poverty serves to forestall jealousy. The technical requirements of hand gardening, in the careful planting of seeds in rows rather than by broadcasting them, in weeding and hoeing, in the manuring of individual plants, in husbanding all refuse for the compost heap, are congruent with a moral calling to act out hard work as a way of demonstrating one's righteous claim, against envy, to one's own share of scarce resources. The Green Circle constitutes a community of spirit only insofar as it acts as a jury, adjudging the toil and thrift of its fellow members in a constant watch of mutual suspicion. A tedious manicuring of the crops does not make them grow better but it does make for better human relations.

The *Sacred Edict* devotes the whole of section V to the cause of peasant diligence, economy, and simplicity. Here again the intellectual handlers of high culture shape the facts of rural life and elevate them to the status of the directive: "Set store by economy as a means to the careful use of property." Simple living in the Green Circle thus has political meaning for the ruling class.

The disadvantages of peasant life, carried to cultish extreme, serve as a form of adjustment to both the local situation and to the outside world. The peasant cannot work his land in security from the malicious gossip and envy of his neighbors unless he acts out toil, thrift, and simplicity on a histrionic scale; but he cannot serve the Cult of Poverty unless he pretends ignorance of the leisure and luxuries available to the men of high culture.

These aspects of peasant morality are in line with the one-sidedness of the village economy. The Green Circle, embedded in civilization, is not self-sufficient as it was in Neolithic times before its transformation. It is not self-sufficient morally or economically. The peasant knows that the "men who know" hold a moral judgment about the values of folk life, but he has no voice in formulating this judgment. Similarly, his market dealings for cash, which complete his household budget, give him no claim on the economic controls that the local gentry exercise over him. The peasant's need for cash in a village penny economy is greater than the market's needs for his commodities. What the peasant produces is on such a small scale, squeezed out of a domestic economy, that failure to market his cotton or silk or tobacco hurts no one more than himself, a circumstance underlined with the advent of the dual economy.

The Cult of Poverty is the unwritten charter of the Chinese peasant family. It points to a condition of family anarchy, the amoral striving of families in the absence of a community charter. Be that as it may, the Cult of Poverty is necessarily served by a small family, not by a big family. That folk life tends to reduce itself to the economic cooperation of a conjugal family is made vivid in the short story, "A Country Boy Withdraws from School," by the Chinese humorist Lao Hsiang.

The boy in the story is sent to school under a compulsory regulation unique to an experiment in rural reconstruction begun in 1930 among sixty-one villages in Ting Hsien, Hopei province, by the Chinese National Association of the Mass Education Movement. The association started in 1923 as a literacy movement, but expanded its goals to achieve no less than a pilot program for the transformation of the Chinese peasantry into an agricultural estate of true farmers. Lao Hsiang's experience at Ting Hsien is the basis for his story, and for his pessimism.

The experiment defined the problems as "ignorance, poverty, disease, and civil disintegration." Reconstruction took four lines of attack, "cultural, economic, health, and political." But the sorry fact is, these were no solutions. Education in literacy, scientific farm management, public health measures, and political consciousness were promoted under the political status quo. Scientific seed selection could not guarantee land ownership under conditions of widespread tenancy; increased production could guarantee against no hike in rents under the dual economy; literacy could guarantee no relief from a tax structure disallowing recapitalization of agriculture; new marketing cooperatives could not guarantee that customs officials would not allow the dumping of foreign goods at prices lower than native products. All of these forbidding circumstances continued to contain peasant morality within the Cult of Poverty, making of "ignorance, poverty, disease, and civic disintegration" not causes but symptoms of what the reformers wanted reformed.

The family in Lao Hsiang's story is a small family of five individuals, composed of two elderly grandparents, a married couple, and their nine-year-old son. The boy is already part of the family labor force.

> He is expected to help in the pulling of haystubs in the spring and in the weeding of the fields in summer; he should be able to carry bricks during the building of farmhouses or dig ditches for the irrigation of the garden, thus making himself worth half the labor of a grown-up man.

In sending the boy to school, his father has to hire a day laborer to take his place.

> Returning from his first day at school the boy announced that his textbooks cost a dollar twenty cents. Everybody is stunned. It is the grandmother who breaks the silence. "We are forced to send him to school, and now we are to pay for his books as well. Why, on the very first day he spends over a dollar. Who can ever afford that? Even if we stop burning oil-lamps and go without lights for half a year, we can't save that amount. Why, it is the price of eight bushels of maize!"

After lengthy family council it is decided to pay for the books out of a little cash recently taken in from sale of the mother's earrings, which had been set aside for buying cabbage seedlings.

The father warns the boy:

"We're sparing your help in the farm, and sending you to school. You know it is hard for us. You are nine years old. You owe it to us to work really hard at school and learn something."

The boy does indeed learn something.

Six days have passed, and according to the regular school routine, the teacher has already taught Ah Chuan his first lesson. The text of the lesson is four characters: *"This is mamma."* Ah Chuan is really a good boy, for from the time he comes home till supper time, he keeps on reading *"This is mam-ma."* He presses his book with his left hand, and points at the characters with his right hand while he reads, as if the characters would fly bodily off the pages of the book at the slightest relaxation of his finger.

But his mother is sitting by, and every time he repeats *"This is mam-ma,"* her mother's heart feels a slight tug until she really cannot stand it any longer, and she snatches the book from Ah Chuan's hands and says, "Let me see. Which one is your mamma?" Ah Chuan tells her in all honesty that the one with high-heeled shoes and curled hair and a long gown is the mamma. On hearing this, the mother breaks out into a cry, which is a howl. Ah Chuan's father and grandparents all come round, thinking that a devil has gone into her, and ask what's the matter, but she only cries and will not explain. At long last, she only says, "Whoever did see such a monster in our village for a mother?"

So they all begin to understand that she is crying because of a sentence in the school book.

And there is the continued trouble of expenses. To cover the cost of paper, Ah Chuan's mother has to sell her hair decorations. But when Ah Chuan comes home and says the class is going to hold a tea party and everybody must contribute ten cents for oranges and apples and chocolates, his father gives him a scolding.

"Look here! I'm sparing this money, which I earn with the sweat of my brow, for you to go to school to buy books, to get you educated. I am not going to give you money for you to squander on sweets. Whoever invites you to tea must pay for it as well."

Now the whole show has been given away. Ah Chuan's father aims a good kick at him, but luckily for him, there is a table in between, and the table turns, crashing five or six bowls to the ground.

The family holds another long council to decide whether Ah Chuan should stay in school or not. Grandmother is so terrified that the boy's learning to learn about the outside world is wrong that she fears he will be arrested. But in the end, the family agrees to let him try for a few more days.

After this disgrace, Ah Chuan makes up his mind to work hard and recover his favor with the family. Every afternoon after he comes home from school, he keeps working over his lessons until dark, unaware that Fate is lying in ambush for him in the form of a new lesson, and that his days at school are numbered.

For the grandmother has been feeling that since her son's marriage, her position in the family has not been quite the same, that her words are not listened to the way they were before. It happens that Ah Chuan has come to a new lesson and the words are: "In the family, there are a papa, a mamma, and brothers and sisters." There is no mention of the grandfather and the grandmother. The realization penetrates into her old soul with all the force of accumulated anger and resentment. "Now, I am not wanted any more. I know I have no place in the family." And in her bad temper, the old woman picks up a brick and dashes the iron cooking pot to pieces.

At this point, the father brings the boy's brief career at school to a halt.

"Oh, don't be angry, mamma," says Ah Chuan's father. "I have decided that we shall not send Ah Chuan to study books of this kind any longer. I would rather go into the district jail."

And the next morning, Ah Chuan's father dismisses a hired farm hand, and the teacher makes a cross against Ah Chuan's name in the pupil's register.

The grim reality behind the humor of this story lies in the fact that in the peasant farm family, agriculture is a cooperative enterprise of husband and wife, and that children are put to work as soon as possible. Labor is the only factor of production the family is free to maximize beyond the fixed limits of the little land and capital in its possession. Labor is thus not cost-accounted but is expended on a self-sacrificing basis. Any increase in other expenditures can only be met through a decrease in personal consumption. The least that the grandparents in the story can do is to share in a united family policy to eat less.

The grandparents attached to Ah Chuan's father are not relieved of hard labor out of filial piety, which enjoins care of parents by the son, but because they are too old for hard work. Filial piety is rather the ethical support of a father-son relationship important to joint families of the elite. These families hold property in trust among several generations, and it is important for a chain of managerial authority in the male line, reaching up to the family head, to be respected. Peasant families cannot build the power structure that goes with filial piety because the family is a production unit based on husband and wife cooperation. Elderly parents in a peasant family may feel very keenly the shortcomings of their marginal tasks, such as Ah Chuan's grandfather, who is described elsewhere as sweeping the yard. The grandmother's anxiety is openly expressed in her reaction to the boy's textbook, a Chinese version of Dick and Jane, which excludes grandparents and mentions only a father, mother, brothers, and sisters. She thus shows sharp awareness that the crucial axis of peasant life is husband and wife solidarity, not intergenerational solidarity.

Had not the boy been required to attend school, his family would have been spared the expense of his replacement by hired labor, textbooks, paper, and tea parties. The pots, broken in anger over these expenses, emphasize how upsetting learning about elite culture can be to the folk way of life. As it was, the textbooks alone cost the sale price of eight bushels of corn or the purchase price of enough kerosine to provide illumination for half a year. (The kerosine lamp, a foreign import, made rapid inroads into the peasant household economy because it allowed extension of the working day for further self-exploitation.) The family bore the boy's school expenses the same way it originally planned to buy cabbage seedlings, and that was by giving up something. In this case, the something given up was the wife's earrings, her cosmetic property, the little property a woman inherits and keeps after marriage. Without the proceeds from the cosmetic property to fall back on, the boy's family would do without light or corn, or without salt, as the family next door is mentioned as doing.

"Doing without" is a normal aspect of consumption among peasants, part of the pattern of self-exploitation that includes unpaid expenditure of labor. Control over personal consumption is as much a form of mutual aid within the family as agricultural teamwork.

What is more, restrictive consumption has a moral point to make as part of the Cult of Poverty. Doing without also means a denial of gentry norms of consumption, even to the point of turning down the attractiveness of such trivial items as sweetmeats. Peasant thrift acts to preserve the identity of folk culture as well as to defend against jealous neighbors.

The solidarity of the Chinese peasant family is a defensive solidarity against the encroachment of high culture and against the jealousy of neighbors. Such defense measures are best handled in the smallest of kinship units, the conjugal family. The smaller the family unit, the easier it is to control consumption as a unit, just as it is to command unpaid labor as a unit. Elderly parents attached to the family may be a handicap, but the joint family is out of the question in the pursuit of these tasks. The shared motivations of defense and mutual aid that belong to the Cult of Poverty cannot easily be extended very far beyond the conjugal relationship of a single man-and-wife team.

CHAPTER 7

STARS IN HEAVEN

No ordinary villager will gainsay the proverb, "All walks of life are lowly, only the scholar stands high." Both educated and uneducated as readily accept the equation of scholarship with power as ignorance with meanness.

The proverb is a garbled version, filtered down to the peasantry from high culture, of the thoughts of Mencius:

> Inequalities are in the nature of things. There is the business of superior men and there is the business of little men. Hence there is a saying, "Some work with their head; they govern others. Some work with their hands; they are the governed. Those who are governed feed the others; those who govern are the fed." This is a just arrangement. [*Meng Tzu,* III:i:4]

One of the principal tasks of high culture is to rationalize the gap between elite and nonelite status. The literati do so by speaking of class differences in terms of a division of labor between harmoniously working parts of society. The *Sacred Edict* says that "The upper and lower classes form one body" (XIV:6). This body, in the native model of stratification, contains four parts:

1. Scholars
2. Farmers} The Fundamental Occupation
3. Artisans ⎫
4. Merchants ⎬ Accessory Occupations

At the top of society are the scholars, the literati, that is, the spokesmen for the ruling class. Heading the lower class are the peasant farmers, the fundamental producers. Not so honorable are the artisans and merchants because their activities depart from physiocratic essentials. In theory, the farmer is given an honorable place by way of putting down the big merchants. In reality, farmers are treated with no less contempt than any other members of the lower class, all of whom are

A scene from Lu Hsun's short story, "The Divorce." Original.

regarded as so much "meat and fish" supplying the energy
needs of the governing class. The governing class actually includes wealthy and powerful merchants, but they are classified
with lowly artisans and petty merchants by the literati as a
method of demonstrating that only the scholastic portion of
the ruling class holds the right to classify who is who. The
men who do the rationalizing of high culture take themselves
as its superior product, and they are able to make everybody
else believe this.

A related task is to persuade the nonelite to accept inequality. The *Sacred Edict* says:

> Reflect—all you people, whether scholars, farmers, workmen or merchants, have an occupation handed down in a family. The scholar wishes that his sons should succeed to his literary fame; the farmer that he should plow, weed and reap. [XI:5]

The *Sacred Edict* cautions that "persons must on no account abandon the Fundamental Occupation" because agriculture is the "Source of Power" (IV:5). It is wrong for "those now in humble circumstances to seek wealth and honor in some future day" (VII:15). The peasant is asked to "seek no happiness that does not pertain to your lot in life" (VII:15).

But clearly, a peasant's contentment with his humble lot is self-enforcing; it proceeds not from his being enjoined against upward mobility by the state, but because his fellow villagers call for a Cult of Poverty that denies mobility. The statesmen of high culture thus are allowed to draw a static model of stratification, in which these scholars may count themselves a birth elite, while the nonelite likewise have their status "handed down in a family." Actually, upward mobility does occur, but it is more than offset by a net mobility downward into the Sink of Death.

Elite status is unambiguous. Either one attains legal title to it or one does not. If the scholar alone stands high, it is because there is no middle ground to declare. Naturally, variations in wealth occur in the elite sector, but the important thing that members of the elite take note of among themselves is the variation in political status. This ranges from the holder of a *sheng yuan* degree (or its purchased equivalent) taken at the district examinations, to the highest civil officer in the land. It is the peasantry, legally powerless as a nonprivileged class, that is left with differences in property ownership as the sole basis for stratification within its own ranks. But even here the Cult of Poverty tends to level off the show of these differences. When the peasant looks upward to the ranks of the elite, all are for him equally statesmen of the realm, from local gentry to government officials.

It is in recognizing the unequivocalness of elite status that the peasant recognizes the nonprivileged status of his own world. The route of social mobility up and out of that world calls for shedding the values of folk culture and assuming the values of high culture, a profound change. Mobility is an all-or-nothing proposition, one reflected in the proverbial saying, "Overnight the poor student becomes a somebody."

The famous eighteenth-century author, Wu Ching-tzu, found something ridiculous to satirize in that overnight vault into fame launched by graduation from the examination halls, in his epic novel of manners, *The Scholars*. He has one of his characters, Fan Chin, finally pass the provincial examinations at the age of fifty-four after twenty trials in the district preliminaries.

Fan Chin returns home, before the results are posted, to find his wife and mother faint with hunger. No food has been in the house for the last two days. Taking a hen under his arm, he goes out in search of a customer. In the meantime, government heralds come riding up to the door, plant banners announcing Fan Chin's success, and press into his hovel of a house to demand a tip and their share of a victory feast. More horsemen gallop onto the scene as neighbors rush out to fetch the master home. Other neighbors pour in gifts of eggs, chickens, wine, and rice. In disbelief, Fan Chin is dragged home by main force to read the announcement, whereupon he is transported by a fit of delirious joy and runs screaming from the house, straight through a duck pond and on back into the market area, dripping slime and frothing at the mouth. A search party led by his father-in-law, Butcher Hu, finds Fan Chin in the middle of the street still crowing, "I've passed! I've passed!" The appearance of Butcher Hu, the one person Fan Chin most fears in life, snaps him out of his fit, and he returns home to dismiss the heralds. No one is more proud of the honor done the family than Butcher Hu.

But until that sensational moment, Butcher Hu did nothing but ceaselessly revile his son-in-law for his ambition. After Fan Chin passed the preliminaries at the district halls,

> Butcher Hu spat in his face, and poured out a torrent of abuse. "Don't be a fool!" he roared. "Just passing one examination has turned your head completely—you're like a toad trying to swallow a swan! And I hear you scraped through not because of your essay, but because the examiner pitied you for being so old. Now, like a fool, you want to pass the higher examination and become an official. But do you know who those officials are? They are the stars in heaven! Look at

the Chang family in the city. All those officials have pots of money, dignified faces and big ears. But your mouth sticks out and you've a chin like an ape's. You should piss on the ground and look at your face in the puddle! You look like a monkey, yet you want to become an official. Come off it! Next year I shall find a teaching job for you with one of my friends so that you can make a few taels of silver to support that old, never-dying mother of yours and your wife—and it's high time you did. Yet you ask me for travelling expenses! I kill just one pig a day, and only make ten cents per pig. If I give you all my silver to play ducks and drakes with, my family will have to live on air." The butcher went on cursing at full blast, till Fan Chin's head spun.

Fearing his father-in-law more than ever after this yeasty diatribe, Fan Chin had secretly traveled to the provincial examinations on funds begged from his fellow candidates.

Now that Fan Chin has succeeded, no reader of the novel can miss the crude irony of Butcher Hu's celebration:

"Why should I go on killing pigs? My worthy son-in-law will be able to support me in style for the rest of my life. I always said that this worthy son-in-law of mine was very learned and handsome, and that not one of those Chang and Chou family officials in the city so much looked the fine gentleman."

After the heralds depart, the next visitation is by the head of that very Chang family with whose dignified face Butcher Hu previously had compared Fan Chin's with an ape's. A retainer is in the advance.

"Mr. Chang has come to pay his respects to the newly successful Mr. Fan."

By this time the sedan chair was already at the door. Butcher Hu dived into his daughter's room and dared not come out. While the neighbors scattered in all directions, Fan Chin went out to welcome the visitor, who was one of the local gentry. He was wearing an official's gauze cap, sunflower-colored gown, gilt belt and black shoes. He was a provincial graduate and had served as a magistrate in his time.

Once inside, ex-magistrate Chang cultivates a distant social connection with Fan Chin, who is now on the official waiting list for appointment. His influence is worth capturing.

"Sir," he said, "although we live in the same district, I have never been able to call on you."

"I have long respected you," replied Fan Chin, "but have never had the chance to pay you a visit."

"Just now I saw the list of successful candidates. Your patron, Mr. Tang, was a pupil of my grandfather; so I feel very close to you."

Mr. Chang seals his claim on Fan Chin by giving him enough material possessions to start a new and prosperous life.

"Sir, you are certainly frugal." He took from his servant a packet of silver, and states, "I have nothing to show my respect except these fifty taels of silver, which I beg you to accept. Your honorable home is not good enough for you and it will not be convenient when you have many callers. I have an empty house on the main street by the east gate, which has three courtyards with three rooms each. Allow me to present it to you. When you move there, I can profit by your instruction more easily."

After that, all manner of people offered Fan Chin presents of land and shops, and "some poor couples came to serve him in return for his protection."

The episode concludes with the dawning realization by Fan Chin's mother that her new house and all the goods and servants in it do in fact belong to her.

When the old lady heard this, she picked up the fine porcelain and the cups and chopsticks inlaid with silver, and examined them carefully, one by one. Then she went into a fit of laughter. "All mine!" she crowed. Screaming with laughter she fell backwards, choked, and lost consciousness.

It is clear, for all the author's satire, that successful mobility is measured by power, and that power in turn is conditional upon holding political status, either as a ranking or retired bureaucrat in government or as a titled candidate. Power is given by association with government, and wealth follows power. Inlaid chopsticks and porcelain cups come after the fact. Wealth has neither prestige nor security without power. Upward mobility is achieved only when the motivated social climber comes to stand among the rulers or among those eligible to rule. Arrival is marked by holding one or more examination degrees, won or purchased from the state or conferred by the state. "Only the scholar stands high."

Elites, therefore, are first of all power persons. Power, in the name of empire, enables them to draw income from land, service, business, or office; to find security of property; and to enjoy prestige and well-being of person. Rank, not wealth, is the social measure of elite status. Rank is formalized in terms of academic degrees and official titles, for which paper diplomas and certificates (displayed in the ancestral temple) and different costumes (worn on public occasions) are the visible evidence. Mr. Chang wears the dress of a county magistrate in calling upon Fan Chin.

Strictly speaking, the elite are not merely one socioeconomic class within Chinese civilization. They are, in their own view, the very carriers of civilization; the peasants are just so many energy slaves. Such a broad interpretation of self-interest rules out any political unity among the elite beyond identification as Chinese. It would be a presumptuous peasant who allowed himself cultural identity of similar scope.

Gentry families necessarily live off the peasant landscape in their own localities. But the power to do so is gained on a translocal basis. Each family centers in a tissue of influential connections. Reaching out from home base, the approach to power is personal. Mr. Chang, a retired official, comes to make a claim upon Fan Chin, a new candidate for official position.

The Chinese name for the potential to mobilize power-oriented relationships is "face." Peasants lack face altogether. They share power at the zero point. Their response to the presence of elites is flight or avoidance. When ex-magistrate Chang called upon Fan Chin, all the neighbors scattered and even Butcher Hu went into hiding. But the same neighbors were not afraid to approach Fan Chin himself. They brought him gifts, entreating his patronage. The mode of address to a gentleman of their own locality is supplicating.

Elite persons rank each other in terms of power differences. But for peasants there is no face to measure; property is the only basis for measuring status differences. Differences in wealth divide the peasantry into roughly three groups: rich peasants (they have surplus to spare), middle peasants (they manage to make ends meet), and poor peasants (they live in a debt economy). There are also farm laborers, nonagricultural workers, tradesmen, artisans, shopkeepers, petty merchants, all with varying income. But while economic inequalities exist, the display of economic advantage carries no prestige.

Quite the opposite. A new parcel of land, patterned ceiling paper, glass windows, or an added wing on the house—if expenditures on these do not excite envy, they will invite blackmail. The village bully may place a bag of salt in the doorway of a rich peasant and then inform the salt inspector of a violation of the state monopoly, for which the enterprising tattler will be paid his tip.

Such is the insecurity of property unshielded by face. The peasant does not long to grace his daily life with porcelain cups or inlaid chopsticks even if he can afford them. At most he will sport a set of dress-up clothing on ceremonial occasions. Sumptuary laws pronounced by the state are in agreement with the custom of a self-enforcing Cult of Poverty, with its self-exploitation and sanctimonious thrift. Plain living, acted out in the fear of envy or of the bag of salt planted in the doorway, makes for the appearance of economic leveling among the nonelite.

No more emphatic spokesman for the Cult of Poverty can be found than Butcher Hu. His spirited abuse of Fan Chin, in advance of his son-in-law's success at the provincial examinations, is completely in keeping with peasant sensibilities. He spits on a *sheng yuan,* a district graduate licensed to move on to the next stage, the one that really counts, in the quest for office. Butcher Hu regards his son-in-law as unworthy to aspire to that. There were about a million *sheng yuan* degrees extant in Wu Ching-tzu's time, a third of them purchased. Most of them were acquired by wealthy commoners in order to protect themselves from extortion. Neither Butcher Hu's nor Fan Chin's family is nearly wealthy enough to require such protection. So Butcher Hu is unimpressed with Fan Chin's license. He wants Fan Chin to hire out as a tutor to some landowning family and get on with the business of earning a living.

Butcher Hu knows full well that the examination system is an open door to all who wish to achieve privileged status. He acknowledges the Chinese version of the log cabin myth that "overnight the poor student becomes a somebody." The door to mobility is open; perhaps for most it takes wealth to enter it. But for all it takes ambition. Butcher Hu curses Fan Chin's ambition. His cursing instructs Fan Chin that ambition is a product of high culture and does not belong to the Green Circle. Peasant life aims at contentment—that is, at staying above the expendables on the one hand and avoiding elite values on the other. Face and ambition go together as part of high culture. Lack of face and the Cult of Poverty go against mobility aspirations in folk culture. The peasantry does not need persuading by the *Sacred Edict* to accept social inequality.

Butcher Hu's imagery is eloquent. Officials are Stars in Heaven. Fan Chin, reaching high, is a monkey. His words dramatize the fact that the imperial system of stratification has only two strata. Moving from the bottom to the top means renouncing the values of folk culture for those of high culture, or as Butcher Hu would say, the mutation of monkey into star.

CHAPTER 8

THE KITCHEN GOD

PEASANT religion is not the religion of a complete society. There is no village solidarity for religious sentiments to take as an object of worship because folk society by definition is a partial society. The folk community is merely a setting for the life of conjugal families, not for any village-wide collectivity. What is validated by folk religion is each family's mistrust of fellow villagers. And the symbol of family anarchy—the striving of families in the absence of a community charter— is Tsao-shen, the kitchen god.

Tsao-shen is the supernatural inspector and policeman of the family in all respects throughout the year. The god is represented by a paper image and an inscription to the effect that he is the "eyes and ears of Heaven above." He receives burning incense twice a month, the first fruits of the harvest, and a birthday celebration at his altar place above the kitchen stove. At the end of the year the paper god is burned and sent on his way to report family behavior to the Jade Emperor, at which audience the new year's fortune will be decided.

The mythological charter of the god and his mission in the world, however, is almost completely unknown to the people with the greatest stake in his surveillance. Yet the myth is as much a part of the total religious complex surrounding the kitchen god as is the worship of him. The myth is known only to the literati, in a work titled *The Sacred Book of the Original Vows of the Kitchen God*. In defaulting knowledge of the myth to the elite, commoners are left with the observance or nonobservance of certain taboos that will please or displease the god.

The kitchen god belongs to a class of beatific spirits called *shen* that includes earth gods, door gods, gods of city walls and moats, spirits of the hills and rivers, and the like. *Shen* bring good and protect men against the bad inflicted by *kwei:* specters, demons. *Shen* are manifestations of the Yang principle of the universe, *kwei* of the Yin principle. Yin and Yang

Tsao-shen. After a woodcut in Clarence B. Day, Chinese Peasant
Cults, *Shanghai, 1940.*

express the order of the macrocosm, or Tao, which is made immanent in each man at birth. Man is a microcosmic version of Tao. From Yang comes man's intellect and virtues, from Yin his passions and vices. The balance of these principles within him is conditioned by the interplay of the same kinds of soul-stuff, *shen* and *kwei,* that populate the rest of the universe. *Shen* animate all celestial bodies and all natural objects and events; and *kwei* swarm everywhere in numbers innumerable. The Yang principle, identified with Heaven, is elevated over the Yin principle, identified with earth. This is the same Heaven that the emperor, as Son of Heaven, worships in his exclusive act of ancestor worship on behalf of the realm. Heaven, then, is the chief *shen* or god, who animates all spirits, good and bad. No gods visit good nor specters bad on men without Heaven's authorization or its silent consent. In the *Shu Ching* it is written:

> It is Heaven's way to give felicity to the good and bring misfortune upon the bad. [IV, iv, 8]

Heaven's distribution of rewards and punishments is anthropomorphized in the person of the Jade Emperor, a heterodoxical Taoist conception, who holds supreme power over this world and the next. Souls of the deceased pass in review before his Tribunal of Ten Judges. It is in the domain of judgment that the spirit world touches upon the eschatology of Buddhism (an imported religion) and ancestor worship (a native cult of the dead absorbed by Confucianism). Balancing a lifetime's accumulation of merits and demerits, the Judges decide which human souls will be reincarnated, which sent to the Western Paradise or to its opposite, the Buddhist Hell, whose eighteen circles are presided over by King Yenlo and his complex underworld machinery. In the eschatology of ancestor worship, the fate of the soul is decided not alone by individual merit, but by a concerted show of filial piety on the part of descendants, whose concern for the agnatic line will earn them blessings from the departed. Proper burial calls for geomantic divination of the most auspicious currents of *feng-shui,* or cosmic breath, which circulates in the vicinity of the grave site. Souls not so cared for may not only bring misfortune to the impious family, but cause indiscriminate trouble as revanchist specters who seek out the soul-stuff of luckless victims for renewed life. Like all other *kwei*, these specters may be exorcised by shamans or scared away by setting up emblematic representations of the appropriate *shen*, such as door gods, whose left and right stations at the entranceway defend the household within. Souls of commoners become servants of the Jade Emperor's retinue; those of the elite receive official posts in the celestial bureaucracy. Eminent scholars, statesmen, and generals may be deified and become the objects of special cults. The state cult of Confucius is the preeminent example.

Scholars stand high, among other reasons, because they are pillars of Tao. They know the Confucian classics. Therefore they know the order of the world. They by definition are beyond the reach of specters. Officials are even more immune from evil. For they are appointed to office by the Son of Heaven, who shares with Heaven a lordly mastery over all spirits in heaven and on earth. His appointees are delegates of his power over the spirit world. Hence the peasantry looks up to gentry and officialdom as powerful allies in the eternal war against specters. Indeed, it is part of an official's duty to take the lead in exorcising work in times of epidemic disease, whether they believe in specters or not. The Dutch ethnographer, J. J. M. DeGroot, observes of these officials that

> The stupid confidence of the people in their exorcising capacities goes so far as to ascribe these capacities to characters or signs written with red ink pencils which they have used for writing their letters and decrees. Such pencils are fixed over doors, or placed on the sick to cure them; underlings in tribunals and offices sell them to the people and to shopkeepers for a goodly price, as also visiting cards of mandarins, impressions of their seals, waste envelopes, and so on, in particular those of viceroys, provincial chief judges, and other dignitaries of first rank. Such things are also burned to ashes, mixed with water, and given to patients to drink. The poor, who cannot afford to buy them, content themselves with those of schoolmasters or other members of the learned class, even of schoolboys; or they invite these persons to draw small circles of red ink around the pustles and ulcers from which children in all parts of China so commonly suffer.

DeGroot's opinion of the peasantry as "stupid" for its literal faith in the power of the elite to chase demons or specters is not far wide of the mark. The same view is held by the elite.

The exact word would be "superstitious." Superstitions are cognitive relics of systematic doctrine. Only men of high culture comprehend a global knowledge of the spirit world. They quite rightly treat the garbled fragments of belief that filter down to the Green Circle as unreflective superstition.

The intellectual difference between coherent doctrine and superstition makes for a power difference between the upper and lower classes. Take the Fox Woman as a case of belief in were-animalism. P'u Sung-Ling (d. 1715) in his novel of domestic manners, *Hsing-shin Yin-yuan Chuan* (*The Tale of a Conjugal Union to Arouse the World*), casts the Fox Woman in the role of an agent of Buddhist retribution. A shrewish wife, Su Chia, is given to tormenting her husband for his having killed an Immortal Fox in his former life, which fox Su Chia is the reincarnation. The husband lives in fear that Su Chia will expose his shameful secret, that he bribed an examiner to pass him. Here the idea of Buddhist retribution, together with a strict sense of Confucian morality, is used as a mere literary device on which to hang a string of sensational episodes in which Su Chia tortures her husband. P'u Sung-Ling also appeals to the Fox Woman theme in many of his short stories collected under the title, *Liao-chai Chih-i,* which is widely known in the West as *Strange Tales from a Chinese Studio.* The scholar who squanders his patron's money on drinking and wenching and who then fails to pass his examination draws the observation of his fellows that he must have been bewitched by the Fox Woman, who entered his bed unbidden and seduced him out of a bent for trouble making. Here demon possession serves only a minor explanatory function, giving an interesting and perhaps amusing gloss to the mishandled affairs of scholars without implying their surrender to literal belief in were-animalism.

But peasants take the idea of possession by the Fox Woman at face value. In *Children of the Black-haired People,* a well-researched novel by Evan King, a peasant couple try out the freedom-of-marriage reform advocated by the new revolutionary government of the late 1920s. They arranged the marriage between themselves without the aid of a go-between, a thing unheard of except among expendables. What is more, the bride showed herself at the wedding feast instead of sequestering herself. Neighboring villagers went before the local

gentry and accused her of being the incarnation of the Fox
Woman from the village after having her feet cut off.

Peasant fear of the woman was triggered by her violation
of marriage customs. Life in the Green Circle is conservative
with a vengeance. The constant vigil of mistrust that villagers
keep on one another, ever alert for signs of advantage to attack with malice and envy, makes for conformity not alone
in customs of hard work and conspicuous underconsumption.
All traditional usages call for zealous observance. The strong
feelings aroused by nonconformity are made public in the
imagery of demon possession.

But the educated men of high culture are more enlightened
in matters of demonology. For them, the Fox Woman is little
more than a literary cliché. They act as magicians in the
peasants' war against specters not out of naïve belief in evil
spirits but out of political expediency. The ruling elite depend
on folk conservatism. Demonology keeps life in the Green
Circle self-regulating. The cost of administering public affairs
for peasants, in return for exploiting them, would abolish
privilege.

The unreflective ideas of the folk strike the elite as stupid.
Of course. Peasant religion is no religion at all. It is a fraction
of superstitions and taboos dropped from the full theology
of Tao expanded by high culture. But the full theology itself
was expanded out of folk religion in the first place, using
materials that derive from prehistoric times when folk society
was still a complete society, before civilization absorbed it.
From the very beginnings of their rule, the men of high culture have converted Neolithic dumb shows into sophisticated
numbers, which in turn have been directed downward for unreflective assimilation. Theological doctrine is continuous with
folk superstition because high culture in the Agrarian State has
no other option than to contrive its doctrinal formulations out
of unformulated folk culture. The literati hold the content of
contents. They can explicate one set of ideas in the religious
realm in terms of another, the political, as in the case of the
gentlemen who drove out the Fox Woman.

Political control is instituted in a number of official temples
throughout all districts of the empire on the principle of
"instruction through worship." The invocatory texts read at
these temples contain the same moralistic injunctions to be

found in the *Sacred Edict*. There is the added promise that what disobedience escapes the bamboo rod of the magistrate will surely meet with "unseen punishment" of the gods in the next world.

In these proceedings the government has attempted to universalize local gods and thus to measure the power of all gods to reward or punish human behavior in terms of good or bad subjects. About one-quarter of the *shen* worshiped by the peasantry fall within the imperial calendar, which schedules two sacrifices a year at the beginning of spring and autumn. The other *shen* are worshiped on their birthdays. The state recognizes the two calendars of worship in its designation of *kuan-ssu* (official cults) and *min-ssu* (people's cults). There is some overlapping. Those *shen* captured for the *kuan-ssu* are put up as spiritual exemplars of the imperial order, those who are said to uphold the literary tradition, military strength, government, agriculture, the arts and crafts, and moral goodness. The *min-ssu* take their gods as objects of worship for private blessings: prosperity, good health, protection from specters.

In acknowledging the job of rationalization done by high culture, the peasant also acknowledges the continuity of theological doctrine with his own folk superstitions. This is evident in the annual round of festivals that all villages of the empire celebrate whatever the other differences in local culture. But the Green Circle is only a setting for the religious practices of families. They enact no public affirmation of community life. The village is an incomplete religious unit. Its practices are completed in doctrines formulated by the elite. The peasant knows that the literati know whatever needs to be known about theology.

In times of agricultural crises, caused by specters, the magistrate is obliged to act as district magician. In time of drought he may publicly beat the idol of Ch'eng-huang, the city god, for failure to bring rain. With the advent of the Republican regime, magistrates ceased to carry out such practices. This was a loss for the peasantry who now had no access to the best supernatural remedy. In some areas they took to praying for rain while parading one of their local gods from the *min-ssu*, the water god. This was less effective, in the peasant view, but commoners have no access to Ch'eng-huang, which belongs to the imperial pantheon of the *kuan-ssu*, without official intercession. Peasants cannot take this god for their own any more than they can usurp the authority of the government. Not only that. They are ignorant about the myth connected with the god. Deference to the mythological formulations of high culture is another sign that folk culture lacks a power base of its own.

Thus, while the doctrinal content of high culture is continuous with the superstitions of folk culture, the peasant does not participate in high culture. He knows only that elite persons hold a monopoly on theological knowledge. Insofar as the folk are ignorant of state-managed doctrine, to that extent have they abdicated their mythological charter as a people with a collective identity and a sense of communal oneness in the Green Circle. Were folk religion to underwrite community integration, it could not at the same time function to admit the community, as a part-society, to the civilization. Folk society lost its basis for group consensus in its transformation from an isolated state of Neolithic culture to a nonisolated one. The resulting surrender of religious self-sufficiency has set limits to a sense of communal solidarity within the Green Circle. The peasant is thereby allowed to have his culture two ways: community oriented, looking inward, away from civilization, but yet being part of civilization. The result is family anarchy.

The religious anarchy of families is expressed in the worship of a household god, Tsao-shen, the kitchen god. Tsao-shen symbolizes the rightness and legitimacy of each conjugal family to pursue its own good with no concern for others in the same community. Indeed, the others are regarded as potential competitors. One family's gain is another's loss. If Tsao-shen acts as an agent of material prosperity, he must do so at the expense of others. Small wonder that he at the same time acts as a protector against demon possession. Fear of specters is a public realization that fellow villagers are capable of heartless competition and malicious envy.

On the surface it appears that the Green Circle enjoys some show of community spirit in the cooperative building of village temples. Of the many temples to be found in most Chinese villages, a few belong to the *kuan-ssu*, erected from tax moneys at the direction of the magistrate. These temples, however, do not stand in the name of the village as do altars to She, the god of the soil, which stand in the name of administrative units at the provincial, district, or prefectural levels. The village is not an administrative unit. Temples belonging to the *min-ssu,* undigested by the state, are built from moneys raised by private subscription. The same is true among urban neighborhoods filled with folk migrated to the city. Typical of *min-ssu* temples in the village are those dedicated to the T'u-ti, the paired gods of earth and grain, whose birthdays fall in the early spring, and to Hua-kuang, the god of fire and hearth, whose birthday comes in the late fall. Gods such as the T'u-ti certainly touch upon the ecological fundamentals of peasant life and they make sense as objects of common concern. Temples to them are raised from public subscription. But worship there is individual, not collective. What is more, temple contributions may be described as an instance of ceremonial extravagance whose function is to reduce the tensions of mutual suspicion by allowing economic surplus to be spent on a display of merit.

Lists of contributions are kept in the temples; donors get their money's worth by seeing their names posted in a conspicuous place, as subscribers of such and such an amount. (The ability to recognize one's name is not incompatible with the functional nonliteracy of peasant culture.) In some regions the amount subscribed is inflated by a factor of four or five, or whatever, according to the customary fiction. The number of temples in a village may reach a ratio as high as one to every ten families. It is a common saying that the more temples a village has, the poorer it is. Temple building serves the Cult of Poverty, not the community, with a form of ceremonial expenditure that has the effect of leveling wealth in appearance if not in fact.

Ceremonial spending to the same effect is done on marriages and funerals. The debt caused by these extravagances is enjoined by the fifth section of the *Sacred Edict.*

> On marriage:
> Although it is your duty to fit out your sons and daughters in marriage, you must at the same time have an eye to your means, and do what you are able. Why go out of your way to act beyond your proper positions, and aim at all sorts of display—stylish silk festoons, gems, embroidery, sedan chairs, umbrellas, drums, music; killing pigs, slaying sheep till you are up to your eyes in debt? [V:7]

The ceremonial accessories referred to are rented ones. All the tinsel and glass and other embellishments are supplied by sedan-chair rental shops for whatever degree of show is wanted. Music making is by hired road troupes.

On funerals:
Even if parents die, while to give them burial is the first duty of the living, you should simply prepare funeral requisites up to the measure of your means: all that is needed is that parents should be interred in peace; these are the only requirements of filial piety. Why do you not apply your mind to matters of such great importance as these, instead of calling in Buddhist and Taoist priests to chant the Liturgy and go through the ritual of Penitence? You invite guests, get up feasts, have theatricals and music, making the skies ring with your noise, culminating in acting stories and performing plays, some dancing, others capering, till it seems as though the death of parents were a matter of extreme joy. [V:7]

The *Sacred Edict* criticizes these expenses by way of backing up the state's sumptuary laws. But the renting of silks and sedan chairs is no imitation of gentry consumption habits. Ceremonial extravagance is part of the Cult of Poverty, a defense against mutual suspicion. The underlying formula is: "Behold, you neighbors of mine, how it is that I spend my wealth not on personal luxuries but only in the discharge of my social obligations. I have done nothing to enrich myself at the expense of others. I have, rather, spent my substance meritoriously."

Ceremonial extravagance serves to act out a denial of the very selfishness worshiped in the person of the kitchen god. The men of high culture view this self-seeking worship of the kitchen god with contempt because it only goes to reveal once again the powerlessness of nonpersons. The elite say that peasants merely worship (*pai*), seeking individual material welfare. But the elite themselves conduct elevated sacrifices (*chi*) by way of thanking Heaven for blessings given to a collectivity in the form of a great family or a powerful alliance of families. Peasants merely play an animistic lottery, as at dice. This is viewed as no more ethical than gambling on the murder and theft of a rich man to advance one's fortune, a common practice where upward mobility is restricted and which further explains why property is insecure without a position of power to protect it. The elite hold this power by definition. It is based in elaborate kinship organization, which takes ancestor worship as its chief ceremony. The sacrificial rites of ancestor worship, conducted out of formulated theory, offer up thanks for blessings given to that collectivity. That is to *chi,* to make sacrificial offerings as a group for a group. But to *pai,* as peasants do, is to seek individual gain out of superstition and ignorance of Tao. If peasants were to make sacrifices in the interests of the village collectivity they no longer would be peasants, subordinate to exploitation by the ruling elite, but an interest group with its own power base. Worship of the kitchen god is a sign that in surrendering to family anarchy they have surrendered their mythological charter as a people in their own right.

CHAPTER 9

SANCTIMONIOUS HUSBANDRY

IN *Peasant Society and Culture,* Robert Redfield, the late professor of anthropology at the University of Chicago, wrote that the good life of peasants everywhere includes:

> . . . an involvement of agricultural labor with traditional, often reverential, sentiments about the land; the connection of that labor with ideals as to personal worth; the inculcation in the young of endurance and hard work rather than a disposition to take risks and to perform personal exploits; the acceptance of arduous labor, yet with a great enjoyment of its surcease.

The imagery is pastoral: the cheerful rustic who loves the soil, who reverences ancestral ways.

Redfield contrasts the sacral attachment of the peasantry to the soil with the economic expediency of industrial man. In this contrast he sees a polarity of world view in attitudes toward natural resources. The natural piety of the peasant makes for a "moral order" different from the "technical order" of industrial civilization with its instrumental address to nature, which is exploited with confidence and rational efficiency. The technical order involves man in an I-It relationship to nature, the moral order in an I-Thou relationship. The lack of technical mastery in the folk world accounts for the I-Thou approach. Men in folk societies extend to nature the same concern for personal values that they hold for each other. Redfield's theory correctly calls attention to the importance of personalized relationships in peasant society. It does not follow, however, that because relationships are personalized they must be pious in tone; they may be grievous. Folk society in China most certainly is not welded together in cooperative harmony against the hardships of peasant life.

Nor does the moral order require the sanctification of husbandry as such. Peasant love of the soil is ambivalently maintained. Power, privilege, leisure, wealth, luxuries, all these are recognized as benefits of high culture. But the peasant learns not to learn about them. Such preventive ignorance of the outside world makes for ambivalence toward folk culture, which is the keynote of the Cult of Poverty.

The Cult of Poverty induces the peasant to work more and consume less. The morality of hard work does not allow for a display in daily consumption of the economic advantages won by hard work. Poverty, real or feigned, is elevated to a principle of the good life. In *Peasant Life in China,* Fei Hsiao-t'ung writes:

> Thrift is encouraged. Throwing away anything which has not been properly used will offend heaven, whose representative is the kitchen god. For instance, no rice should be wasted. Even when the rice becomes sour, the family must try to finish it all. Clothes are used by generations, until they are worn out. Those worn out clothes will not be thrown away but used for the bottom of the shoes. . . .

The shabbiness of the peasant costume is worn as a uniform. Good clothes are saved for wear during ceremonial occasions, when ritualized spending is required to neutralize suspicions that one is hoarding wealth in a secret effort to get ahead of others. Any deviation from acting out a daily poor-show may, in addition to exciting local envy, even attract the attention of the district magistrate. A. H. Smith noted in his late nineteenth-century classic, *Village Life in China,* that:

> In a time of intense excitement over alleged kidnapping of children, we have known a man to be apprehended in open court and examined as a bad character, because the color of his clothes was unusual.

Uniformity of costume among peasants in their own market area contrasts with the exotic outfit affected by the local bully, who gains his éclat from a studied combination of accepted tatterdemalion with deviant accessories. A. H. Smith notes the effect:

> His outer leggings are not improbably so tied as to display a lining which is more expensive than the outside; and his shoes are invariably worn down at the heel, perhaps to make an ostentatious display of a silk embroidered heel to the cotton stocking—a touch of splendour adapted to strike awe into the rustic beholder.

Significantly, the *Sacred Edict* has cause to mention these bullies. In reproving their mischief, it uses a euphemistic term, *hsiang-tang chung hao-chieh* (III:6), which literally means "strong heroes of the village." The real meaning is "tough guys around the village." Bullies are commoners who do not accept the low ceiling placed on ambition by the Cult of Poverty. Frustrated by the stratification system that allows true mobility to be realized only by a quantum jump to the ranks of scholar-statesmen, they find their outlet in bullying and dominating their fellow villagers. Achievement of success in this way of life comes with winning the title, "village king." Bullies are strong and may cultivate their strength through the exercise of "fist and foot" gymnastics, Chinese boxing. They may be hired in gangs, by local gentry and others, to settle quarrels by force. The *Sacred Edict* refers to them in delicate terms, knowing full well that in times of government weakness, these "heroes" can lead bandit gangs or play an important role in rebellions.

Village bullies form a floating population that neither owns nor cultivates land. The *Sacred Edict* gives this description:

> They associate with some of the underlings at the law courts, and learn how to draw up an indictment containing some ambiguous phrases—how to make use of a few expressions that will hoodwink and blind the mind. Wishing to do the community out of money and wine for their own use, at every turn they beguile and excite others to wrangle over the least thing, adding the remark, "Lose money but not reputation." They stir up strife in all sorts of ways, perhaps by perfecting some artful device to set people at variance, or else acting contrary to all reason and right, scare them into giving money. [III:8]

Or, as Smith observes:

> The yamen is the spider's web, and the bully is the large insect which drives the flies into the net. . . . [He] will not let others alone, but . . . is always inserting himself into their affairs with a view to extracting some benefit for himself. . . . There is always about one of these villages bullies a general atmosphere of menace, as if he were thirsting for an opportunity to issue an ultimatum. . . . [He] is able to hold in terror the man who has property to lose, by an open or an implicit threat of vengeance, against which the man of property cannot defend himself.

The presence of the village bully thus adds to the pressure of mutual suspicion in making for a Cult of Poverty. The

propertied peasant had better play poor lest he be marked
for the bully's threat to beat people, burn houses, or destroy
crops.

Redfield's moral order does indeed promote a moral connection between agricultural labor and personal worth, but it
does not promote a sense of community in any case because
the community defaulted its ethical charter to high culture
when folk culture was absorbed by civilization. The moral
order of the peasantry promotes family anarchy. The connection between labor and personal worth is made for each
family in its claim to its own share of limited resources. In a
closed economy the striving for material gain—for land, for
irrigation water, for goods—is a disturbance to the social
order. Gain means plunder of others. Therefore, contentment
with one's own limited share, without striving for more, is
essential—at least in appearance. But the malicious suspicion
that others are actually striving for more behind the appearance of contentment is inevitable. One's own sense of worth
and attachment to the soil always is at odds with another's.

In irrigated areas such as the Yangtze River valley, mutual
suspicion characteristically revolves around disputes over water
rights. Small plats may adjoin in the same field without de-
marcation by retaining walls or dikes. The different parties to
such a field then share its water resources, but not without fear
that someone has not done his fair share of pumping. To make
up for cheating on the part of others, always a good excuse to
make some gain on the sly, one may dredge deeper channels
to one's own plat in order to receive the greater water reserve.
And there is always the trick of tapping water from a higher
field for a lower one. Conflict over rights to the natural
products of the feeder canal—fish, grass, and shrimp—may
excite intervillage hostilities in the form of litigation or even
combat. It is easy to see why voluntary cooperation within or
between villages is impossible to muster for the sake of local
water control. Hence the villagers' appeal to local gentry, for
a fee, to manage their own labor in the construction of waterworks. Mutual suspicion moves peasants to supplicate gentry
with the plea: "Tell us what to do."

Mutual distrust may also arise between brothers immediately
they divide their father's estate. A. H. Smith describes the
process:

The middlemen who have to conduct operations, begin by taking an inventory of the numerous pieces of land, the buildings, etc., which they appraise roughly, endeavoring to separate these assets into as many portions as there are to be shares. A certain part of the land is set aside for "nourishing the old age" of the parents; and perhaps another section is reserved for the wedding expenses of unmarried daughters or younger sons. What remains is to be divided, which is accomplished by grouping the portions, and writing the descriptions of the several pieces of land, houses, etc., on pieces of paper which are rolled up and placed in a rice bowl. This is shaken up and it is a courtesy to allow the youngest son to draw first. Whatever is noted on his bit of paper represents his share, and so on until all are drawn. The household furniture, water jars, utensils of every kind, and all the grain and fuel on hand must all be taken out in public in the presence of middlemen to be sure nothing is secreted. We have known a particularly obstreperous son to come to his father's house the day after a division, and under the pretense of looking for something he had lost, to feel in every jar and pot to be sure no beans or millet had escaped him.

Perhaps it was unnecessary for Smith to add:

A Westerner is constantly struck with the undoubted fact that the mere act of dividing property seems to extinguish all sense of responsibility for the nearest kin. It is often replied when we ask why a Chinese does not help his son or his brother who . . . has nothing in the house to eat, "We have *divided* some time ago."

With dismay, the *Sacred Edict* notes the same thing:

All the squabbles that arise among brethren in the present day are on account of property. Some squabble about money, some about land, some about houses, some about food: all sorts of things. What if there is a little unfairness in dividing the family estate, the advantage is still in the family, not shared by an outsider. [I:8]

The *Secret Edict* also comments:

Farmers are accustomed to squabble over their fields. One says, "You have encroached upon my boundary." Another says, "You have plowed over the corner of my ground." And it is needless to say that mutual recriminations ensue when cows, sheep, and other animals have trampled down one's crops. [IX:4]

The state enjoins against such squabbles, between families and neighbors, because it expects family and community to carry the burden of nonadministrative social control in the countryside. But this end actually is served by mutual suspicion. The state in practice elevates mutual suspicion to a legal device of police surveillance (*li-chia*) by redefining it, in the words of the *Sacred Edict,* as "mutual espionage."

> All in the various *li* without exception must be enrolled on the register. Within the *li,* aid each other by diligent search. In the evening ask who is at home and who is absent, which family has anyone coming or going. All questionable persons must be reported at once. The *li-chang* will forthwith notify the magistrate. If everyone lived in quietude, would not things be delightful? [XV:4]

The Confucian state thus draws on an old Legalist theory that the people ought to be organized in groups and be obliged to denounce each other's crimes. But in point of fact, the state organizes nothing below the level of the district magistrate's office. The *li-chia* system of police surveillance is merely a rationalization, flattering to a sense of despotic power on the part of the state, of mutual suspicion, mistrust, jealousy, and envy held between villagers. In the *Sacred Edict* the state piously speaks out against mutual suspicion, but slyly takes advantage of it in the hopes that local quarreling will throw up for prosecution any local wrongdoing threatening to the state. The malice of mutual distrust is so intense—it is the measure of family anarchy—that it actually involves the enjoyment of loss and misfortune on the part of others, as the *Sacred Edict* correctly notes.

> If there be calamity, by all means render assistance; if sickness, by all means ask after the patient; if there be litigation, exert yourself to bring about a reconciliation, and do not accent the quarrel by tale bearing; if there be robbery or fire, combine to give assistance. Do not take pleasure in calamity. Do not undervalue life and scheme, by committing suicide, to incriminate another. [III:3]

The anomie abjured here is a description of what really happens. The fact is that people *do* commit suicide in anger at others. Another trick, a family may place the body of a dead relative on the doorstep of a rival and thereby charge him with murder. The bully can get a bag of salt to plant, but the ordinary villager at least may find a corpse among his own to plant to the same end.

Mutual suspicion is one more factor tending to reduce the size of the peasant family unit to a conjugal family. The conjugal family is the unit that can get the most work out of the least numbers. The meaning of self-sacrificing cooperation in this small group goes beyond economics; it is also a means of defending title to property in a hostile social environment riven with mutual jealousy. The Cult of Poverty has priority over "incense and fire," or biological continuity over the generations. No elaborate cult of ancestors, as in gentry families, interposes a father and son axis between husband-and-wife alliance. Yet the peasant states his claim to his property in terms of filial piety. Fei Hsiao-t'ung reports that, "To sell a piece of land inherited from one's father offends the ethical sense." But the institution of kinship is an expensive one for the peasant to maintain, costing him heavily at weddings and funerals without bringing in any revenue as do the ancestral temples of the gentry, those symbols of powerful joint-family corporations and their organization into lineages or clans. Indeed, peasants claiming membership in a clan are expected to contribute to the building and maintenance of clan temples in exchange for little more than the right, denied nonmembers, to rent land from propertied members. For the peasant to justify his own property rights in the name of kinship can be nothing but platitudinous, witness the fact that in the same name he spends with ritual extravagance in order to be rid of the suspicion that he is accumulating wealth and hiding it.

Filial platitudes regarding the land are necessary. The villagers view each other as rivals in a struggle for limited resources. Family anarchy therefore disallows sentimentalizing about common adversity. Everybody must show his total commitment to his share in order to justify his claim to it. In this way, land is a means of self-assertion. Fei writes:

> The villagers judge a person as good or bad according to his industry in working his land. A badly weeded farm, for instance, will give a bad reputation to the owner. The incentive to work is thus deeper than the fear of hunger.

No one can say of a man, if he exploits his own labor to the limit, removing every weed, dressing every row; if he goes hungry, if he wears tatters; if he embraces poverty as a way of life—no one then can say that he has not demonstrated his rights of ownership to his land. As he wades knee-deep through the flooded rice fields, too busy at planting down the line to pick off the leeches from his calves, the ever-enduring peasant of Redfield's moral order—wedded to the soil, rejoicing for all men at the right turn of the season—is acting out the message for his neighbors: "Hard work makes my land mine against all envy, jealousy, and blackmail."

Yes, the peasant loves the soil. But someone makes him do it. The sanctification of land is a sanctimonious play to a critical audience. The peasant is obliged to assert his claim over what is rightfully his. And the guideline of his behavior, establishing his security in a universe divided by mutual suspicion, is the ambivalent world-view directive, "Love the soil—or else!"

Part Two

High Culture

CHAPTER 10

RIVERS TO GLORY

DYNASTIC government does not make the welfare of the people its object. Unlike the nation-state, the Agrarian State does not administer services. The emperor seeks only to impress regional power persons with his majesty and to make them feel inferior as exploiters of the peasantry unless dependent on the throne for their cultural glamour. Such are the politics of culturalism: political unity depends on the willingness of local elites to borrow ritual forms of imperial glory.

The Ch'ing dynasty, like all other imperial dynasties before it, depends for the support of its culturalism on the most productive region of the realm, enclosed by force from the start, and the transport of its harvest to the metropolitan center. The glories of imperial unity are centered there. The waterways, natural and artificial, that transport the grain tribute to that place are the Rivers of Glory.

Imperial unity means control by the emperor of a Key Economic Area (KEA), that is, the control of a region superior to any other in both agricultural productivity and transport facilities. The KEAs are four in number, two primary ones and two secondary ones.

Primary
A. The Yellow River basin, including the Hwai River system
B. The Lower Yangtze River basin
Secondary
C. The Upper Yangtze River basin (Red basin)
D. The Hsi River system

The strategic importance of these river systems has been stressed by Chi Ch'ao-ting in his classic of Chinese geopolitics, *Key Economic Areas in Chinese History*. Unity exists when the emperor controls either area "A" or "B," with or without areas "C" and "D." No empire can stand on the resources of the latter two, alone or together. See Map 2.

The merit of Chi's work is in demonstrating a close connection between the glorification of imperial authority and the advantage it takes of regional geography. Periods of unity express the throne's control over one KEA where facilities for agricultural productivity (irrigation) and for transport (navigation) permit supply and defense capabilities superior to any other area that rivals might control.

The emperor's geopolitical problem, then, is to make regional powers feel inferior to his own magnificence. This is problematic because he has to look abroad for the means of nourishing that glory. Peking, the capital city, is not located in an especially productive area but rather is near the northern border because of the emperor's prior concern for deploying his military machine against the threat of invasion by steppe nomads. It would therefore be easy for any of the provincial capitals, located along navigable rivers in productive regions, to match the splendor of the metropolitan center if Peking were restricted to its own vicinity for the collection of grain tribute.

The geopolitical history of the empire is the history of the emperor's ability to feed his court by river and canal with supplies from a distance, and to make it the grandest cultural center on earth. Dynasties, however, come and go. These fluctuations measure the pulse of imperial majesty. Dynastic history, including times when the throne has been captured by non-Chinese, is the account of three Unities and two Partitions. See Figure 4.

In the view of Chinese historians, every Partition is a time of chaos, confusion, corruption, and immorality. But Unity is only a unity of cultural authority over elite persons, and centralization is centralization only in political control over government officials. Partition means nothing more than disunity in the realm of high culture. The Green Circle remains intact throughout, except where irrigation is dependent on government waterworks.

At least half the landscape of the Green Circle is irrigated or protected from flooding by dikes, river embankments, and organized flood watching, some of this undertaken by Peking. But where there is government-directed flood control, it is a by-product of navigational maintenance for the sake of the grain tribute. Where there are government-built irrigation facilities, these have been installed for the sake of raising pro-

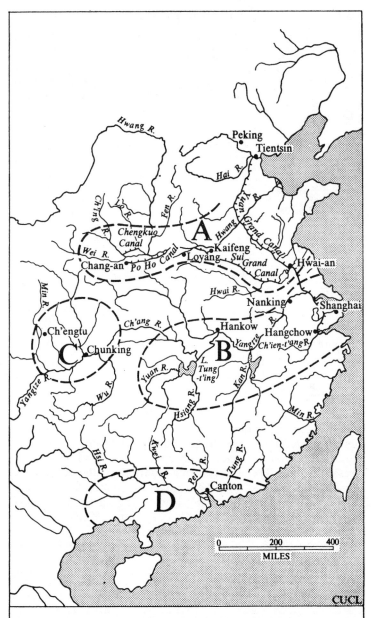

Map 2. Rivers, canals, and Key Economic Areas during various periods of Chinese history. "A" is the KEA for the First Unity, "B" for the Second and Third Unities. "C" and "D" are secondary areas that make for important regional divisions. Adapted from Chi Ch'ao-ting (1936).

FIG. 4 *Major regimes during the era of Cyclical Imperial Conquests*

	Native	Foreign	Foreign and/or Native Partitions
(First Unity)	Ch'in 221–206 B.C. Former Han 206 B.C.–A.D. 25 Later Han A.D. 25–220		
(First Partition)			Three Kingdoms, Western Tsin, Northern and Southern Dynasties 220–589
(Second Unity)	Sui 589–618 T'ang 619–907		
(Second Partition)			Five Dynasties, Sung, Liao, Hsi Hsia, Chin 907–1279
(Third Unity)	Ming 1368–1644	Yuan 1280–1368 Ch'ing 1644–1911	

duction in the KEA enclosed by the throne for its granary, its source of grain tribute for the supply of the metropolitan center. Most irrigation systems are actually built to a smaller scale under the managerial supervision of local gentry for peasant clients. The water source from which the feeder lines are drawn, however, may be a government canal. But again, those major artificial waterways are first and foremost navigational canals. The Grand Canal, uniting KEA "B" with Peking, is named *Yun Ho,* Transport River.

The Manchu government's handbook on the Grand Canal explains:

> The capital stands at the northern part of the empire. The demands for state worship and for the supply of the court,

AT RIGHT: *Driving piles in a river embankment. After a Chinese print.*

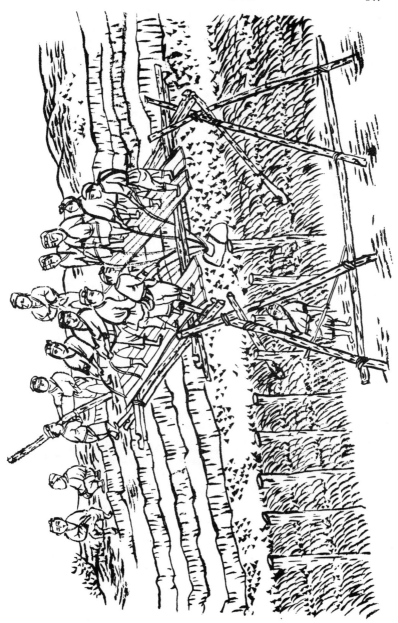

the salaries of officials and stipends for scholars, and, above all, the commissariat for the army, all depend upon the grain tribute. Civil and military officials, and their servants and soldiers whose names are registered in the commissariat records, number 170,000. Assuming that each has a household of eight persons, the total number of persons dependent on the grain tribute would be 1,360,000.

The annual quota of grain moved up the Grand Canal to meet these needs is four hundred thousand tons.

The history of the relationship between the imperial capital and its grain supply, via canal transport, is outlined in Figure 5.

FIG. 5   *Transport canals*

	Imperial Dynasty	KEA	Transport Canal	Route	Imperial Capital
First Unity	Ch'in	A	Chengkuo Canal	E to W from Lo to Ch'ing in Wei valley	Hsien-yang
	Former Han	A	Chengkuo Canal	Same as above	Ch'ang-an
	Later Han	A	Po Ho Canal	W to E from Ch'ang-an on the Wei to the Yellow River	Loyang
Second Unity	Sui	B	Sui Grand Canal	SE to NW from Hangchow to Kaifeng on the Yellow River	Ch'ang-an
	T'ang	B	Sui Grand Canal	Same as above	Ch'ang-an
Third Unity	Yuan	B	Yuan Grand Canal	SE to NE from Hangchow to Peking	Cambaluc (Peking)
	Ming (to 1402)	B			Nanking
	Ming (after 1402)	B	Yuan Grand Canal	SE to NE from Hangchow to Peking	Peking
	Ch'ing	B	Yuan Grand Canal	Same as above	Peking

The imperial nerve center, always contesting with regional power, depends on its transport canal to supply enough glory

and magnificence to win that contest. The contest is one between the unsubstantial culturalism of the emperor and the
substantive power of his governors over men and materials.
The Dragon versus the Local Snakes. Provincial rulers, before
provinces were brought into the empire, used to be lords of
their own kingdoms of similar geographic scope. When kings
became governors, they gladly took up the imperial concept as
a useful aid in enhancing their own local sway. The force of
the emperor's culturalism is strictly derivative: the emperor
impresses men of high culture who, in turn, defer to his glory
because it adds dignity to the business of exploitation in their
home localities.

The political system of empire, which transformed kingdoms into provinces, was initiated by Ch'in Shih Hwang Ti,
the First Emperor. The Ch'in dynasty lasted for only fifteen
years, but the imperial order, founded in 221 B.C., lasted for
over two thousand years.

Province is an elastic translation of several Chinese words
for the maximal administrative unit of empire. Ch'in created
about forty of them, which took the name of *chün,* military
commanderies. These were smaller than the eighteen provinces
of China Proper in Ch'ing times, but some of the geographical
boundaries have remained the same. The minimal unit of empire is the district or *hsien.*

Ch'in Shih Hwang Ti, however, did not originate the *chün.*
He took this unit of organization as it existed in preimperial
times, and made it subordinate to his capital city at Hsien-
yang, across the Wei River from the present-day city of Sian.
Neither did he originate the unit he subordinated to his provinces, the *hsien.*

The *chün* originated in Eastern Chou times as a means of
governing territory captured from the northern barbarians by
the border states of Wei, Chao, Yen, and Ch'in itself. *Chün*
were not hereditary fiefs. Military officers were appointed.
Their job was to hold state frontiers against invasion by the
Hsiung-nu and other Tartar tribes. It was along these frontiers
that the northern states built the defensive walls that Ch'in
Shih Hwang Ti connected to form the Great Wall. During
the Warring States period, *chün* also came to be established
along state frontiers where these had expanded to touch upon
one another. A free peasantry cultivated the wasteland between the feudal holdings belonging to the smaller states of

Fusion China, and government followed this expanding population in the form of military commanderies.

Hsien originated as a means of annexing states defeated in war. The victorious states liquidated the ruling aristocracy of the vanquished states, then replaced it with professional administrators, town by town. These civilian appointees coexisted, where they did not enfeoff their office, with feudal authority in the person of the ruler.

Hsien are the basic building blocks of both the feudal and the imperial order: a central town with its populated countryside no more than a day's cart ride away from the center. The empire expands by adding more of these modular units after the fact. A self-densing peasantry swarms into transformable wasteland and establishes a Chinese landscape of cultivated fields and nucleated settlements. A local elite wins mastery over *hsien*-sized parts of this landscape, the territorial limit of exploitation with overland haulage of grain. Aspirations of the elite are captured for alignment with imperial glory. The emperor's glory is the greater because he can sustain a more magnificent establishment based on long-range haulage of grain by canal.

Ch'in Shih Hwang Ti gave birth to the imperial system when he set up thirty-six, later forty-one, *chün* throughout All-China. Of these commanderies, eighteen were in existence before his time, six in his own state. The transition to empire was complete when he doubled the number and subordinated all of them, by means of personal representation, to a single capital city at Hsien-yang, the capital of All-Within-the-Wall. To each *chün* he named three incumbents, a civil administrator, a military governor, and an overseer. The overseer reported directly to the First Emperor the doings of the other two, who themselves communicated by imperial post with their respective departments at Hsien-yang. But joint administration never failed to cast up its kingpin, a fact of political life openly acknowledged by the terminal Ch'ing regime when it assigned a *hsun-fu,* or coordinator, over each provincial apparatus.

In the First Emperor's design, each province was to be headed by a triumvirate that repeated the triplex functions carried out in the capital city: administrative, military, and supervisory. The play of men out in the provinces was meant to forestall the rise of regional machines based on the enfeoffment of office. After all, provincial governors are the political descendants of the self-styled kings (*wang*) who held sway, with a title usurped from the Chou regent, over regions of provincial magnitude during the Warring States period. Governors are not kings only because they are appointed by the emperor. But they are still kings for all that, for a triennial turn of office, at least. They may enjoy whatever revenues accrue to them out of the royalties of governorship.

The Ch'in empire shortly fell to a coalition of feudal lords. The Han emperors restored the provincial system. They patronized Confucianism with the result that an examination system was instituted for the recruitment of officeholders on the basis of scholastic merit, not birth. The examination system in time fixed the terms by which the organs of central government appointed most provincial officers. The imperial capital came to sustain a magnificent scholarship that made learning stand high for emulation by whomever was motivated to seek office.

What follows is the geopolitical history of empire that lurks behind its constitutional history.

FIRST UNITY

During the first period of imperial unity, the capital received grain from short canal systems running east to west within the same region occupied by the capital itself. This was Kuanchung, the western half of KEA "A."

The Kuanchung region was the scene of Neolithic and Bronze Age cultural evolutions, and also the place from which Ch'in launched its conquest of empire. Ch'in's geographic position is significant. It was in the northwestern corner of China during the time of the Warring States that the ecological interface between steppe and sown land first made its conflict felt. The rise of civilization south of the interface contributed to the realization of a barbarian culture to the north of it.

It was Ch'in Shih Hwang Ti who erected the Great Wall against the Tartar tribes, whose barbarism was specialized enough in his day to cause them to plunder civilized communities. But plunder, the wolf upon the fold, is only a dramatic highlight in the course of regular dependency in the form of trade. Once the Chinese committed themselves to intensive farming, with its displacement of stock breeding, they looked to the steppelands for wool and leather, and for horses. On the other side, it took all the animal products the northern barbarians could muster to exchange for items even more strategic to themselves, namely metal and grain. This is not to mention tea, ceramics, and woven fabrics. The possibilities of trading and raiding for grain, in particular, had led the steppe peoples to gradually abandon the supplementary farming of their ancestors. Long before the building of the Great Wall, Neolithic culture had spread to both sides of this boundary. But rising population densities to the south tested unintended limits of the environment, eventually making for an irreversible divide between the steppe and the sown. Mixed farming on the sown became one-sided horticulture. Mixed farming on the steppe either remained that way, as it did for the Manchus, or it became one-sided stock breeding on a nomadic basis as it did for the Hsiung-nu, Toba, Ch'i-tan, and the Mongols. The steppe and the sown evolved into the obverse and reverse of each other, rather evenly matched in war.

The steppe horseman, however, was no threat to the sedentary cultivator until after the Spring and Autumn period. Up until that time, from the beginnings of the Eastern Chou, the Chinese charioteers moved against horse breeders who had not yet learned to ride their stock. Both sides were more evenly matched when they adopted cavalry during the Warring States period.

The Chinese military machine successfully held out against barbarian insurgency during the First and Second Unities. When the machine weakened, the Chinese still could hold out against the superior cavalry of the barbarians by retreating in depth through cultivated land, as they did in Sung times. The steppelanders may always have been outnumbered forty to one, but they had the advantage of mobile striking power. When the Chinese war machine broke down completely against this threat, the barbarians took over, as did the Mongols and Manchus. They in turn had to man the frontiers against fresh competitors from their own side of the Wall.

Barbarians were enabled to conquer China, or part of China, for their own dynastic houses because their border contacts instructed them in Chinese political institutions. With all that military pressure, counter pressure, negotiation, and the bestowal of Chinese titles on barbarian chieftans—the Khanate, for example—the steppe leaders achieved regular participation in organs of Chinese government even when they were not installed as conquerors. The lessons learned in sparring were applied in times of takeover, which happened for the first time on the part of the Liao during the Second Partition.

But if civilization created barbarians, the barbarians in turn stimulated the military and administrative powers of civilization. The military conquest of empire by Ch'in owed in great part to its adoption of fighting tactics belonging to the mounted warriors of neighboring steppelands. And the administration of empire, following victory, was made possible by the extension to All-China of the *chün* that Ch'in invented for its early border contests. It was these military commanderies, with their nonhereditary leadership in the service of defending feudal properties, that inspired political sociologists of the Legalist school to generalize a policy hostile to feudal privilege. The cause of feudal privilege in the rival school of Confucianism was argued in Lu and Ch'i, states whose borders touched upon the lands of no Tartar tribes and for whom the style of *chün* administration had no political relevance.

The geopolitical position of Ch'in and Han, dynasties of the First Unity, is unique in Chinese history. Like all unified imperial dynasties, they had to locate their metropolitan center in the north where the greatest military strength could be moved against barbarian attempts at conquest. The north at all times is the Key Strategic Area (KSA) for military defense of China's inner Asian frontier. During the First Unity, the KSA coincided with KEA "A." At that time, a continuing stream of colonists were going forth into the southern wastelands of the Yangtze area, following the lead of the Lung-shan pioneers, but area "B" was not yet ripe enough for plucking by the state.

FIRST PARTITION

By the end of Han times, the Yangtze River valley began to resemble the northern landscape, whose density of population had enabled imperial government to attract cultured men to its cause during the four and one-half centuries of the First Unity. No longer was the Yangtze territory sparsely populated with fire-and-water agriculturalists, Tai peoples who burnt off virgin forest cover, flooded the ashen land, and then seeded wet rice. Now the nutritional density had risen enough to invite the attention of aristocrats. These rallied around the glory of their own regional courts. The same thing happened in the Red basin, where one of the Ch'in governors earlier had irrigated the Chengtu plain and had made of it a "sea on land." These two natural areas, "B" and "C," came to rival "A" and weakened its supremacy. The result, without benefit of barbarian invasion, was a ternary partition of the Han empire. Lo Kuan-chung, a fourteenth-century historical novelist, made the events of this partition famous in his *San Kuo Chih Yen I* (*Romance of the Three Kingdoms*).

The three kingdoms were the houses of Shu, Wu, and Wei. Shu occupied secondary area "C," based on the irrigation and transport systems of the Chengtu plain, with its capital at Chengtu. Wu based its power on the navigable and productive facilities of the middle and lower Yangtze (KEA "B"), with its capital at Chien-yeh (renamed in the Ming dynasty as Nanking). Wei occupied the historic environs of KEA "A," with its capital at Loyang, seat of the later Han emperors.

In the three-way competition among Shu, Wu, and Wei for the inheritance of imperial glory, Wei, in area "A" to the north, clearly had the advantage. By later Han times, the north had been widely open to government control, from Kuanchung in the east to Honei in the west. Kuanchung covers the ancient and fertile region of the Yellow River where it receives the Ch'ing, Lo, Fen, and Wei. Honei covers the alluvial loessland of the lower Yellow River and the entire Hwai River drainage down to the East China Sea, the region of northern Honan, southern Hopei, and western Shantung. The house of Wei centered in this region, where it bordered on Wu. Wu's capital was located near the mouth of the Yangtze, close enough to the Hwai drainage that a short canal pushed up through the lake country for one hundred miles could have linked areas "A" and "B." It was this very linkup, completed for the dynasties of the Second and Third Unities, that Wei anticipated by favoring Honei over Kuanchung. The episodic Tsin empire that followed the San Kuo period managed to actually connect the Yangtze and the Hwai by such a canal, but did not survive to profit from it. The benefits for empire were first realized only when it was connected as a section of the Sui Grand Canal. Meanwhile, the Hwai basin was overrun as a battlefield in a north-south contest for passage between the Hwai and the Yellow.

The kingdom of Shu was held by an independent ruler in

San Kuo times, as it has been for seven or eight times in Chinese history. This explains why KEA "C," the Red basin of Szechuan, is a secondary area. Like all the KEAs, area "C" is able to stand alone with its own glorious court when the glory of the imperial court fails to attract All-China. But when the imperial throne attracts the loyalties of all powerful men *except* those in the Red basin, the idea of empire is not diminished. The first time Szechwan appropriated and concentrated grain tribute in the name of its own dynastic glory was during the few years, A.D. 25 to 86, that marked the interregnum between the Earlier and Later Han dynasties. The second was during the San Kuo period, under the house of Shu, from 221 to 263. The third was during Western Tsin, so brief an imperial unity that it must be listed with the First Partition. The fourth was during the Five Dynasties period of the Second Partition. The fifth was from 1362 to 1371, at the start of the Ming dynasty, and the sixth came at the end of it. The seventh was during the T'aip'ing rebellion, from 1851 to 1863. Chungking was China's wartime capital in that remote mountain basin, sustaining all that remained of Free China during the Japanese occupation, after the Sino-Japanese conflict of the 1930s had merged with World War II.

The three-cornered struggle of San Kuo times reduced less to a battle with swords and spears than to combat with spades, hoes, and carrying baskets. Each party to the contest aimed at maintaining the most glorious court in its region. Population distributed something on the order of twelve to five to three for Wei, Shu, and Wu. Wei's population numbered about twenty-nine million, supporting well over a million in the capital city—evidence of well-organized grain transportation. Wei applied its strength chiefly in the building of canals, dams, and reservoirs in the Hwai River basin, a strategic area of passage between the old established north of KEA "A" and the newly developing south of KEA "B." It was strategic because the Yangtze evolved to become the richest of all the KEAs and because its produce had to be passed to the north, to a capital city located in the KSA, out of consideration for military defense against barbarian invasion.

The Western Tsin dynasty inherited twenty-seven years of imperial glory from the victorious campaigns of Wei. Western Tsin's capitals at Loyang and then at Ch'ang-an fell to the Hsiung-nu and the house was driven south, and there held a fraction of its empire a while longer, as the Eastern Tsin, with its capital relocated at Nanking. From that time onward, until China was reunited under the Sui, the north remained barbarian. The south remained Chinese under a melange of local courts denominated by Chinese historians as Nan Pei Ch'ao, the Northern and Southern Dynasties.

The inclusive name for the whole of the First Partition is Liu Ch'ao, or Six Dynasties. All capitals were at Nanking. These six dynasties (except for Wu) are the Chinese houses that kept the south during Nan Pei Ch'ao against the day when a Chinese emperor would again shine his glory over All-China. The barbarian pretenders to the Han throne included assorted Turkic, Mongol, and Hunnish peoples whose initial, petty states based on plunder Chinese historians have dismissed as the Sixteen Kingdoms. These were followed by a rather more durable and extensive Toba Wei dynasty whose tribal rulers, originating in eastern Mongolia, soon were forced out by further barbarian infiltration and political fragmentation.

The short-lived barbarian houses of the Sixteen Kingdoms did not exploit the Chinese environment in the Chinese way. This accounts for their quick turnover and limited jurisdiction. To the west they sat astride the great silk route and taxed the caravan trade. To the east they impressed grain with armed troops and trundled it off to court in carts, as did the Toba Wei on a larger scale.

With no imperial cause to dignify office holding, few of the Chinese elite chose to serve under the petty governments of the barbarian kingdoms. With capital cities emptied owing to a decline in riverine transport of grain, traders lost a source of wealth in providing food and commodities to urbanites. The absence of urban security under a centralized imperium was compensated for by the elite in fortified manors, organized by rich and powerful clans against barbarian strong-arm levies of grain and men: Attracted to these private citadels, miniature city-states, were peasants who exchanged their vulnerability in the open countryside for immured roles as tenants and soldiers. Several of these self-sufficient estates, each numbering thousands of retainers to complete its economic and military base, moved to south China where they had the effect of sinicizing the native population.

These manorial estates kept the life of a new aristocracy going until Sung times.

SECOND UNITY

The southern dynasties of Nan Pei Ch'ao fully landscaped the lower Yangtze with wet rice and irrigation installations while barbarians reduced the north by plunder. The north still retained the larger population in KEA "A," but had lost many refugees to the south and the burgeoning of KEA "B." The north still held its greater political importance, however. It was the oldest area to experience cultural fusion and thus it most easily rallied to the cause of imperial glory. And it bordered on a hostile barbarian frontier that called for constant exercise of the imperial war machine. But the south had gained in productivity. This benefited the Nanking governments, to be true. Colonists from the north acculturated native peoples to the self-densing methods of Chinese horticulture and thus to an immobility convenient for taxation. But refugees of wealth and power, however, looked to the time when China would be reunited and they could return home to the civilized lands of the north.

When unity came again under the Sui dynasty, the graniferous capital was located in the political north, Ch'ang-an, but its granary in the productive south. The Sui Grand Canal linked the two.

Like the Great Wall, the Grand Canal was constructed or rebuilt in part from older sections. A strategic section, running north and south between Hwai-an and Yang-chou, connecting the Yangtze with the Hwai River, had been cut during Eastern Tsin times. The Sui Canal continued south to Hangchow. From Hwai-an it turned northwest for the long stretch along the Ssu tributary of the Hwai, and beyond, to Kaifeng. There tribute boats could head up the Yellow River for the remaining journey to the capital city, Ch'ang-an. The canal route was lined with elm and willow. An imperial highway, with postal stations, paralleled it.

Like the Great Wall, again, the Grand Canal was built with corvée labor. On one stretch alone it is recorded that 3.6 million laborers were assembled under the local conscription of all able-bodied men between fifteen and twenty years of age. A child, old man, or woman from the same locality was drafted to bear food and cook for each laborer. With police and section chiefs, the total numbered 5.5 million. Earth-moving equipment was limited to hoes, baskets, and shirt bibs, a primitive technology that gets the work done when millions of men are organized to apply it. This despite heavy losses from death and flight.

The Sui Grand Canal was an economic and military necessity for the Sui and T'ang empires of the Second Unity. Economic because the productive rice lands of the Yangtze were located in the south; military because the barbarian threat came from the north. During the First Unity, the KEA and the KSA both lay inside area "A." By the time of the Second Unity, the KEA of empire had shifted to area "B," but area "A" still remained the KSA, given continued military stress along China's steppe frontier. The Sui Grand Canal prompted a dependence on the growth of area "B" that, from the T'ang dynasty onward, permanently settled the location of the KEA for imperial China.

SECOND PARTITION

T'ang regional commanders set themselves up as "princes," "kings," and "emperors" over territories large and small of the former imperium. Like the First Partition, the parts of the Second can be grouped in a north-south division. Initially, the north carried the legitimate succession of states, the Wu-tai or Five Dynasties. The Five Dynasties, then, supply the name for this brief period even though it embraces a decade of other states in the south, the Ten Kingdoms. Eventually a succession of two Tartar tribes, the Liao and the Chin, occupied the north while the Chinese held southern and central China with the native Sung dynasty.

Each one of the successive Five Dynasties held KEA "A," a resource base larger than that held by all the Ten Kingdoms put together. Heavy fighting to the northwest in Kuanchung, however, so decimated the region that it remained weak and underpopulated until well into Sung times. The effective economic base for the Five Dynasties, then, included only the Yellow River plain and the Hwai basin—large enough at that. Capital cities were located either at Kaifeng (four times) or at Loyang (once), both accessible by water transport. The old capital area of Ch'ang-an to the west had by this time sunk in the ruins of war.

Chinese historians have assigned dynastic succession to the

north despite the fact that they detest the Wu-tai as the worst example of licentious military dictatorship on record. Peace, prosperity, and Confucian culture obtained in the south—but only among the nonsuccessive territorial regimes of the Ten Kingdoms. Area "A" still held its reputation with historians for unitary control over the Yellow basin, the oldest—and once the most productive—center of the civilization.

Greater productivity already had passed to South China by T'ang times, but not a matching capability for political unity. Even the glory of the T'ang court failed, during the latter half of the dynasty, to persuade estate-owning officials of the south to render up their tenants for twenty days a year for corvée labor on the Grand Canal. In a self-defeating countermeasure, the T'ang government had to send down its own transport workers to haul in the tribute grain for Ch'ang-an. South China, under the Ten Kingdoms, was by far the most productive, but its internal culture differences disallowed unity, much less enduring attachment to a northern throne. It is not merely that the south is a younger area (it had to be pioneered from the north). The dissection of the Yangtze landscape by mountain and valley encouraged a greater persistence of local political cultures, more so than in the wide plains of the Yellow River, which long were open to easy translocal communication, including the movement of mounted warriors.

The Ten Kingdoms were founded by military governors who took over the southern provinces of the T'ang empire. But while these local rulers had failed to find a continuing equation of interests with an imperium, neither had they found any necessity for interstate rivalry in support of their regional claims. For one thing, these southern kingdoms were able to accumulate great wealth under peaceful conditions by associating with great merchants, in governmental monopolies, in the trading of tea, salt, and porcelain whose markets extended as far as India, Indonesia, Western Asia, and Japan. And, of course, each kingdom provided ample rice and adequate river transportation to deliver food to its capital city.

The regions into which the Ten Kingdoms were divided approximate to those natural areas that go to define the boundaries of imperial provinces, or combinations of these, such as the vice-royalty of Liang Kwang (Kwangtung and Kwangsi). Six natural regions lie behind the power of the ten different states listed in Figure 6.

FIG. 6   *The Ten Kingdoms and their Rivers to Glory*

Natural Region	Transport Rivers	Kingdoms, with Dates	Capital Cities
Red Basin	Min	Former Shu 901–925	Chengtu
Red Basin	Min	Later Shu 934–965	Chengtu
Yangtze Delta	Lower Yangtze	Wu 902–937	Yangchow
Yangtze Delta	Lower Yangtze	Southern T'ang 937–975	Nanch'ang
Southeastern Coast	Fuchun	Wu-Yueh 908–978	Hangchow
Southeastern Coast	Min	Min 909–944	Foochow
Canton Hinterland	Hsi system	Southern Han 917–971	Canton
Central Yangtze Plain	Ch'ang	Southern P'ing 925–963	Chingchow
Central Yangtze Plain	Hsiang	Ch'u 927–952	Ch'ang-sha
Shansi Basin	Fen	Northern Han 951–979	T'ai-yuan

Note: The Ten Kingdoms are smaller in regional size than the contemporary Wu-tai, or Five Dynasties, of the North China plain. The
Wu-tai, with their capitals located either at Loyang (once) or at
Kaifeng (four times), dominated the entire Yellow basin and drew
upon the Yellow and Hwai Rivers for transport. It is perhaps the scope
of this regionalism that has moved Chinese historians to assign royal
succession to them rather than to the more culturally acceptable Ten
Kingdoms.

Each region supported a local court on the basis of its chief
river system. Each provided alluvial soils for the conduct of
intensive farming by a dense peasantry, and natural waterways
for the transport of grain to the capital city.

Regionalism was defeated finally with the end of the Sung
dynasty and the beginning of the Third Unity. Sung culture
marks the divide between a second aristocracy and the mature
Agrarian State. Thereafter, China never fell into disunity for
long. Even barbarian conquests eventuated in imperial unities.

The military dictatorships of the north came to an end
when soldiers proclaimed a general of Later Chou, last of the
Five Dynasties, as their emperor. His dynasty he named Sung.
The Wu-tai regimes are rated as imperial only in retrospect by
way of preserving the fiction of unbroken succession. They are

listed as the fourteenth through the eighteenth of the twenty-
two official dynasties. All are listed in Figure 7.

FIG. 7   *The false continuity of dynastic succession*

I	Hsia	[1989–1558 B.C.] *	
II	Shang	[1558–1051]	(Preimperial)
III	Chou	[1050]–249	
IV	Ch'in	221–207	
V	Former Han	206 B.C.–A.D. 8	(First Unity)
	Later Han	25–220	
VI	Shu-Han	221–263	
VII	Eastern Tsin	265–420	
VIII	Liu Sung	420–479	(First Partition)
IX	Southern Ch'i	479–502	
X	Southern Liang	502–557	
XI	Southern Ch'en	557–589	
XII	Sui	581–618	(Second Unity)
XIII	T'ang	618–906	
XIV	Later Liang	907–923	
XV	Later T'ang	923–936	
XVI	Later Tsin	936–946	
XVII	Later Han	947–950	(Second Partition)
XVIII	Later Chou	951–960	
XIX	Northern Sung	960–1127	
	Southern Sung	1127–1279	
XX	Yuan	1206–1368	
XXI	Ming	1368–1644	(Third Unity)
XXII	Ch'ing	1644–1912	

* Dates in brackets are traditional.

Sung armies annexed the southern regional territories of
the Ten Kingdoms and imperial unity, at least in name, was
achieved. No transport canal between north and south operated for much of the Sung period, however. What is more,
North China had fallen to barbarian conquest.

During the Sui and T'ang dynasties, the Chinese imperial
armies had kept the northern frontiers guarded by a constant
play of defensive and offensive action. The struggle was lost
under the Five Dynasties, when a good portion of North China
was infiltrated by a confederation of Tartar hordes out of
southeastern Mongolia named Ch'i-tan or Khitan. They occupied Manchuria, Mongolia, and the northern part of the north
China plain.

In 946 the Ch'i-tan ruler proclaimed overlordship of the Chinese under the dynastic name of Liao. Of the Liao dynasty's five residencies, the southernmost was Peking, beginning that city's history as a capital located in the KSA. Rather than advance their military conquest any farther south, the Ch'i-tan demanded and got exhaustive payments of "protection money" from the Sung in the form of gold and silk. The Sung armies were at a disadvantage because the enemy occupied the border-lands where horses could be raised.

Of all the "protection money" extracted by the Ch'i-tan from the Chinese, none of it reached nomadic tribesmen to the rear of the frontier in the region of the Amur River. These disadvantaged members of the confederation, the Jurchen Tartars, Tungusic forefathers of the Manchus, rose up against their rich living brethren and captured Peking for themselves in 1125, ending the Liao dynasty. One escaped prince fled to the west with a small band of followers and founded the Kara-Khitai state among the Uigurs of central Asia, in the oasis country in the vicinity of Kashgar and Samarkand.

The Jurchen set themselves up as the new rulers of China and took the name Chin or Golden. The Golden Hordes swept to Kaifeng and captured the Sung emperor and his entire court, bringing to a close that period of Chinese history known as Northern Sung. A new capital was set up in the south, at Hangchow, for the Southern Sung. Whereas the Chinese frontier with the Ch'i-tan Liao during Northern Sung times was located somewhere along the Yellow River, with the Chin during Southern Sung times it was located along the Hwai. The Chin did not stop fighting for further penetration until they were swept away by the Mongols in 1234 under Chinghis, who also wiped out the Western Liao in 1211.

The conquests of Chinghis in Central Asia, preparatory to control of China Proper (which came about under imperial title by his grandson, Khubilai) included destruction of the Tanguts in 1227. The Tanguts were a Tibetan pastoral people who had built a kingdom athwart the Old Silk Route along the upper reaches of the Yellow River, in the arid regions of Kansu and Ninghsia. In 1038 the Tanguts stopped paying tribute, out of their tax on trade, to the government of the Northern Sung and proclaimed their own empire, that of Hsi Hsia. Without sufficient horse for the Chinese armies, denied them by control over the steppeland on the part of the Liao and later by the Chin, Sung troops had no means to counter the Hsi Hsia threat to Chinese imperial sovereignty. The fact of the matter is, that if the Chinese mean to control for themselves their own agricultural economy in China Proper, within the Wall, they have to hold enough pastureland without the Wall to supply their cavalry. Only then can they defend against the mobile striking forces of the steppe peoples. Hence the importance of the KSA.

THIRD UNITY

Grandsons of Chinghis expanded his conquests in Central Asia to include four Khanates that stretched across almost the whole of Eurasia from Hungary to Korea. China fell within the Khanate of the Great Khan, that of Khubilai. Elsewhere, the Mongol superempire grew wider by the sheer expedient of sweeping plunder that lasted for a century. After an initial period of destruction in China, Mongol troops there settled in garrisons and Khubilai mastered the traditional Chinese methods of administering native officeholders. In this the Mongol conquest of China Proper repeated the pattern set by previous invasions. Chinese peasants worked the land and Chinese officials taxed the land; barbarians held the supervisory posts jointly with Chinese, leaving the lesser posts—and the life of the local gentry—totally to the Chinese elite. The difference is that the Mongols took over all of China in this manner. So did the Manchus under the Ch'ing dynasty, the second and last of the unified conquest dynasties.

Sandwiched between the Yuan and the Ch'ing is the Ming, the one native dynasty of the Third Unity. Its political arrangements were taken over virtually intact by the Manchus, including the Ming statutes. The Manchus also took over the existing provincial system, except for making a few subdivisions of the fifteen Ming provinces for a new total of eighteen. The Manchus gave every support to Chinese institutions and they broadly supported Confucian learning. Indeed, they posed as a legitimate native dynasty, come to rescue the Chinese from bad government, as evidenced by internal rebellions. This pose is completely in keeping with the Chinese concept of dynastic succession: the bad last and the good first. The badness of the last emperor of the previous dynasty loses the "Mandate of Heaven" for his line, only to invite the first of a new line who will start a new house in goodness. That the Manchus could make their conquest at all depended on internal weakness of the native Chinese regime, as usual in the case of barbarian success. What is different in this case is that the Manchus, like the Chinese, are an agricultural people, albeit with a mixed economy. Manchu culture may be described as a variant of Chinese civilization. The Ch'ing dynasty, in fact, admitted Chinese homesteaders to Manchu territory in Manchuria.

All three dynasties of the Third Unity established capitals at Peking, the Ming doing so after it discovered it could not handle its border problems from Nanking. For the Yuan, Peking was the southernmost of three capitals, including Kara-korum and Shang-tu, the Xanadu of Coleridge and the Ciandu of Marco Polo (modern K'ai-p'ing). The Ch'ing moved to Peking from Mukden on the accession of the first Manchu emperor to the Chinese Dragon Throne.

For the supply of Peking a second Grand Canal had to be constructed. This was done under the Yuan and maintained by the last two dynasties.

The Yuan Grand Canal repeated the course of the Sui Grand Canal from Hangchow up to the Hwai River. But from there, instead of turning west toward Ch'ang-an, it continued north-ward to Tientsin, for a total length of 1,286 miles. Strung along the canal were government granaries that readied grain in stor-age until loaded on canal barges, or until loaded on carts when the water level dropped, as it sometimes did in the drier country of the canal's upper sections.

The bed of the canal is alluvial soil all the way. One section follows an old course of the Yellow River (it shifted south-ward between the twelfth and nineteenth centuries) at a point below Kaifeng, to run with the Hwai. Construction labor in-volved no digging of a deep channel but merely the throwing up of embankments with a hoe-and-basket technology. The sluices were simple enough: thick planks sliding in grooves hewn in stone buttresses, and hauled by men on ropes.

One technical problem, never really solved, was passage of the canal across the Yellow River. The Ho carries so much silt washed into it from the eroded loessial highlands that, by the time its movement slows on the Yellow plain, enough silt drops out of suspension to actually raise the riverbed above the level of the surrounding plain. No important cities have been built here. Periodic flooding has always been a threat. Danger to the canal works at their junction with the Ho is the responsibility of the Yellow River Conservancy to avert, if possible. It devotes itself to flood watching and diking the longer course of the river. Effective flood control, however, must rest with damming the headwaters. Under the Ch'ing regime, the Yellow River Conservancy, with its four hundred officials under three directors-general and its twenty thousand troops, came to cost as much as 10 percent of the central government's revenue. This does not count what it costs to maintain and operate the six thousand forty-five-ton grain junks belonging to the Grain Transport Service.

The combined expenses of the Yellow River Conservancy and the Grain Transport Service moved Commissioner Lin, of Opium War fame—in 1840 he burned chests of British opium in single-handed fidelity to laws against its importation—to consider creating a KEA in the Hai River valley by means of investment in irrigation facilities for the conduct of intensive farming there. The Hai flows through Tientsin in a course used by the Yellow in the tenth century B.C. In the commissioner's time, it cost 125,000 tons of grain to transport 275,000 tons to Peking. In a memorial to the throne, Commissioner Lin argued that the required tribute grain could be raised in the vicinity of the metropolitan center itself, at great savings and to the benefit of self-sufficiency for the court and army. In fact, several like proposals had been submitted from Yuan times onward. The Yuan dynasty went so far as to hire a thousand irrigation farmers from the Yangtze valley to instruct northern peasants in a pilot project. But neither the Mongols nor anybody else has ever been able to revise geography and make area "B" out of area "A."

Steamship transportation in the latter half of the nineteenth century reduced the cost of hauling tribute grain by a factor of ten. But by this time, the economic areas began losing the controlling significance they exercised when agricultural productivity and water transport were the combined measure of the Dragon Throne's power to outshine rival courts set up on the basis of smaller natural regions. With the advent of industry and trade, electric communications, railroads, steamships, and overseas commerce, the economic areas figured as but one factor among others in deciding the role of central government.

A symbolic turning point might be made of 1842, when the first paddle-wheeled vessel from the steamboat powers of the

West entered Chinese waters. Through various treaties signed afterward, these powers exacted rights of extraterritoriality from thirty-eight coastal and riverine treaty ports, pressure points of the dual economy. The ambitious minority from all parts of the land then lost interest in acquiring their wealth and power under the emperor's cultural umbrella as agents of his glory.

The fall of the Ch'ing dynasty ended more than a dynasty. It ended the culturalism of the Chinese Agrarian State and began the nationalism of the Chinese nation-state.

CHAPTER 11

LORDS OF THE SOIL

IN his *Principles of Political Economy,* John Stuart Mill aimed to explain the principles of an expensive market economy. He did so by contrasting his subject with its most exotic opposite: confiscatory appropriation—profiteering—in a stationary pre-industrial economy. He describes the wealth of profiteering as that:

> . . . torn from the producers, either by the government to which they are subject, or by individuals, who by superior force, or availing themselves of religious or traditional feelings of subordination, have established themselves as lords of the soil.

Lords of the Soil may be understood to include everybody in the Agrarian State who is privileged to take advantage of those "traditional feelings of subordination" that cause the peasantry to yield up its substance.

In relationship to folk culture, the Lords of the Soil all share a single character of exploitation as a corporate elite. Government, in the first instance, reduces to taxation. Because the supply of grain and manpower coming out of the Green Circle is inelastic, taxation is paradigmatic for a style of profiteering by all privileged persons in all fields of exploitation.

To take an example from fiscal policy. Money circulates in China's agrarian economy, but it exists in both private and public forms. The only coinage of universal currency, accepted everywhere at face value and not by weight, is the copper cash of imperial mintage. But this public coin, rated across the empire at about twelve hundred cash to the tael, circulates mainly in the penny economy of peasant life. Should transactions be made on a larger scale—across localities and in big amounts—no coinage of face value will avail, not even Mexican dollars (416.5 grains) or American trade dollars (420 grains) marked with the rated fineness of silver content. The one public medium of exchange is spent locally by the little people in little amounts. Big merchants and officials spent private monies by weight of silver. These units carry no face value. If they did they would not be believed. The craft of the merchant includes the ability to weigh and assay ingots and shoes of silver for parity with others differing by region, trade, or government agency. Mistrust among commercial dealers, displayed in their steelyards, is appropriate where the fiscal usages of Bronze Age trade missions still prevail in the transport of bullion by armed troops at 10 percent of its cost just to move it from one place to another.

The tael is the ounce of China, and sixteen of them make a Chinese pound, the catty. The tael varies between 540 and 583 grains of silver, or on the average of one and one-third ounces of silver. The government ordinarily reckons the tael at 575.8 grains of 1,000 fine silver, known as the Kuping tael. The Kuping tael may be counted as banking money in a country where no partity exists in the bankbooks of bankers. The rate is artificial except for those in charge of making the exchange, which is customarily 0.2 percent lighter in the paying than in the receiving rate. The whole system allows of currency manipulation to the disadvantage of those who traffic in public currency, taken at face value, by those who traffic— with their knowledge and scales—in the various weights of precious metal.

Public money belongs to the weak and private money to the powerful, another example of the power gap between non-privileged and privileged persons in the Chinese Agrarian State. Men of privilege belong to the following sectors of the imperial Establishment:

1. Central government
2. Local government
3. Commerce
4. Gentry

Note that merchants belong to the privileged Establishment, in fact if not by social definition. The scholastic portion of the ruling class defines merchants as lower class by way of keeping intact their own very special privilege of being the arbiters of social value. The literati claim this intellectual prerequisite on the grounds of physiocratic doctrine, which allows that officials

AT RIGHT: *An official supervises the production of salt, a state monopoly. After a Chinese print.*

and landlords, who live off taxes and rents, are more elegant than those who gain their income from commerce, a step removed from the soil.

CENTRAL GOVERNMENT

The imperial center transacts administrative business with its provincial bureaus. Its executive or financial department records the intake and outgo of these transactions in detail. Beyond that, however, comparison with bureaucratic government in the nation-states does not apply. Revenue is collected into no "common purse." What is more, the statistics of revenue and expenditure are ritual statistics.

To westerners, accustomed to a common purse instituted in the government treasury, the ritual format of the Chinese imperial budget drawn up by the financial department must appear to be a facade erected by wheedling provincial officials to conceal hanky-panky from the throne. This is not the case. Office itself is a commodity.

The official at his post maintains himself by squeezing a fee for himself on every transaction of funds remitted to the imperial center. The center is perfectly aware of this. Indeed, it endorses squeeze. For the salary of the official is so small that it is considered as nothing more than a symbolic pledge given by the throne to equip him with a license to hunt for revenue in the territory belonging to his post. But there is, however, a "bag limit" in effect. Some of the take must reach the center in exchange for the license. This portion moves upward in the form of bribes and gifts from the lowest ranking officer to his superiors. The imperial budget of intake and outgo, phrased in terms of taxes put to public service, is the ritual cover for the real transactions. This budget is the emperor's prerogative to draw up; the glorious array of statistics, attesting to the range of his sovereignty, is his claim to that sway.

The most glorious set of ritual statistics is that of the permanent appropriations. It lists the order of priorities for expenditures, but it does not come close to reflecting actual monetary expenditures. See Figure 8. Some private incomes are bigger.

The total of 32 million taels does not include emergency outlays. In 1911, just before a revolution overthrew the monarchy, a true budget estimate on the western model was tried. Expenditures were calculated at over 376 million taels, revenues

FIG. 8   Native classification of expenditures (1911)

			Taels
I.	Military		21,884,763
	Regular pay of officers and men	14,862,929	
	Additional pay of military officers	1,398,755	
	Sundry expenses in the army	274,523	
	Regular pay of Chinese and Manchu troops in Peking	5,348,556	
II.	Civil		5,042,443
	Regular salaries of civil officials	1,908,086	
	Additional allowance of civil officials	2,937,369	
	Salaries of civil and military officials in Peking (Manchus excluded)	196,988	
III.	Imperial		394,694
	Tomb furnishings	106,861	
	New Year expenses	180,000	
	Silk manufactures	107,833	
IV.	Intelligence (imperial post)		2,147,961
V.	Hydraulic (waterworks and water conservation)		1,618,081
VI.	Educational (public worship, charities, scholarships, and examinations)		625,784
VII.	Unaccounted		415,957
	Total		32,129,683

at only 297 million taels, making for a deficit of 79 million taels. By that time, certain extraordinary outlays had exceeded the totality of the traditional permanent appropriations. Examples are the 56 million taels for interest on foreign loans, and another 55 million taels for administration of government railways and telegraphs. Military costs were up to a whopping 137 million taels, one-third of the real budget. The old ritual appropriations were heavily put upon by very real extraordinary outlays. The deficit—the concept of deficit as well as the fact itself—was a novel fiscal category and must be accounted for by the elastic demands, under the pressures of culture contact, on sources of revenue inelastic in the native economy. As the Ch'ing dynasty came to a close, alternate sources of income for local officials, coming from outside the Chinese economy, enabled them to build regional machines stronger than central government. During the Republican government that followed collapse of the dynastic house, local governments did not acknowledge their agricultural taxes as lifted in the name of central government. Indeed, thirteen provinces declared themselves under warlords as independent economies. The grain tribute stopped. The Republican government accordingly relinquished the land tax in name as well as fact to the provincial governments, and itself learned to live off the maritime customs, excise taxes, and the old salt monopoly.

The salt royalties had not failed. When the fledgling Republic contracted for the great "five power loan" in 1913 from Germany, Britain, France, Russia, and Japan, it was secured on the *gabelle*. Foreigners from the five powers, with their service-oriented handling of bureaucracy, then entered the administrative works of the salt commission in order to police it. Here is an example of semicolonialism at work. It helped save the salt royalties for the claim of central government under the Republic. But it also pressed the Republic to continue taxing its economic base, including the modern sector, in the style of central government under the emperors, which was elemental profiteering. Profiteering is archaic, and it displaces risk investment in productive enterprise.

Central government in the Agrarian State lives off three types of confiscatory taxation. They are taxation of cultivated land, taxation of salt (royalties), and taxation of commodities (duties).

The agricultural tax includes a land-and-head tax and a special shipment of unhulled rice from the lower Yangtze provinces (the grain tribute from KEA "A"). By Ming times, the normal agricultural tax had been more or less combined in one levy—the corvée part in money (which is paid out for a permanent labor force in place of a seasonably drafted one), and the land part in both money and kind. This fiscal reform followed upon the absolute increase of silver brought to the realm by way of a reluctant but gathering trade with the West. No commutation to money payments is made in the case of tribute grain, however.

All government revenues are collected in the emperor's name, but few reach him. The tax revenues owed the center by the provincial governments are divided into a transporting fund and a reserve fund. Of the transporting fund, the money part of the land tax is one-fifth of it owed to Peking; the other four-fifths, the reserve fund, is retained in the provincial treasuries. Officials in each province receive a part of their salaries from the reserve fund, another part from produce in kind collected in their territory. What makes a valuable commodity of an official post is the unofficial increment collected beyond that called for by central government in the transporting and reserve funds. Except for a nominal amount actually transported to Peking, these funds rather serve to specify the bag limit set on official profiteering, always exceeding by more or less. Central government at Peking has to live off its own catch, the grain tribute for one thing, taken from the imperial granary that the founder of the house was careful to secure with his sword with the conquest of his dynasty.

Royalties accumulate from the universal consumption of about eighteen pounds of salt per year per person at a light assessment per unit of weight. Central government earns about half its income from this source. If Peking did not assert a monopoly over the production and distribution of salt, the profits would go to bandits, rebels, and other claimants to regional power.

The salt itself is produced by the evaporation of seawater from coastal salt pans and is distributed from there. Interior brine wells, salt lakes, and some mines account for the remaining part of the inland supply. Production and distribution is divided into ten districts, the same ones declared under the Sung dynasty.

The customs duty is a general excise tax on merchandise collected from customhouses located along the seaboard, rivers, inland waterways, land routes, and land frontiers. This tax is called the regular customs to distinguish it from the novel maritime customs that evolved out of western contact. The latter is collected on freight arriving in China by steamship.

LOCAL GOVERNMENT

The salary paid the district magistrate by central government over his three-year term of office, three or four thousand taels, will just about cover the cost of his official robes. It is understood that the magistrate is to maintain his retinue of deputies, secretaries, servants, and assorted understrappers out of his own pocket. The magistrate, and every other provincial official, must collect fees for the expenses of his office as well as for his income and profit. The western objection is that the fees are collected but the work not done. But what work? The Chinese official is not a civil servant, an executor of the community, paid out of public moneys to help the public. His office is an emolument of privilege.

Faithful to post-Enlightenment ethics, westerners regard Chinese officials as venal, hypocritical, deceitful, and time-serving. One Chinese writer, educated to the same viewpoint, promises to reveal scandal in high places by means of thin fiction in a work titled, *The Reminiscences of a Chinese Official.* This calls to mind *The Scholars,* by Wu Ching-tzu. Written from a viewpoint from within the system, *The Scholars* attacks wicked men who fail the system. *The Reminiscences,* written from a westernized viewpoint, attacks the system itself.

The scandal in the *Reminiscences* reduces to a description of squeeze in all manner of situations. The author means to expose the misuse of public funds. In this the author is justified because the squeeze system, from which officials used to draw their rightful incomes, came to be dysfunctional at a time when the call for nation building really required the honest administration of public funds. China had to become enlightened like the West or be swallowed by enlightened westerners.

An interesting example of squeeze is given in chapter IX, which scornfully is entitled, "How to Get Rich Through Relief Work." The reference is made to flood relief. The banks of the Yellow River have burst below Chengchow for a length of thirty *li,* or for about three hundred miles. Central government has laid out two hundred thousand taels to repair the break. Repair work is done under the director-general of the Yellow River Conservancy. In emergency, extra subdirectors are appointed. One Chia Taotai is appointed director of the Upper Section.

> Under his able management, for he was really an able man, the works made rapid progress. Within two months the breach was narrowed down to the width of half a *li.* By that time the flood had subsided, which made the process of construction much easier. At the same time, Chia Taotai's accountants were busy making or rather inventing accounts. The number of coolies employed on the works each day was easily made to swell from 3,000 to 10,000, and their wages increased, only in his books, from 100 cash to 180. The old half-rotten timbers he bought from the drift-wood collectors at 20 tael cents apiece were charged 70 tael cents. He also paid the salaries of fifty or more men on his staff whom he never employed. During the critical periods when the coolies had to

work extra shifts, he gave them 10 extra cash as reward instead of 20. As for himself there were cart and horse allowances, body guard allowance, staff allowances, food allowances, extra allowances and what not. In short, he made no less than 150,000 taels out of his four months' work as Director.

(It must be understood here that although the amount allotted for the repair of the broken embankment on this occasion was 200,000 taels, the actual amount spent, including the remittances from the Provinces and the charitable institutions of Shanghai, amounted to something like 500,000 taels. Not more than 200,000 was actually used for the works proper, as there was really very little repairing to do. The directors simply waited till the water subsided and then filled in the parts which had been washed away. The rest of the money went into the pockets of the officials.)

At last the breach was repaired, and a day was selected formally to close the gap. This was done, as usual, early in the morning. Chia was carried in a chair to the spot where the last bit of the gap had just been filled. A small mat shed was specially erected, under which was placed a make-shift table with candles and incense sticks burning on top of it. With Chia Taotai in the front the officials all knelt before the table and kowtowed nine times to thank the God of the river for his mercy. It would be difficult here to say whether the country people or the river-works officials were more thankful to the God of the river. It would be still more difficult to tell whether they thanked him for his power to break the embankment or for his mercy in letting the breach be easily repaired. Perhaps they thanked him for both, as the former helped them to get a fat job and the latter gave them a wider margin for the artificial accounts.

Chia Taotai is made out to be activated solely by greed, as if the whole imperial system were but a simple projection of his personal brand of wickedness. In fact, his name is taken after the title of his ambition, *tao-t'ai,* the better from which post to enrich himself. A *tao-t'ai* is an intendant of a *tao* or circuit, the lowest ranking provincial official permitted to address dispatches to the throne. A *tao* is a subprovincial unit of administration that subsumes a number of *fu* (prefectures), which in turn embrace several *hsien* (districts or counties), that final outpost of empire where the magistrate presides.

Squeeze works in the absence of a common purse. Officials draw income by the sheer act of remitting funds through a great many channels of transaction. The chances for profiteering are distributed equitably, making for a coefficient of squeeze of about 10 percent throughout the system.

For example, suppose central government wants a given province to collect five hundred thousand taels from *likin* duty for the year. This money goes into no imperial treasury for reapportionment under definite heads of imperial expenditure. Rather, central government will specify that a series of remissions be made directly to such as the following services:

	Taels
To the Shanghai *tao-t'ai* in payment of the foreign debt	100,000
To the same official on account with legations abroad	50,000
To the Yellow River Flood Prevention account in Honan	200,000
For the renewal of coastal defenses in the home province	50,000
To the imperial household in Peking	50,000
To Peking for upkeep of the royal tombs	50,000
Total	500,000

Each of the above accounts is the target of piecemeal remission from a variety of other sources. Each transaction allows two officials at either end of the line to squeeze off their customary share of it. *Likin* duty itself is a squeeze on trade—an expropriative taxation of internal transit.

Or again, in the case of land tax quotas, about one-fifth of the officially collected revenue goes into the transporting fund and four-fifths into the reserve fund. It is from the reserve fund that central government assigns outgo to certain categories of expenditure in each province. The assignment serves to set up more channels of transaction for those who handle the accounts to squeeze.

In a squeeze economy, salary is a mere perquisite. If the wages of a day laborer are five taels, the annual salary of a magistrate, a seventh-rate official, is forty-five taels, nine times as high. But the cost to the magistrate of keeping his office is much higher. The profits are higher still. One official, the governor of Honan in a dispatch to the K'ang-hsi emperor, requested the legalization of squeeze.

It is impossible for any magistrate to support his family and to pay for the services rendered by his secretaries and servants, without charging a single cash in excess. A magistrate charging ten percent in excess of the regular taxes may be considered a good official. If he were not excused from impeachment, it seems to me, it would be irksome to inflict the same penalty on so many of your subordinates.

The emperor disallowed the request on the grounds that he would be acceding to an illegal tax on the people. He had his Confucian benevolence to uphold. Meanwhile, the invisible costs of government—the very business of empire—battened on the people as usual.

Confucian talk about government accountability is a formality, as are the ritual statistics of empire. The real business is profiteering, as everybody knows. Confucian ideology is not a facade hiding some unpleasant truth. For the reality is no more concealed than a cat in a cellophane bag, least of all from peasant folk, who have no power to protest hypocrisy, in any case. Rather, the ideology is a battleground where the Dragon struggles with his Local Snakes.

COMMERCIAL

No merchant class ever evolved in traditional China to encroach upon the economic prerogatives of government. This is so because Chinese merchants, bankers, brokers, usurers, and traders are themselves allies of government. For example, merchants are organized in guilds, in which business disputes are settled without the need of going to court and which pay taxes for their members as a unit. Yet government appoints guilds as agents for the distribution, transport, and sale of commodities belonging to its state monopolies, notably salt and foreign trade.

This is to dismiss the small-scale commerce of local traders, peddlers and tradesmen. They are little folk serving little people. Peasants have not much to offer each other. Even for big merchants there are not many lines of profit to pursue, given the repetitive landscape of the Agrarian State. The possibilities of translocal trade are sufficient to occupy only 1 percent of the gentry, which altogether number no more than 1.9 percent of the total population. But commercial profits are so high that the few who make them gain the equal of all the income squeezed out of government service by all officials, or half the income earned on rentals by all landlords. This immense wealth, derived from nonphysiocratic sources, invites officials to either invest in business or to squeeze business. Either way the merchant is tied in with a community of interests with officials. He works in partnership with officials, or he pays government an exorbitant fee for an official title that protects him from squeeze.

The classical community of interest between commerce and government revolves around salt. Central government aims to protect its royalties, and merchants to protect their profits under government license, in the translation of salt from producing centers to consumption centers. Both parties make their gain by profiteering on the model of agricultural taxation.

The peasants who produce the salt are known as stove men. The merchants who dispose of the salt produced by the stove men are known as field monopolists when their business is limited to the sale of salt on the salt fields, or to government or to other merchants who hold the monopoly on distribution. Another class of merchants, when they combine the field monopoly and the monopoly on distribution, are known as monopolistic distributors. Stove men labor for the field monopolists or the monopolistic distributors as does a tenant for his landlord. As the tenant's labor is requited with a claim to the land he labors on, so is the stove man requited with a market on which to sell the produce of his labor.

Merchants secure the appropriate license or monopoly certificate on a yearly basis from the department of finance upon payment of a stipulated tax, and then procure the salt at the appointed place. The government thus exacts fixed royalties on salt in advance, irrespective of the amount distributed in sale. But no risk is entailed. The merchant profits at no cost of venture capital but rather from the sure benefits of protection money paid out to officials who see to it, in requital for their share of the commercial profits, that certain merchant families be allowed to perpetuate their claims to the limited quota of certificates. The more wealthy the salt merchants, the more heavily government will press them for donations, donations often reciprocated with the award of honorary degrees. Big

I. Boat traffic on a canal in the lower Yangtze area near Nanking. (*Photograph by Lucy Calhoun*)

II. Acrobat performing in the marketplace of Ling-fu-ssu, Kwangsi province. (*Photograph by Lucy Calhoun*)

III. Portrait of a merchant-gentleman. Note books on the teapoy.
(Courtesy of the Smithsonian Institution)

IV. Conjugal family belonging to the peasantry, here located in
a folk neighborhood within a city. (Courtesy of the Smithsonian
Institution)

V. The Tartar Wall around Peking, with camel caravan from the border lands passing by. (Photograph by Lucy Calhoun)

VI. Joint family of three generations belonging to the gentry. (Courtesy of the Smithsonian Institution)

VII. Brass brush case; brush holder of carved bamboo stalk cut near the root, holding hair and reed or bamboo brushes (Ch'ing); ceramic tile disc for ink pallet (Han). (Courtesy of the Chicago Museum of Natural History)

VIII. Confucian temple at Peking. (Courtesy of the Chicago Museum of Natural History)

IX. A merchant's steelyard. (Courtesy of the Chicago Museum of Natural History)

X. A scholar's study. (From artwork directed by Professor Uchida Michio of Tohoku University. Gift of Professor Uchida)

XI. Imperial troops, armed and drilled by western powers, march over the Lion Bridge leading to the Cho Yan gate of Peking. (Photograph by Lucy Calhoun)

XII. A scene within the walls of the Forbidden City. From left to right: a prince of the blood (indicated by the striped costume under his fur coat); a palace eunuch hurrying by; Mrs. Calhoun; a high Chinese official, the viceroy of Chihli; Manchu prince; Chinese official with mandarin square partly showing; another Chinese official. (Photograph by Lucy Calhoun)

XIII. A Manchu princess. (Photograph by Lucy Calhoun)

XIV. The patriarch Li Hung-chang as viceroy of Chihli and superintendent of trade for the northern ports. From A Photographic Album of The Japan-China War, *Hakubundo, Tokyo, 1895.*

merchants are part of the state apparatus, as agents of government monopoly and as holders of government degrees or titles.

Government control over the disposal of salt, through direct sales or through the licensing of monopolistic distributors, is incomplete. Of all possible sales, the salt revenue service accedes to only 50 percent. The other 50 percent of the market is in the hands of salt smugglers. Central government tolerates such an incomplete monopoly because it has not the power to enforce a complete monopoly. In any case, the government can afford to default half its potential salt revenues. This tolerance is reflected in the penal code, which allows that no penalty can be inflicted on a smuggler unless the person *and* his illegal salt both are taken in evidence. A 50 percent monopoly by central government is sufficient to defend salt revenues against regional interests because each regional power will be able to lay claims to less than that.

LOCAL GENTRY

Historically speaking, the gentry represent a new sector of the Establishment that emerged to power from Sung times onward. Although Fusion China evolved the concept of a bureaucratic elite, the gentry as officeholders and office seekers did not come into their own until aristocratic power vanished utterly. The Ch'in emperor had defeated or bought out the military aristocracy of the Warring States. But a second aristocracy arose to last on through T'ang times during the first half of the Era of Cyclical Imperial Conquests.

The second aristocracy fell from power with changes started during the Second Unity. The Sui Grand Canal opened communications between economic areas "A" and "B." These translocal communications favored identification by manorial heads with an imperial glory made all the more magnificent by the wealth brought to its center via that canal. For the first time rich and powerful men reached out in earnest for the rewards of the examination system, which at last prevailed over the emperor's appointment of landed aristocrats to office. In Sung times, the *Peking Gazette* began publishing to meet the growing interest of local elites in court affairs. The *Gazette*, published until the end of the Ch'ing dynasty, is a record of official acts, promotions, decrees, the emperor's replies to memorials, sentences, executions, and torturings. It is sent by mail under the war ministry to the provinces where it is distributed to interested parties.

But the men who started looking to the *Peking Gazette* for news of imperial glory were not merely attracted to it. They were pushed out of their landed estates by relentless demographic pressures: more births than the aristocracy could accommodate. Men of the warrior nobility in Eastern Chou times kept their kind by dividing the feudal patrimony among sons who were able to open geographic frontiers by conquest. Men of the second aristocracy, when that frontier closed, divided their landholdings among sons in the practice of homoiogeniture. Soon after that, the Sung government enacted homoiogeniture into law. The Sung law aimed at breaking the power of the aristocracy, but the law merely stated what had become a fact. Private estates were no longer self-sufficient because they were reduced to smaller holdings among more numerous holders. When the law went into effect, the dying aristocracy was already looking for new economic frontiers as an alternative to ever subdividing patrimonies.

One frontier was government service. Successful candidates of the examination system were placed in posts far from home, in fresh territory to exploit.

Another frontier was commerce, opened up by the release into the open market of all the little people who had been clients of the great estates. Printed currency and a money economy had already evolved with the T'ang dynasty. A genuine commercial revolution resulted during the Sung period of the Second Partition. Wealth could be made in trade as in government office, or in both. Trade promoted the growth of towns and cities. No longer were urban centers merely double-walled fortresses—administrative buildings within the inner ring, huddles of peasant huts within the outer ring. New homes of the new gentry were located there, and in new towns unassociated with administration. Merchant gentry, bureaucratic gentry, scholastic gentry, landed gentry—these were the different faces of the new corporate elite that had replaced the second aristocracy. Now the towns contained amusement quarters—wineshops, tea shops, restaurants, geisha houses, and theaters. This is not to overlook bookshops, a service industry of some importance to scholar-statesmen. Accommodation of the urban gentry rested, of course, with peasant manpower removed from the folk culture of the villages to the folk neighborhoods of cities. Inevitably, an urban equivalent of the expendable "grass-and-ashes" peasantry appeared in a coolie proletariat, another route into the Sink of Death.

All in all, this new urbanism set the appearance of the mature Agrarian State. If high culture is urban culture, it is because the two main economic resources of the gentry came to be located in cities, centers of trade and office. It is only in post-Sung times that the countryside came to be romanticized in art and poetry: rural appreciation from the shelter and comforts of the city.

Political power in the mature Agrarian State came to follow office, and wealth followed power. The illusion that the gentry is merely a class of landlords is created by the high turnover of office. Officials do not generally pursue a lifelong career in government. They hold office for a brief time, make the most of it, and then retire, often investing their profits of office in land. But they also invest in business. Land is the more prestigious because it is nostalgic of the country estates belonging to the second aristocracy. Also, land cannot be taken away and movable wealth can. Officials do not choose to remain in office long because they may be driven out after a short time by the despotism of the system. The higher a man rises in the ranks, the closer he gets to the person of the emperor. His position gets more exposed and vulnerable. He can make highly visible mistakes and rivals can use influence to unseat him. The trick is to get out with one's political connections intact for application to one's private economic life back home.

The biggest source of gentry income is government, formal and informal. Informal government includes the arbitration of disputes, the management of local irrigation works for peasant clients, and the organization of local defense. Next in importance is landholding, and then mercantile activities, money lending, investments and service fees. These three sources of income—government, land, and business—return income in the ratio of about three to two to one.

Few members of the gentry serve formal government at any one time. The bulk of income from government is from informal government, about two-thirds of it. The total income from informal government equals that of formal government, which means that office holding is very profitable. A great amount of wealth is divided among the few who win appointments. Income from informal government is divided among greater numbers in smaller per capita amounts.

Gentlemen hold one-fourth of the land, taking 40 to 50 percent of the yield in rents. Total rents equal total income from office. This again indicates a large gain from office for a select few, and a relatively low return on land, especially if taxation is taken into account. But gentry status carries with it immunity from taxation, thanks to an equation of interests between local government and the local gentry. The main burden of taxation falls on the peasants. Lucky ones find it convenient to register land under the name of some patron who will pretend to play the role of landlord. He collects a fee for this service, an amount less than his client would pay the government in taxes, and pockets it as a clear profit. The pretended landlord is also in a preferential position to buy land if it comes up for sale, at which time he becomes the real owner with a policy of rack-renting.

Chang Chung-li of the University of Washington in Seattle has calculated the gentry's share of the Gross National Product for the 1880s. This is somewhat later in time than our ethnographic present, when the number of gentlemen had increased at the expense of claims on the economy by the nobility, but the fact remains that only a tiny fraction of the population is privileged to consume the products of peasant toil without labor on its own part. The number of privileged persons holding degrees in the 1880s was 1.5 million. These men hold gentry status de jure. They are the *shen-shih,* the scholar-statesmen: men licensed to take a higher degree, men qualified for office, men in office, or men retired from office. With their dependents, the gentry de facto, the total number of privileged persons comes to 7.5 million, or close to 2 percent of the population. Of the gentry de jure, only 1.6 percent, or 23,000 men, actually hold civil office at any one time. Add to this another 1.1 percent, degree-holding assistants who act as secretaries. The others, living in their home communities, are the local gentry. According to Chang's calculations, the gentry as a class—officeholders, local gentry, and dependents—accounts for 24 percent of the GNP. Perhaps we ought to say the Gross Imperial Product, or GIP.

It is true that the wealth of Cathay is concentrated in a few at the expense of the many. But gentry income is distributed over an immense range of inequality. This distribution shows, once again, that it is not wealth that determines privilege. It is a matter of legal definition. The gentry class includes everybody from a rich merchant with a purchased degree, to an official with an earned degree, to the poorest licentiate who will avoid manual labor at the expense of his standard of living. Peasant farmers, artisans, and tradesmen also earn incomes that vary from high to low, but these men are all equally nonprivileged by definition. It is nonprivilege that defines the peasantry, whatever the occupation or income, income that averages out to twenty to twenty-five taels per annum among some four hundred million peasants.

If John Stuart Mill speaks of the riches of Cathay as being "torn from the producers" by the Lords of the Soil, the exact rate of tearing in the Chinese Agrarian State can be calculated as the most the Green Circle can yield up and the most the gentry can get. Discounting the nobility, the Neolithic landscape of the Green Circle can sustain close to 2 percent of the total population in parasitism with 24 percent of its substance.

The parasitic metaphor is not wholly adequate, however. The Neolithic host is actually part of a transaction. Exploitation by the gentry is not a one-sided affair. It involves an exchange of things of unequal value, perhaps, but an exchange nonetheless. Peasant production for gentry consumption amounts to a bargain of sorts between two parties.

If there were no gentry to exploit the peasantry, there would *be* no peasantry. The very process of exploitation brings an isolated Neolithic folk culture into civilization as a nonisolated folk culture. Just as the Miao would revert to a primitive state of culture if their trade contacts with the Chinese were cut off, leaving them without metal, so would Chinese peasants revert to tribal culture if not exploited by men of high culture.

It would be folly, then, to sneer at the self-serving justification of state power by the literati. The *Sacred Edict,* in explaining why the peasantry ought to render up its quota of grain and labor with right good cheer, advances the argument that moneys and proceeds received will be reinvested in the improvement of the peasant condition. Nothing, on the face of it, could be further from the truth. Yet this is what the *Sacred Edict* has to say:

> There has been arable land from time immemorial, and taxation in consequence. Taxes are of extreme importance:— the State depends on them to meet all its expenses: in the nature of the case they should be collected by the State from the people, and rendered by the people to the State. In all history, which Dynasty has not thus levied them? Besides, the fact is, these taxes are not for the private use of government, but are used for you people. For example, they are used to sustain the numerous officials, that they may look after you; and to support numerous troops that they may protect you. With regard to the purchase of grain, and storing it in granaries, this also is simply for fear of years of famine, that you may be relieved. And not to stop mentioning this, there are also cities, canals, embankments, boats and granaries to be built and kept in repair—uses without number; all beyond question simply applying your taxes to promote your interests: never has the State oppressed the people for its own gratification. [XIV:1]

The farrago of lies and half truths indited in this statement of policy is obvious. The state claims to be dedicated to servicing the needs of the people when in fact it merely lives off them.

Yet, for all that, a bargain between nonprivileged producers and privileged consumers does exist. And perhaps it is not too lopsided, after all. The *Sacred Edict* is candid:

> To put it briefly:—if none of you owes taxes, the official will not come to enquire after you, nor the underlings to search for you. You will be able to dwell together with your wife and family in peace and safety, without the slightest annoyance. How delightful! [XIV:3]

How delightful, indeed! In effect, what the men of high culture are saying to the little people is this: "Let us exploit you and we will let you have your folk culture."

CHAPTER 12

THE MIGHTY DRAGON
AND THE LOCAL SNAKES

SYMBOLICAL of the emperor and all that pertains to him is
the dragon, a kind of reptilian dachshund: a serpent mounted
on four short legs. The imperial dragon often is portrayed in
skyward progress, its pythonic folds humping along through
a mass of heavenly clouds.

The emperor represents the transcendent power that keeps
the universe in balance. It is said:

> Heaven speaks not, explains not, yet the four seasons follow
> in regular succession, and all things follow in their turn. [*Lun
> Yu,* XVII:19]

If the emperor be infinite in wisdom and complete in virtue,
his subjects will bow to his sway without uttering a word. But
only the sage kings of old were so endowed with heavenly
principles.

> Shun is an example of government without effort. He gravely
> and reverently occupied his royal seat, facing due south. That's
> all he did. [*Lun Yu,* XV:4]

And so it is that the imperfect emperors that followed Shun
must render up to Heaven a prayerful apology for any floods,
droughts, plagues, murrains, earthquakes, comets, and eclipses
that are the signs of incomplete virtue and faulty personal
example.

For this act of cosmic piety the emperor at the time of the
winter solstice repairs to the Altar of Heaven and there faces
north, into the light of the pole star, Heaven's hinge on which
the world hangs. Having accounted for his weakness of personality over the past year, he turns around, ready once more to
occupy his throne, facing south, as Heaven's vice-regent. In
the words of the sacerdotal *I Ching,* government is a matter
of right ritual making the ruler's "character worthy of imitation" (hexagram XVI). Or, as Confucius says:

Frontal view of a bronze dragon, dating from the late Chou period.

When the ruler himself is upright, things will get done even without his giving orders. [*Lun Yu*, XIII:6]

From the highness of his south-facing Dragon Throne, the emperor confers office on his mandarins. They come before him in the imperial audience chamber, in tune with solemn music and high ceremony, to receive their appointments as representatives of the crown. They abase themselves before him, falling to their knees three times, and at each bow touching their foreheads to the ground three times for a total of nine knockings. Installed out in the provinces they receive each imperial dispatch, placed on an altar in a special room decorated in royal yellow, with burning incense and further prostrations as if in the presence of the emperor himself.

But for all these terrifying rituals of subordination, the more truckling, the less despotism. The emperor's despotism is the plight only of those exposed to it in the throne room, where they have entered voluntarily in quest of patents of rank. The majesty of the imperial person is elevated, not on account of any power to make the earth tremble, but for his duties to Heaven. In these duties he acts as a scapegoat for his subjects as the result of a liturgical failure to harmonize man and nature with his personal example as expressed in right ritual.

> The sovereign who follows reproof becomes a sage. When the sovereign thus becomes a sage, as wood by the use of the line is made straight, his ministers without being charged anticipate his orders. When the ministers see that the sovereign yields himself to be molded by them, who among them would not dare to act in respectful compliance to his Majesty? [*Shu Ching*, IV:viiia:11]

The emperor, by allowing himself on scriptural authority to be reproved not for political but for liturgical error, is thus made captive of the very cosmological majesty that illuminates his officials in their control over more substantive matters.

The emperor presides over central government, a miniature state in itself, fed by the Grand Canal and centered in Peking. Of the 40,000 civil and military officials that make up the imperial bureaucracy, 90 percent of them belong to central government and work in the capital city. The other 10 percent, together with the local gentry, who number about 1.5 million, control the eighteen provinces of China Proper, which cover about 1.4 million square miles. The saurian conceit that pictures the emperor as a high-flying Dragon is appropriate to a ruler whose all-mighty powers are granted rather more in Heaven than on earth. An irreverent proverb puts it this way:

> The Mighty Dragon is no match for the local snake, which knows the ins and outs of the place.

The Dragon may be in charge of keeping man and nature in harmony, and he may be the richest and most spectacular man in the empire for doing so, but the Local Snakes, i.e., local officials and local gentry, are in charge of running the empire.

But this political reality is not verbalized as such with straight talk. It is rather verbalized with certain conventions of double-talk that insist that provincial governors and magistrates are appointed by the emperor as his deputies on a mission to extend the reach of his authoritarian powers. This is not true in practice. The proverb hits home. The proverb even hints at the tension that exists between the two domains, that of the Local Snakes looking for more autonomy and that of the Dragon trying to limit it.

The official version of dynastic government's mission is well phrased in the words of one examination candidate, who writes that "the emperor at the head of the bureaucracy, as a general of his armies, will lead the world forward to the practice of social virtue." This is the one unsubstantial mission of government all can agree on—putting oneself up as a good example for the commoners—seeing that so few gentlemen of the realm fall under the administrative discipline of central government. This mission is also congruent with the fact that commoners are politically passive, i.e., they generally lack the mobility aspirations to enter the ranks of the ruling elite, either in the formal government of officialdom or the informal government of the at-home gentry. In upholding the idea of the Great Society, it is to the Mandate of Heaven that the emperor looks, not to peasant votes. His Neolithic subjects look to the Green Circle for their place. Given the deculturated, broken tribal wholeness of folk life, the emperor may well boast of his taking the lead in pacifying it with the cosmic power of his example.

> The ruling elite is like the wind, the little people like the grass. When the wind blows, the grass bends. [*Lun Yu,* XII:19]

So it is that talk about the Great Society is given to morality, not enforceable statutes.

The Dragon Throne has meaning only for those persons who seek office—or are prepared to—by way of adding imperial dignity to the vast areas of public affairs they already control. It is the local gentry who arbitrate disputes and manage the labor for the digging of irrigation ditches for peasant clients, and they do so on their own without being appointed as agents of central government, and they educate themselves to this idea of public service through self-hired tutors. These are the men who get the work of empire done in the countryside, and who cooperate with the magistrate in getting it done. With all this privilege and responsibility taken into their own hands, there is little more they can do without taking away *everything* from the emperor's central government. The 1.5 million educated men of high culture so completely dominate the rural economy and control jurisprudence in the countryside and towns that dynastic government can collapse and life in the provinces will go on as before; and when dynastic government is restored, these same gentlemen bring to it a continuity of the traditional order. Only a few of them take up posts in that 10 percent of the bureaucracy making up local government. But when they do, they acquire yet other autonomous powers in the fields of administration, fiscal management, military power, and political authority in general. What is it, one might ask, that the Dragon controls out in the provinces that is not invaded by the Local Snakes?

The answer is: not very much in substantive matters. Apart from his right to appoint civil and military officials, draw up the ritual budget, and establish the criminal code, it is imperial dignity that the Dragon has to offer. Gentlemen seek titles, degrees, and posts because they are attracted by the glamour and cultural brilliance of the emperor's court, where consumption reaches its peak, scholarship its brightest, and ritual its perfection. Ambitious men have only to duck under this cultural umbrella to find something glorious beyond their own localities to bestow: the name of the emperor and his cause. The cause is culturalism, the idea that the only collective goals men of power throughout the Great Society can share are the nonadministrative ones of liturgical conformity—the imitation of imperial models and the display of high culture before peasants. These goals are nonetheless political because they reflect a difference between peasants and elites, and a power contest between elites and the throne.

In the Great Society, power persons from all over the realm belong to a common hierarchical order capped by the emperor. When the Local Snakes don their imperial robes, indicating rank in office or academic degree, they illuminate a ceremonial status system headed up by the Mighty Dragon. The pageantry of office and dignity of scholarship work to awe the Neolithic peasantry into yielding up its quota of tax and arms to the Local Snakes who know the ins and outs of the place.

Despite the fact that local gentry and local officials accept the emperor's status system, with his robes, rituals, and scholastic titles, they are constantly pushing for more autonomy, for more power to influence appointments to both central and local government. This political activism, in the form of petitioning and clique activities, is somewhat checked by the fact that the Local Snakes have to compete with the Dragon's hereditary brood of reptiles, the royal clansmen and other members of the nobility. At the end of the Ming dynasty, sixteen emperors over 277 years had delivered over one hundred thousand clansmen to the inheritance of an imperial income, a ratio of ten to one against the number of civil officials at that time.

The emperor thus must take some steps to keep local officials from enfeoffing their posts in competition with the nobility. Therefore, no local official (always posted at least five hundred *li* from home) is allowed to marry in his bailiwick, or own land in it, or permit relatives to hold office under him, or generally to hold office for more than one or two terms of three years each. In those few years an official is expected to make the best possible use of his franchise for profiteering, within the bag limits of his rank, of course.

Local officials, if they are to hold appointments in the emperor's name, must then sacrifice some of the autonomy they enjoyed at home as members of the local gentry. It is this exchange that keeps Chinese culturalism in balance. The transactions involved may be summarized under three points for each side.

FROM LOCAL OFFICIALS TO THE EMPEROR

Perhaps the single most important obligation owed central government is the requirement to send a contingent of examination candidates to Peking for the triennial palace examinations. Here is the substantive basis for the emperor's control over the top goals of upward mobility within the Great Society. The men sent there to be certified by the emperor as the elite of the realm also get a chance to appreciate—in the imposing palace architecture and monumental art, in the bustle of official life at its busiest, and in the universal attendance upon the court—the magnitude of imperial glory that attaches to the franchise awarded them.

The second obligation is fiscal, and the fiscal obligations of local government are satisfied by courier. These take the form of a series of ritual statistics that guide, shape, and protect local vested interests. From most provinces, little if any actual revenue is transported to the metropolitan center.

The third obligation is deference. Twice monthly all ranking officials in the provinces are to report themselves to the emperor on a salutary card of yellow paper, to the effect that (say) "Lin Tse-hsu, viceroy of the two Kwangs, humbly presents his duty to the throne, wishing His Majesty repose." The emperor acknowledges in vermilion ink, "Ourself is well." Here there is no real substance to the transaction, but in such ritual formalities as these reside the essence of imperial culturalism. The one man at the apex of the hierarchy has the power to call forth ritual deference from his inferiors in the Great Connected Whole, and it is such transactions that build up and maintain the imperial cause. Such ritual deference as prostrating oneself before the emperor is a small price to pay in exchange for a kingly role glamorized from on high.

FROM EMPEROR TO LOCAL OFFICIALS

Most important of all the emperor's duties in upholding the imperial community he heads is the granting of patents of rank and office to his civil and military officials. He determines the bag limit for each rank and defines the term of office and geographical range within which spoils may be sought. This makes the emperor a powerful patron to a wide number of clients, a remarkable organizational achievement given the primitive communications technology of the Chinese Agrarian State. Of course, he or his close aides get a chance to scrutinize all clients when they come to Peking. There the need to fight through the rigors of influence peddling works as a harsh but effective sorting system in selecting the most determined candidates. The others may be retired from consideration.

Second, the emperor's board of revenue makes up an All-China budget. But there is no centrally devised budget including all provincial accounts, i.e., there is no common purse for imperial collection and disbursement. The budget made up by the financial department merely specifies along which lines the traffic of funds is to be handled. This is no empty gesture on the part of the throne. Ritual budget making is the essence of culturalism, the establishment of models to imitate, not orders to obey. The emperor shapes the pipelines through which local officials squeeze their booty, and everybody agrees to talk about the transactions in the language of strong centralism. This is what is meant by "serving the imperial will."

Finally, the emperor must control a military machine if he is to hold power over the idea of empire against possible usurpers. The Manchu throne has in its pay three hundred thousand bannermen armed with pike, bow, and sword. Their position in the imperial guard is inherited by right of conquest. Half these troops are stationed in Chihli for defense of the capital. A part remains in the Manchurian homeland. The rest are divided among small garrisons in the provincial capitals. The provinces themselves supply troops for their own local defense in the native armies of the Green Standard.

The payrolls of the Green Standard carry six hundred thousand Chinese soldiers, a figure perhaps padded by half for the increase of the commanders' income. Just as civil officials appropriate taxes for their own local establishment in the name of empire, so military commanders of the Green Standard squeeze the payroll in the name of provincial defense. Civil officials by the nature of their franchise can violate the customary norms of profiteering to a great extent before appearing disloyal to the system they serve. Troops on the rampage, on the other hand, are more visible than a peasantry extorted by bureaucrats. Perhaps the contempt held by civil officials for the military lies in this odious distinction. In any event, as soon as a commander uses his soldiery for a feat of brigandage or a power play, his "official forces" are defined by the throne as "bandit gangs." The problem of the emperor is to keep some balance between troops defined as "official" and those defined as "bandits." The leverages used by the emperor in this balancing act are the promotions, stipends, and other awards he can deliver. Military officers alone are recipients of old feudal titles, dating from Chou times, such as duke, marquis, and earl. These are hereditarily bestowed, although no land grants are given. Only imperial clansmen are given fiefs with their feudal titles.

The authority of the emperor in all these transactions rests with initiating communications and in the duty of his officials to receive them with uncritical, passive respect. It is for the ruler to

> . . . issue decrees as if from a spring of flowing water. [*Kuan Tze*, I:3]

And it is for his servants to reply only in formulas fixed by him.

> Words which the first kings did not prescribe, those the ministers and officers of state dare not speak. [*Hsiao Chung*, IV]

It is sufficient discharge of his duty for an official to promulgate an imperial order; feedback is disrespectful of authority. Should an official address a message upward to the throne, he is required to couch it in the apologetic language of confession for his misdeeds, asking to be "pulped from head to heel" for venturing the humblest suggestion. The punishment is for ritual insubordination. Uncritical receipt of imperial messages is a sincere demonstration of personal loyalty—sincere because it permits the emperor to exercise his moral sway, that is, his liturgical influence. There is no dialogue of information and reply. For information the official is dependent on his clique or faction. From the emperor's point of view, cliques are conspiratorial against his authority because they weaken his power to elicit ritual subordination. Proper subordinates receive messages in silence and do not discuss them with others.

If the emperor means to lead the world to social virtue, it is a virtue very close to realization: the peasantry already pays up without much complaint. Thus is government said to be accountable to the people—people *do* pay up in return for moral instruction. In terms of fiction, the flow chart of empire would be diagramed as in Figure 9.

The actual flow chart of empire is shown in Figure 10.

But the fiction has a logic of its own. Its aim is not to *explain* the politics of empire but to *boost* the politics of empire. It does so by giving reasonability to the idea that government

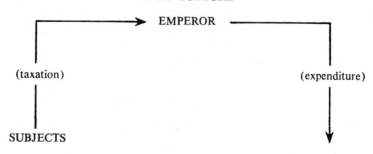

FIG. 9   *Fictional flow chart of empire*

is a service when it is not; and this is believed because the idea is a useful point of contention between the Dragon and the Local Snakes. Who has the right to be responsible to the people translates as, Who has the right to exploit them in whose name?

Actually, the power of the emperor is in the hands of a small clique of high officers who have his ear. For the time a given clique is united under its privileged communications with the emperor, it may impose its will on others competing for the place. It is within these cliques that the real push and pull between the interests of the Local Snakes and the Mighty Dragon takes place.

Privileged clique members, always high officers, are advanced in age. In this they are unusual. Most officials serve only one or two terms of three years each before retirement. It is over these ranks of high turnover that the patriarchs exercise control. They appoint, promote, dismiss, demote, and punish. The emperor periodically reads off a catalog of these actions by way of making the men care for their official standing as against their private interests. The emperor's role is to force officials to care for their standing in the imperial hierarchy, but the emperor's clique distributes the actual material and power benefits of office.

The contest between local and central government, then, passes through a few key officials at court, who are highly visible to the emperor and therefore highly vulnerable to the emperor's despotic whims. The danger of privilege is threat of its loss. Thus, the venerable old officials at court are in a sense hostages for the loyalty of their followers to the imperial cause and a check against the loyalty of "pupil" to "teacher." The patron/client relationship on which cliques are

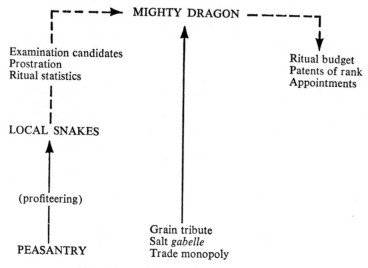

FIG. 10   *Actual flow chart of empire*

built the Chinese phrase in the language of a teacher/pupil relationship. But pupil can get together with teacher against the throne only in Peking, and so the emperor makes sure that the pupils are widely separated out in the provinces. The balance of interests between center and parts thus reduces to a struggle of the patriarchs to maintain their clients and to the emperor's struggle to alienate them.

Beyond that, one of the greatest concerns of the emperor is to maintain the legitimacy of royal blood. Officialdom agrees most readily to this concern, for in a sense, the emperor is a captive of this concern. The Manchu emperor ought not to impregnate Chinese females. Just as certainly no Manchu woman in the harem, or among the emperor's wives, is to be impregnated by anybody *but* the emperor. All children born to the emperor's four wives and to his concubines are legally his (ranked according to the rank of their mother). To cast doubt on the father of any of these children would be to cast doubt on the royal line, whose blood purity is the mainstay of the emperor's mandate. From the earliest imperial times only castrated males or eunuchs have been allowed in the residential quarters of the imperial palace. In Ming times their number reached one hundred thousand; toward the end of the Ch'ing dynasty, eunuchs numbered only three thousand, confined only to the Forbidden City. In the autobiography of Aisin-Gioro Pu Yi, the last of the Manchu emperors under the reign name of Hsuan T'ung, the numerous tasks of the eunuchs are detailed as follows:

> In addition to being in attendance at all hours, carrying umbrellas and stoves, and other such jobs their tasks, according to the *Palace Regulations,* included the following: Transmitting imperial edicts, leading officials to audiences, and receiving memorials; handling official documents of the various officers of the Household Department, receiving money and grain sent by treasuries outside the palace, and keeping a fire watch; looking after the books of the library, the antiques, calligraphy, paintings, clothing, fowling-pieces, bows and arrows; keeping the ancient bronzes, the *objets de vertu,* the yellow girdles granted to meritorious officials, and fresh and dried fruit; fetching the Imperial Physicians to attend in the various palaces, and obtaining the materials used in the palace by outside builders; burning incense before the records and precepts of the emperor's ancestors, their portraits, and the gods; checking the comings and goings of the officials of various departments; keeping the registers of the attendance of the Hanlin academicians and of the watches of the officers of the guard; storing the imperial seals; recording the actions of the sovereign; flogging offending eunuchs and serving women; feeding the various living creatures in the palace; sweeping the palace buildings and keeping the gardens tidy; checking the accuracy of the chiming clocks; cutting the emperor's hair; preparing medicine; singing opera; reciting classics and burning incense as Taoist monks in the City Temple; becoming lamas in the Yung Ho Kung as substitutes for the emperor; and many other duties.

The eunuchs are a successful instrument in keeping the purity of the ruling house, but the instrument introduces another element of factionalism, as between officials versus eunuchs. The eunuchs effectively monopolize communication channels to the emperor, bought off by this or that clique. Even royalty itself is at the mercy of the eunuchs. Pu Yi reports that his uncle, Huang Hsu (the ninth and next to last emperor of Ch'ing house), had to bribe one of the top ranking eunuchs to announce his visitations to Tzu Hsi (regent in control), to whom he owed respects. Not announced, in the elaborate code of court etiquette, he couldn't enter.

Just how effectively eunuchs act as gatekeepers to the emperor is described by Pu Yi. Pu Yi, the tenth and last of the Mighty Dragons to sit on the Ch'ing throne, continued to live like an emperor on the palace grounds after his abdication of 12 February 1912. He was treated this way and given expenses in accordance with Articles Providing for the Favorable Treatment of the Great Ch'ing Emperor after His Abdication, courtesy of the provisional Republican government headed by President Li Yuan-lung. Pu Yi writes in his autobiography about his demand to have a telephone installed. He had learned about telephones from his English tutor, Reginald F. Johnston.

> When I was fifteen an explanation from Johnston of the uses of the telephone aroused my curiosity, and when I heard from my brother Pu Chieh that my father's house had one of these toys I told the Household Department to have one installed in the Mind Nurture Palace. On receiving this order the head of the Household Department, Shao Ying, turned pale with horror. He did not utter a word of protest, however, and withdrew with a "yes, sire." But the next day all my tutors came to offer advice.
>
> "There is no precedent for such a thing in the ancestral code. If a telephone is installed anyone might talk to your majesty, a thing that never happened in the times of your ancestors. . . . The ancestors never used these foreign contraptions. . . ."
>
> I had arguments with which to retaliate: "The chiming clocks, pianos and electric lights in the palace are all foreign things that have no place in the ancestral system, but did not my ancestors use them?"
>
> "If outsiders can make phone calls whenever they like will they not offend the Celestial Countenance? Will this not damage imperial dignity?"
>
> "I have been offended by outsiders often enough in the press. What difference is there between reading insults and hearing about them?"
>
> Perhaps even my tutors did not understand at the time why the Household Department asked them to dissuade me. What really frightened the Household Department was not that the "Celestial Countenance" might be offended, but that the telephone might enable me to have more contact with the outside world.

Pu Yi finally got his telephone installed, complete with directory. He then proceeded to call Dr. Hu Shih, the famous

Chinese scholar that Johnston had talked about. This is the same Hu Shih who led the literary revolution in China, who was ambassador to the United States 1938–1942, who was bold and powerful enough to uphold the ideal of a free press against the policy of the Nationalists' refugee regime on Formosa, and who died there in 1962.

Pu Yi called Hu Shih:

> By a piece of luck he answered the phone himself.
>
> "Is that Dr. Hu?" I asked. "Excellent, guess who I am."
>
> "Who are you? I have no idea."
>
> "Ha, ha, no need to guess, I'll tell you. I'm Hsuan T'ung."
>
> "Hsuan T'ung? Is that Your Majesty?"
>
> "Right, I'm the emperor. I've heard your voice now, but I haven't seen you. Come round to the palace when you have time so that I can have a look at you."
>
> This casual joke brought him along. Johnston told me that Hu Shih had come to see him especially to confirm the telephone call as he had not expected "His Majesty" to phone. He anxiously asked Johnston about palace etiquette and decided to come when he found out that I was a reasonably good-tempered emperor. I had forgotten all about our conversation and had not told the eunuchs to inform the guards, so that when Dr. Hu Shih arrived at the palace gate no amount of talking would get him in. Not knowing whether to believe him or not the guards referred the matter to me, and only let him in when I gave the word.

Indeed, the very rituals celebrating the cosmic majesty of the Mighty Dragon work to hinder his communicating with anybody outside the court. Pu Yi writes about the daily pomp in his life:

> Whenever I went for a stroll in the garden a procession had to be organized. In front went a eunuch from the Administrative Bureau whose function was roughly that of a motor horn: he walked twenty or thirty yards ahead of the rest of the party intoning the sound "chir . . . chir . . ." as a warning to anyone who might be in the vicinity to go away at once. Next came two chief eunuchs advancing crabwise on either side of the path; ten paces behind them came the centre of the procession—the Empress Dowager or myself. If I was being carried in a chair there would be two junior eunuchs walking beside me to attend my wants at any moment; if I was walking they would support me. Next came a eunuch with a large silk canopy followed by a large group of eunuchs of whom some were empty handed and others were holding all sorts of

things: a seat in case I wanted to rest, changes of clothing, umbrellas and parasols. After these eunuchs of the imperial presence came eunuchs of the imperial tea bureau with boxes of various kinds of cakes and delicacies and, of course, jugs of hot water and a tea service; they were followed by eunuchs of imperial dispensary bearing cases of medicine and first-aid equipment suspended from carrying poles. . . . At the end of the procession came the eunuchs who carried commodes and chamber pots.

The majesty of the emperor is built out of the numerous services multiplied to serve him. The services and the personnel are a measure of the glamour at the royal heart of the court. Pu Yi describes the extravagant display put on at mealtime:

When it was time to eat (and the times of the meals were not set but were whenever the emperor felt like eating), I would give the command "Transmit the viands!" The junior eunuchs of the presence would then repeat "Transmit the viands" to the eunuchs standing in the main hall of the palace in which I lived and they would pass it on to the eunuchs standing on duty outside the hall; these would in turn call it out to the eunuchs of the "imperial viands room" waiting in the Western Avenue of the Forbidden City. Thus my order went straight to the kitchens, and before its echoes had died away a procession rather of the sort that used to take a bride's trousseau to her groom's house had already issued from the "viands room." It was made up of an imposing column of several dozen neatly dressed eunuches hurrying to the Mind Nurture Palace with seven tables of various sizes and scores of red-lacquered boxes painted with golden dragons. When they reached the main hall they handed their burdens over to young eunuchs wearing white sleeves who laid out the meal in an eastern room of the palace.

About one hundred main dishes were laid out on the tables, aside from tables of cakes, rice, porridge and salted vegetables.

According to the record of one month of the second year of my reign, the Empress Dowager Lung Yu, the four High Consorts and myself used up 3,960 catties of meat (over two tons) and 388 chickens and ducks every month, of which 810 catties of meat and 240 chickens and ducks were for me, a four-year-old child.

This is not counting the monthly allocation for all the numerous other ranking personnel attached to the palace. The monthly expenditure, "wasted in order to display the grandeur of the emperor," came to almost fifteen million silver taels.

Imperial grandeur also calls for constant garment making. In the records of one month in some forgotten year, Pu Yi found that "eleven fur jackets, six fur inner and outer gowns, two fur waistcoats, and thirty padded waistcoats and pairs of trousers" had been made for him. This ever-burgeoning wardrobe was the target of a complicated schedule of costume changes as laid down in regulations in the charge of eunuchs of the clothing storerooms.

> To manage all of this extravagant pomp there was, of course, a suitable proliferation of offices and personnel. The Household Department, which administered the domestic affairs of the emperor, had under its control seven bureaus and 48 offices. The seven bureaus—the storage bureau, the guard bureau, the protocol, the counting house, the stock raising bureau and the construction bureau—all had storerooms, workshops and so on under them. The storage bureau, for example, had stores for silver, fur, porcelain, satin, clothes and tea. According to a list of officials dating from 1909, the personnel of the Household Department numbered 1,023 (excluding the Palace Guard, the eunuchs and the servants known as "sulas").

If the emperor is visualized by officialdom to sit gravely, reverently on his throne, facing south, and nothing more, it is because the pomp and extravagance thrust upon him to magnify his celestial glory immobilizes him. The more pageantry, the less the real power of the emperor, and the less the accountability of his officers.

It is clear that the pomp and extravagance that build up the imperial glory of the Mighty Dragon, in whose name the Local Snakes serve themselves, also restrict him from expanding his personal domain into the provinces. When the Local Snakes come to Peking and prostrate themselves before the Mighty Dragon, they appreciate full well the strength of their side in the everlasting contest between palace and province. Their bowings and abject prostrations are the substance of that strength: the ritual containment of the emperor.

CHAPTER 13

FUNERALS AND ANCESTORS

WHEN King Ch'ing acceded to the Chou regency in 618 B.C.,
he addressed his princes, thanking them for assisting him in
sacrificing at his ancestral temple. Heartfelt thanks they must
have been, for the conduct of the ancestral ceremonies was the
instrument of royal accession by which those under the king
raised him to it. A song written about the occasion has come
down to us in the *Shih Ching*, or *Book of Odes*. Titled "Lieh
Wen," it concludes with these lines:

> The King of Chou is top man
> In war valor. Obey him.
> You all have your fiefs from him.
> None are as strong as he.
> His glory is the brightest;
> All copy-cat his power.

The court poet who sang this panegyric knew from observation that royal virtue expressed itself most eloquently with
catapults and battering rams.

Just as Confucius redefined *chun-tzu,* noble sons of the
ruler, to mean a nonhereditary nobility whose superior bearing
was acquired by education, so he passed on a new meaning
for *jen,* man, the qualities of a king. When the *Odes* were
composed, *jen* meant war valor. Confucian tradition gives man-
liness an altogether different gloss. Here is the same "Lieh
Wen," celebrating the king's accession, translated with a
Confucian bias:

> A man among men, the king!
> The four quarters look to his
> Illustration of glory
> For magical influence.
> With virtue so arresting,
> All parts do imitate him.

The attractive virtue in question is love of parents, which
makes for government by filial piety. This method of govern-

ment is said to have been invented by the pre-Shang culture heroes.

> The first kings displayed their supreme moral power in a vitalizing demonstration of filial piety, by which they made the Great Society obedient. [*Hsiao Ching,* I]

The emperor is said to so love and reverence his father, which is Heaven, that he begets

> . . . the teaching influence of the virtuous moral power imminent among the hundred clans. [*Hsiao Ching,* II]

The effect among the hundred clans—influential families of the same surname; formerly the ducal courts named after their leading families—is such that:

> If funeral rites are performed with great care, and if remote ancestors continue to be recognized long after they are dead, then will the virtue of the people be made excellent. [*Lun Yu,* I:9]

But what has tendance of the dead and devotion to living parents to do with imperial politics? Answer: the Confucian doctrine of filial piety, backed up with a set of classics dating back to feudal times, has *everything* to do with imperial politics. The politics of culturalism again.

On the one hand, filial piety is the model of virtue the emperor presents, in Heaven worship, for imitation among those subjects of his that count—the hundred clans, the politically active and mobility oriented elite. The elite, in turn, set themselves up as moral exemplars among the peasantry, but it is understood that the model at this level is to be avoided. An obedient peasant rejects the life way of his betters. The domestic ritual of the elite, however, takes after court ritual. This is the connection that relates each influential family to the Great Connected Whole under the emperor's cultural leadership.

On the other hand, filial piety is used as a doctrinal weapon by officials to keep a certain distance from the emperor, while still standing under his cultural umbrella. They assert thereby their right to work in the *name* of the throne but not *for* it. This weapon serves the native Chinese aspirants to office by keeping them competitive with imperial favorites among the Manchu nobility. The Manchus, who conquered China in 1644, number ten million, over 2 percent of the population or about the same percentage represented by the Chinese elite, the gentry. Of highest rank, in theory, are the imperial clansmen, some seven hundred descendants of Nurhachi, the founder of the Ch'ing house. To these must be added the blood relations of the emperor, of the empress-mother and grandmother, of the empress, and of the consort of the crown prince. These princes of the blood (twelve grades) give themselves mainly to the material aggrandizements of conquest, provided them through the Imperial Clan Court, and seldom enter administration. The real competition comes from the titular nobility, the Manchu aristocracy of thirty-two grades, insofar as Manchu officials of the first, second, and third ranks are ennobled. For the Manchus, it is usually high office or none at all. The remainder of the Manchu nobility are bannermen, 1.5 million of them, counting dependents. They are scattered throughout the realm, with nearly 500 in Kiangsu province, for example, where the governor is required to raise five hundred thousand taels per annum for them.

It is true that the Manchu elite and the Chinese elite form one governing class given to the preservation of the Confucian state. If the emperor ennobles Manchu officials, this is not to say he is expressly pitting Manchu against Chinese, or even noblemen against gentlemen. Rather more to the point, he is showing the extent to which appointments to positions of formal power are his to make. When he places the stamp of nobility on his choice, he is demonstrating the autocratic strength of his hand against the claims of merit, feudalist claims in a new guise. Because it is a struggle, his power is limited by the force brought to bear on the other side. The emperor thus has to recognize the mobility goals of the Chinese gentry lest these powerful men, who actually control the countryside, combine against him. He absorbs this pressure through the examination system. As the Emperor T'ai-tsung of the T'ang dynasty put it, "The ambitious of the world have fallen within the range of my bowshot." But Chinese pressure for a place in the bureaucracy has steadily displaced Manchu occupants, who started out holding about 40 percent of the posts but who now hold only 20 percent. This still overrepresents the actual proportion of Manchus in the Chinese population. Which is to say, the court to that extent prevails in deciding the make-up of the ruling class. The tag of titular nobility merely highlights this fact. In other words, the struggle between Manchu nobility and Chinese gentry is the old struggle of autocracy versus feudalism, whether it be under a foreign or a native dynasty.

Officers of state manage to satisfy themselves *and* the throne by showing respect for the values of filial piety. The political activism of the Local Snakes is compatible with familism, and familism is compatible with the Dragon's idea of government by filial piety. The Dragon encourages kin groups as interest groups because this localizes the political interests of all those who have no rightful concern for translocal business, the hereditary concern of the throne. Care of the empire is a trust committed to the emperor by Heaven, and it is fitting that he maintain it to the death. An official has only his services to discharge, not a heavenly trust to maintain. When the dynasty fails, the services of the official can no longer be discharged, and he may leave them and save himself, and return home. A quotation from the *Li Chi* in support of this idea is congenial to both the emperor and those of his appointed officials who are not noblemen.

> Therefore, when calamity comes on a state, for the ruler to die for its sacrificial altars is to be regarded as right; but for a Great Officer to die for the ancestral temple is to be regarded as a change of the duty required of him. [*Li Yun,* II:18]

Indeed, the laws of the great Ch'ing empire specifically inveigh against the private worship of Heaven, a treasonable offense. But these laws are self-policing, except among rebel groups dedicated to overthrowing the ruling house in their own name. When the emperor performs his solstitial rituals in worship of Heaven, he worships his royal ancestors as well— their tablets are set up on the topmost terrace of the Altar to Heaven, together with the tablet to Shang Ti, synonymous with Heaven. For others to worship Heaven is to usurp the emperor's own family rites. A pertinent quotation from Confucius on this matter is well-known:

> For a man to sacrifice to ancestral spirits which do not belong to him is presumptuous. [*Lun Yu,* II:24]

Far from being motivated to presume on the emperor's heavenly trust, officials rather receive their appointments by way of working to glorify and enrich their own families. Ancestor worship backs up this aim, which is agreeable to the royal court and to Chinese bureaucrats alike.

It would be a mistake if the word *bureaucrat* in the setting of the Agrarian State called forth a picture of a salaried federal employee commuting from suburban Washington, D.C., to a job in a capital building pushing papers in the public interest, and who then at the end of the day settles down to enjoy his own private home life made comfortable and safe by others as civically employed as himself. The Chinese counterpart of the American government official does not live at home but at his office far away, and for years at a time. Bureaucracy in the premodern economy of the old Agrarian State simply does not allow for the emergence of a professional bureaucratic career apart from the total social and economic context of the official's family life, which is set in the politics of the official's home district. The bureaus of the Chinese Empire do not operate for the distribution of administrative services. There is no need for a bureaucrat to do a job of welfare in exchange for the privilege of his office. Office merely adds dignity to a style of profiteering that can be done at home, from the strength of corporative family organization, even when empire has fallen.

The links that connect Local Snakes with the Dragon in one hierarchical order, which is the culturalism of the imperial cause, are the basic ceremonies of filial piety: funerals and ancestor worship.

The hierarchy is a religious one, embracing court and domestic ritual. The emperor at court worships a nonanthropomorphic sky god, T'ien or Heaven. Heaven requites a universal generosity for *t'ien-hsia,* All-under-Heaven, in response to the emperor's cosmic piety on behalf of mankind. The privileges of court life and nobility thus are justified in the name of Heaven's blessings on all. The privileges of the nonhereditary ruling class are justified in the name of anthropomorphic household tutelaries, the spirits of dead male ancestors. In domestic worship, the ancestral spirits limit their blessings to the family line.

Court and domestic ritual were one and the same in the multistate politics of Eastern Chou. At that time, only heads of state worshiped ancestors, each state being a family corporation. It was a privilege of the power elite to have a family name in which to worship. Each of the feudal states had its court, with its ancestral temple, and so did the royal domain of Chou. In the politics of empire, there is a religious hierarchy. Only the emperor combines ancestor worship with state business. The important families of the empire conduct ancestor worship for family business only.

Filial piety begins with reverencing parents while they are alive, then giving them a big funeral and honoring their spirits after they are dead. Their spirit tablets are added in the family temple to those of previous male ancestors.

A famous story of moral education in the ethics of filial piety comes from Mencius, a story about the sage-king Shun, who had been a worthy minister under Yao before the empire was turned over to him. Shun was unhappy. He wept to high Heaven because his parents did not return his love. But he remained dutiful as ever, tilling their fields. He was emperor, he had married the two beautiful daughters of Yao, and he owned all the riches of the kingdom. Yet he sorrowed. Only reconciliation with his parents would end his grief.

> When young we take our parents as an object of affection; when married, our wife and children; when in the service of the state, our sovereign. If we fail to be appointed, we burn within. But the truly filial man is affectionate to his parents to the end of his life. The great Shun is an example of a man who still was true at the age of fifty years. [*Meng Tzu,* V:i:II]

In the western world, love of parents is regarded as neurotic. But in China, a young boy brought up in one of the gentry families of the empire will find the literature of filial piety part of his education in business management. The great family is a kind of business corporation. The ranks upon ranks of spirit tablets in the ancestral hall are a visible display of the corporation's executives and controllers and ordinaries, high and low. Along the temple walls the boy will see plaques and scrolls indicating government ranks, degrees, public honors, and citations given out to his relatives by government. He will meet with his tutor here, receive his cap of manhood, see the performance of theatrical troops, and as a man he will deliberate kinship policy here. At the ceremonies held in this hall, he will see his kinsmen act out, and later himself act out, the positions they hold in the corporation—at the level of the big family or at the level of a clan organization of families. At the birth of every male child, the marriage of each adult male, the death of each elder, and at the sacrificial ceremonies at spring and autumn, he will find all his relatives, and himself, taking a different part in the ceremonies according to age, seniority, and generation. At funerals, these differences will show up in differences of mourning costume and in the degrees of grief allowed to be expressed. The young boy will see that everybody acts out his position in the kinship structure, and that this position is determined by the closeness to or remove from the dead one. Viewing the sacrificial events given to reverencing ancestors will nurture in him a sense of pride, loyalty, and unity with his family and his clan. Especially will the pageantry of funeral processions, followed by generous mourning feasts, demonstrate the wealth and influence of his clan in comparison with other such units. But most importantly, funerals and ancestor worship function to keep the resources of the big family together as a unit against division after the death of the family's chairman of the board. The rites mobilize family members around a common center.

A description of a sacrificial ceremony held at the ancestral tombs of one wealthy and powerful clan during Ch'ing Ming, a spring festival falling in the first part of April 106 days after the winter solstice, is given an eyewitness account by Robert Morrison in the *China Repository* for 1832. The number of clan members attending, from all the joint families belonging to it, was over two thousand.

> After all things are in readiness, the whole party stands until the director gives the word. He first cries with a loud voice, "Let the official persons take their places"; this is immediately done and the ceremonies proceed.
>
> *Director:* "Strike up the softer music." Here the smaller instruments begin to play.
> *Director:* "Kneel." The priest then kneels in a central place fronting the grave, and behind him, arranged in order, the aged and honorable, the children and grandchildren all kneel down.
> *Director:* "Present the incense." Here stewards take three sticks of incense, and present them to the priest. He arises, makes a bow towards the grave, and then plants one of the sticks in an incense vase in front of the tombstone. The same form is repeated a second and a third time.
> *Director:* "Rise up." Here the priest and party stand up.
> *Director:* "Kneel." Again the priest and all the people kneel.
> *Director:* "Knock head." Here all bending forward and leaning on their hands, knock their foreheads against the ground.
> *Director:* "Again knock head." This is forthwith done.

Director: "Knock head a third time." This is also done. Then he calls out: "Rise up, Kneel, Knock head"; till the three kneelings and the nine knockings are completed. And all this is done in the same manner as the highest act of homage is paid to the emperor, or of worship to the supreme powers, heaven and earth. This being ended, the ceremonies proceed.

Director: "Fall prostrate." This is done by touching the ground with knees, hand and forehead.

Director: "Read a prayer." Here the reader approaches the front of the tomb holding in his hands a piece of white paper on which is written one of the sacrificial forms of the prayer.

The prayer offered was as follows:

"Taoukwang, 12th year, 3rd moon, 1st day, I, Lin Kwang, the second son of the third generation, presume to come before the grave of my ancestor, Lin Kung. Revolving years have brought again the season of Spring. Cherishing sentiments of veneration, I look up and sweep your tomb. Prostrate, I pray that you will come and be present; that you will grant to your posterity, that they may be prosperous and illustrious; at this season of genial showers and gentle breezes, I desire to recompense the root of my existence, and exert myself sincerely. Always grant your safe protection. My trust is in your divine spirit. Reverently I present the fivefold sacrifice of a pig, a fowl, a duck, a goose, and a fish; also, an offering of five plates of fruit; with oblations of spirituous liquors; earnestly entreating that you will come and view them. With the most attentive respect, this annunciation is presented on high."

After the reader finished his prayer, the director called out:

"Offer up the gold and precious things." Here one of the stewards presents gilt papers to the priest, and he, bowing towards the grave, lays them down before it.

Director: "Strike up the grand music." Here gongs, drums, trumpets and clarinets are beaten and blown to make as great a noise as possible.

Director: "Burn the gold, and silver, and precious things." Here all the young men and children burn the gilt papers, fire off fire crackers and rockets.

Such is the sum of a grand sacrifice at the tombs of ancestors. But to many the best part of the ceremony is to come, which is the feast upon the sacrifice. The roast pigs, rice, fowls, fish, fruits and liquors are carried back to the ancestral hall; where, according to age and dignity, the whole party sit down to eat and drink and play. The grandees discuss the

condition of the hall, and other topics connected with the
honor of the clan. . . .

Those . . . who have no ancestral hall eat their sacrifice
on the ground at the sepulchres.

The word *clan* in the above account is an elastic term in
English that will stretch to fit a whole range of Chinese kinship
organizations. At one extreme is the *hsing,* a large aggregate of
people from different localities who acknowledge themselves as
holders of the same surname. At the other extreme, on a smaller
scale, is the *tsu,* a localized descent group or lineage. The *tsu*
may involve just a few families or it may take in a whole settlement, as it sometimes does in Southeastern China. It is rare
in North China. But all levels of clan organization have these
features in common; they keep a register of membership, they
pool some of their property for the upkeep of the ancestral
temple and its services, and they hold ceremonies together, such
as the one carried out on Ch'ing Ming in honor of Lin Kung.

Two thousand people attended the tombs where Lin Kung
was reverenced. To have been at the center of so large a ceremonial enterprise, he must have been a very influential person,
active in clan politics, who was able to build up the Lin clan to
the heights of a *hsing* level of organization. But for most elites,
the maximum unit of kinship organization beyond the joint
family is the *tsu.*

The play of clan politics is an expression of status seeking on
the part of successful families who employ the wealth of their
propertied resources and the glamour of their official political
connections in building up a large, prestigious organization.
The family that takes the lead in organizing a clan will naturally have to pay out something in order to gain its returns, both
material and nonmaterial. The leading family donates the
largest amount of temple land, which serves to finance clan
ceremonies, clan secretaries, the publication of the clan register,
clan charities, and clan schools. Graduates of the clan's private
school who become officials are obliged to bestow their honors
on the clan and to support it financially, much to the special
benefit of the leading family.

The benefits of clanship are not, of course, equally distributed among all member families, which include peasant families
as well. Members who do not pay for the upkeep of the temple
may not enter it, but they are welcome at the open air ceremonies, such as those at Ch'ing Ming; they may partake of the

food offerings after the grandees have departed for banqueting within the temple precincts. The mystique of clanship is effective in winning commoners to the organization as loyal tenants and even as fighting men on those occasions when interclan rivalry comes to the point of violence.

The ability of rich and powerful families to organize massive clans and to mobilize manpower on a large scale obviously poses a threat to government, and a troublesome magistrate may soon find himself put upon by clan pressures in his district, and in rare cases, even physically threatened by a well-directed mob. But in the end, government has the ultimate weapon: the power to deny a troublesome clan the right of its members to take the civil service examinations, success at which, even at the lowest level, grants elite standing de jure.

Clan politics are important in matters of high prestige. But the effective business unit of corporate kinship is the joint family, with its own ancestral altar on the family grounds. The joint family consists of a number of conjugal families combined in a multigenerational unit. The conjugal family consists of a man, his wife (or wives), and their unmarried offspring. This is the same conjugal family unit that makes up the basic household of peasant life. Ordinarily, the conjugal family unit of whatever class dwells in its own living space: that of the peasantry in a one- or two-room farmstead house, that incorporated by the joint family of the elite in a separate apartment or compound in a complex of buildings and courtyards.

The joint family serves the elite as a functional means of securing political and economic advantages for a select group defined by kinship; it has corporately held resources to protect. It typically comprises the paternal grandparents, their unmarried children, and all of the married sons and their conjugal families. All live under one roof, each component family to its own dwelling space. A really large joint family is viewed as the ideal expression of wealth and prestige, but despite this ideal it is hard to find more than from five to thirty persons of three generations made up of three or four conjugal families. The head of the joint family and its priest is the oldest male of the oldest generation. This is usually the paternal grandfather, or if he dies, the oldest surviving son.

The clan does not share in a common purse. Only the joint families that compose it do. But there would be no clan organization of any kind without the member units. Ceremonies at the clan temple and at the ancestral tombs help organize the solidarity of each family member by allowing him to join something larger and more magnificent than himself. Ancestor worship on the part of the elite members of the clan gives a focus to their feelings of personal attachment. The very ritual of acting out their parts in worship helps maintain the status organization of each family that is so rehearsed. Ritual has a binding function, tying people together in a common activity. The language of ritual speaks of group tradition, group pride, group consciousness.

The Chinese elite are quite aware of the function ancestor worship serves. They are conscious of the dangers of splitting up the family estate. Once the sons quarrel over their shares and wish to divide and set up their own independent households, downward mobility is certain. Often the brothers cannot get along with each other, or they cannot stand the intrigues of the wives, secondary wives, concubines, and servants. Life in the joint family makes for bottled-up hostility for the sake of the organization. The rituals of filial piety—ancestor worship and funerals—make for solidarity by redirecting sentiments to a symbolic center, but this does not always work.

That is the psychological meaning of ancestor worship. It also has a political meaning. In this respect it is interesting to note that the rituals of filial piety have descended from Chou times. The public business of statecraft then was not separable from the business of kinship, and ancestor worship was conducted in the ducal court. Ancestor worship then functioned to rally kinsmen around the business of government that vested in them as a family oligarchy. The same rites have been appropriated by the gentry families of joint family organization under empire. These rites direct the prestige, power, and wealth of holding office to the good name of the family and its wider associations.

It is to the emperor's benefit that the elite should be so family centered. He has allowed the ambitious of the world to seek some of the heavenly prerogatives of imperial glory in competition with the nobility. These men are self-elected aspirants to office; they are not invited. They invite themselves to become grandees of the imperial cause. It is best they take their prestige home with them after leaving office.

The Confucian ideology of empire, promoted by scholars of the realm and patronized by the emperor to the interest of both parties, encourages the association of imperial glory with domestic interests. By an edict of 1729, these words of the Emperor K'ang Hsi were ordered to be read on Confucius's birthday to all successful graduates of the palace examinations in Peking:

> Good conduct counts first, and literary attainment comes next. . . . Through these triennial examinations held by the government are accorded the distinctions of "robes of silk" and "bows and flags," by which not only you yourselves are honored but also your grandfathers and fathers share in the glory.

The Confucian ideal of manhood, then, stresses the connection between serving the imperial cause and serving the domestic cause. A man's filial piety (*hsiao*) and his public reputation (*lien*) are two sides of the same Confucian personality. Elites of the realm are indoctrinated, by the very studies that lead to examination for office, to be *hsiao-lien,* "filial sons and honest subjects." Men who are *hsiao-lien* make of the performance of domestic duty and official duty, one duty.

Indeed, the emperor recommends that retired officials wear their robes of office at family weddings, funerals, and ancestral sacrifices. And he sends his officials home for a long period of mourning when their parents die.

Government by filial piety is a metaphor for a power arrangement that keeps things on two planes for peasantry and gentry alike. Peasants are separated from all considerations of power by family anarchy. Gentlemen of the realm are separated from the hereditary domain of the court by familism.

Gentlemen are to consider themselves as holding a certain rank within an overarching status system headed by the emperor. Thus:

> Emperor
> Nobility
>   Imperial Clansmen (about 700)
>   Titular Nobility (all Manchu officials)
>   Bannermen (1.5 million, with dependents)
> Gentry (5.5 million, with dependents)
>   Upper (120,000 holders of the *chin-shih* and
>   *chu-jen* degrees)
>   Lower (980,000 licentiates)
> Peasantry (400 million commoners)

(Note that the number of gentry given here is rather less than it came to be in the 1880s. This numerical increase, plus the increase in proportion of those who bought their status from the government, given its need for extra funds to cope with western contact, is a measure of the inroads made by the ambitious upon the power of royalty to exercise control over the composition of the ruling class.)

Occupying a place in the emperor's scheme of things gives the gentry participation in high culture, in civilization, in the collective goals of empire, in the imperial cause—something denied commoners by definition. Maintenance of this scheme, on its two planes, is what constitutes the politics of imperial culturalism: elites may participate in the emperor's liturgical government and peasants may not.

THE TWO PLANES

in gentry life	*in peasant life*
Court	Court
—	Cause
Cause	—
Family	Family

When the emperor begets the teaching influence in his worship of Heaven on behalf of the people, he is merely acting out virtue already made excellent by circumstances: the virtue of peasant compliance is made so by family anarchy, the virtue of gentry detachment from the court is made so by familism.

Peasants are said to be made obedient to the moral power of the emperor's example of filial piety by showing contentment with their lot; they do not seek mobility goals.

> To follow the seasons and share out the benefits of the earth, and then by rigorous economy in personal expenditure to have food for their fathers and mothers: this is the filial piety of the common people. [*Hsiao Ching,* VI]

Gentlemen are said to be made obedient to the moral power of filial piety by limiting their mobility goals to seeking a place in government, apart from court politics; they seek to dignify their family name with official deeds won in the imperial cause—the emperor's China-wide system of rank and ritual—and do not seek to combine against the throne nor to displace the rights of the nobility.

To acquire for oneself a station in the world and be made famous, one should regulate one's conduct by correct principles, thereby glorifying one's father and mother and transmitting their name to future generations: this is the last word in filial piety. [*Hsiao Ching,* I]

Funerals and ancestral sacrifices are rites of filial piety that direct official status won by the gentry to a symbolic center in their own family life. In this way, politically active men of the realm may find a place in the Great Society, as glorified participants in the royal cause, without trespassing upon the prerogatives of the royal house.

CHAPTER 14

LADDER TO THE CLOUDS

ON the game board of Monopoly, copyrighted by Parker Brothers, players control property and services to win wealth. So it is in real life in the industrial nation-states. A man may accumulate a fortune and with the prestige of wealth go on to win high political office, as did two presidents of top automobile factories in the United States become secretary of defense in their turn. Wealth is the origin of power.

Not so in the Chinese Agrarian State. Power is the origin of wealth. This must be the case. There are no diverse economic interests in competition with each other, and with government, for the investment returns from a diversity of productive landscapes. In the Chinese Agrarian State, there is only one basic landscape to exploit, that of the Green Circle. The grim Chinese reality is represented on the gaming board of *Sheng-kuan-t'u,* Advancing in Officialdom. In one word, the name of the game is Promotion.

The Promotion board is divided into sixty-six squares. Each square (with few exceptions) represents a major bureau of Ch'ing officialdom. Each bureau contains from two to seventeen official posts in it. Players decide what the stakes will be, then put one hundred chips in the pot. When all chips are drawn out, given the combined luck and skill of the players, the game is over. The gamble comes with a throw of four Chinese dice (they have red dots to show the ones and fours) at each move.

To begin with, the players throw for a place in the first square, "Background." From the particular instructions chanced upon there, by way of a combination of numerical and color values shown on the dice, the players are sent in turn to one or another of the other sixty-five squares. Most of these are headlined with the names of bureaus whose subsidiary posts number in the hundreds. Only a few bureaus list no posts. The Bureau of Penalties (square 8), for example, is subdivided by penalties given out to erring officials. This square is like the "Go to Jail. Go Directly to Jail. Do Not Pass Go, Do Not

Collect $200" square on the Monopoly board. A number of graded penalties are exacted there for the unlucky, such as "Stop duty, you are fired," "You are stripped of your title, but stay at your post," or "You face a severe reprimand."

A listing of all the squares is given in Figure 11. Two examples (squares 12 and 58) are given to show how bureaus are subdivided into a series of posts and graded offices.

Fɪɢ. 11   *The sixty-six squares of the Promotion board*

1. Starting an Official Career
2. Beginning of the Examination Life
3. Records Department
4. Military Merit
5. Metropolitan Censors
6. Grand Review of Minor Officials
7. Grand Reckoning of Official Merit (fitness report)
8. Punishment
9. Governors-General (Viceroys)
10. Provincial Governors
11. Tax Grain Office
12. Yellow River and Grand Canal Conservation (with examples of posts)
    a. Director of Rivers
    b. Deputy Director of Rivers
    c. Assistant Director of Rivers
    d. Junior Assistant Director of Rivers
    e. First Class Assistant
    f. Assistant's Assistant
    g. Magistrate
    h. Chief Accountant
    i. Inspector
    j. Sluice Gate Watcher ("unclassified" position)
13. Salt *Gabelle* Office
14. Offices of the Lieutenant-Governors
15. Offices of the Provincial Judges
16. Various Circuits
17. Imperial Commissioners (example: Li Hung-chang)
18. The Metropolitan Prefecture
19. All the Other Prefectures (*fu*)
20. Independent Subprefectures of Chihli
21. Independent Departments of Chihli
22. Departments (*chou*) subject to a *fu*
23. Districts (*hsien*) subject to a *fu*
24. Boards and Courts
25. Peking Granaries
26. Peking Police
27. Palace Examinations
28. Metropolitan Examinations
29. Provincial Examinations
30. Provincial Directors of Education

31. Imperial Academy of Learning
32. Imperial Board of Astronomy
33. College of Imperial Physicians
34. Imperial Equipage Department
35. Dual Titles
36. Board of Civil Office ⎫
37. Board of Revenue   ⎪
38. Board of Rites   ⎪
39. Board of War   ⎬ the Six Boards
40. Board of Punishments ⎪
41. Board of Works   ⎭
42. Colonial Office
43. The Censorate
44. Imperial Supervisorate of the Six Boards
45. Residence for Envoys of the Four Tributary States (Korea, Siam, Tonkin, Burma)
46. Office of Transmission
47. Supreme Court of Judicature and Review
48. Court of Sacrificial Worship
49. Court of Imperial Studs
50. Court of Imperial Banqueting
51. Court of State Ceremonial
52. Review on Titles of Honor
53. Pavilions of the Imperial Palace ("Throne-halls")
54. Grand Council (placed above the Grand Secretariat after 1730)
55. Honorary Titles of Nobility
56. Honorary Official Titles
57. Court of the Imperial Clan
58. Grand Secretariat (with examples of posts)
    a. Grand Secretaries
    b. Assistant Grand Secretaries
    c. Sub-Chancellors
    d. Readers
    e. Assistant Readers
    f. Sub-Assistant Readers
    g. Archivists
    h. Imperial Patent Office
59. Special Favors of the Emperor
60. Granting of Hereditary Rank
61. Hanlin Academy (College of Literature)
62. Imperial Supervisorate of Instruction
63. Imperial Patent Office
64. Imperial Household
65. Office of Purchased Degrees
66. Office for the Transfer of Provincial Officials to the Capital for Lower Posts

With each post under each bureau are listed a series of numerical combinations that can be thrown by the dice. With these are written out instructions for the next move, made with a notched or colored splint. Suppose a player lands on the first post under the bureau of the viceroys (square 9). One of the combinations listed there is *te,* two fours, which if thrown moves the player to the first post under the bureau of provincial governors (square 10). This bureau is easy enough to find because the first post listed there is the governor's office itself. But most of the posts, all written in smaller ideographs, give no indication of what bureau they belong to and the player must know it out of familiarity with real life bureaucracy. If he doesn't know enough about the actual system to know where to go when the dice name a post for him, he must lose his turn (as he also does if he throws certain combinations, or if he throws one not listed at the post where his splint rests). To lose a turn is to lose money. Players draw out chips from the pot according to the rank required of them to occupy the office they are appointed to on each move.

In the Chinese bureaucracy, an official holds title to his office as well as to his personal rank, as calculated on a scale of nine positions in both the civil service and in the military. Each rank carries its distinctive insignia on the robes of the official holding it. The insignia include a round ball or button of some precious material topping the headdress, which is an upside-down lampshade affair with red plumage streaming down the sides (peacock feathers stuck in the hat indicate various imperial honors); an embroidered plaque sewn to the front and back of the costume, figured with birds for civil officials and animals for military officials; and a girdle clasp made of more or less valuable material. These civil and military hierarchies integrate with the nobility in one, unified system of imperial stratification. Princes of the blood are given a sign of their hereditary rank with the same buttons adorning official hats. But players of Promotion, like real-life mobility activists, cannot hope to aspire to nobility, much less to the position of emperor. Each rank, except for a tenth unclassed position (*wei ju liu*), is divided into a principal (a) and a subordinate class (b).

Players of Promotion, therefore, are allowed nineteen different rates of exaction from the pot. High posts, which are the most lucrative, have the highest ranks attached to their incumbents, and low posts are given to men of lower rank. For example, the post of viceroy in square 9 goes with rank 2a, and the post of provincial governor in square 10 is rated at 1b. An example of an unclassed incumbency is the sluice gate watcher in square 12.

FIG. 12   *Insignia of bureaucratic rank*

MANDARIN SQUARES

Rank Button	Civil	Military	Clasp
1. Ruby	White crane	Unicorn	Jade set in rubies
2. Red coral	Golden pheasant	Indian lion	Gold set in rubies
3. Sapphire	Peacock	North China panther	Worked gold
4. Lapis lazuli	Wild goose	Manchurian tiger	Worked gold with silver button
5. Rock crystal	Silver pheasant	Black bear	Plain gold with silver button
6. Adularia	Eastern egret	Mottled bear	Mother of pearl
7. Plain gold	Mandarin duck	Tiger cat	Silver
8. Worked gold	Quail	Seal	Clear horn
9. Silver	Long-tailed jay	Rhinoceros	Buffalo horn
Unclassed —	Chinese oriole	—	—

The players decide beforehand what the money take will be for each rank. They also collect different amounts for honorary titles of nobility if they roll all sixes for duke, all fives for marquis, all threes for earl, all twos for viscount and all ones for baron. At the end of the game, he is a winner who has drawn out of the pot more than he put in.

The game of Promotion reflects the fact that prestige and wealth are dependent on power. The ideal way into power, into one of the twenty thousand or so ranking posts, is to climb, rung by rung, up the Ladder to the Clouds (*pu-pu ch'ing-yun*).

The Ladder to the Clouds is a figure of speech for the imperial examination system by which candidates are graded and licensed with patents of scholarship. These academic degrees bring privilege and, at the top of the ladder, appointments in the clouds. Officials are Stars in Heaven. The Confucian motto behind the system is *chu hsien jen neng,* "Employ the able and promote the worthy."

Worth is moral superiority whose elevation is judged by literary examinations on the philosophical, historical, and poetical classics of the Confucian persuasion and their accretion of learned commentaries. Typically, the candidate is given some quotations from these works that he must treat as a theme in eight steps of rhetorical development as follows:

1. Analysis of the theme
2. Amplification of the theme
3. Explanation
4. Postexplanation
5. Argument, first division
6. Reassertion of theme
7. Argument, second division
8. Argument, third division

These *pa-ku* or eight-legged essays cannot be written passably without extensive reading and memorization. Cribbing takes the form of smuggling miniature editions of the classics into the examination halls. One ingenious candidate is known to have covered his underwear with the classics written in a very fine hand.

Essentially, the Ladder to the Clouds reduces to four rungs. First, an examination in the county seat of the candidate's district, held twice every three years in district cities. Next, an examination in his provincial capital, held every three years in the provincial capitals. Then, on to Peking, for triennial examinations at the imperial capital. The degrees awarded for completion of these first three steps are:

1. At the district level—*hsiu-ts'ai,* "flowers of talent"
2. At the provincial level—*chu-jen,* "promoted scholars"
3. At Peking—*chin-shih,* "entered scholars" ready for office

A fourth step is open to *chin-shih* degree holders who opt for a higher distinction in the *tien-shih* or palace examination taken on bended knee in the presence of the emperor.

The same degrees are awarded to military officers, but for lifting rocks, swinging swords, and shooting arrows from horseback. No literacy is required and even feats of strength are little tested. For this civil officials hold the military in contempt.

The average *sheng-yuan* candidate comes to the district examinations in the autumn at the age of twenty-four, after about ten years of study, pays a stiff fee, and wins his degree after a day and a night of writing in a small cell. This degree provides him with the minimal legal definition of elite status, which exempts him from physical punishment and the venality of government runners. It also licenses him to go on to the second stage in the following spring.

The candidate for *chu-jen* will enter a provincial establishment, supervised by a literary chancellor from Peking and a number of local authorities, covering up to sixteen acres of examination cells arranged along narrow lanes that give access to as many as 8,653 cells. This is the case in Canton. Each open cell measures five feet, nine inches deep, three feet, eight inches wide, and as high as a man's head. It contains two boards fitted into slots at two heights, so that one board placed low will serve as a seat to a desk made of the other board placed at the upper position. At night the two can be put at one level to make a bed. Candidates are virtually imprisoned for a three-day session. They bring provisions, fuel, candles, and writing materials, all searched for cribs. If passed the first time, the candidate for *chu-jen* may be fortunate enough to win his degree by the time he is thirty or so.

The decisive step is the metropolitan examination held the following year in Peking under the board of rites. Decisive because the *chin-shih* degree confers the right to hold office and the privilege of entering the palace examination. From 2,000 to 3,500 *chu-jen* will pursue the *chin-shih* degree, of which only one-tenth—from 200 to 350—will pass. Graduates of the palace examination are admitted to the Hanlin Academy as poets and historians of the realm and are deputed to act as literary chancellors in the several provinces.

Appointments are made to either central or provincial government. The main bureaus of the provincial civil service, with the number of incumbents, are as follows:

FIG. 13   *Provincial government in China Proper*

8 Viceroys	⎰ Hupeh
Chihli	⎱ Hunan
⎰ Kiangsu	Szechwan
⎨ Anhwei	⎰ Kwangtung
⎱ Kiangsi	⎱ Kwangsi
⎰ Shensi	⎰ Kweichow
⎱ Kansu	⎱ Yunnom
⎰ Fukien	
⎱ Chekiang	

15 Governors
   The above provinces, except for Chihli, Kansu, and Szechwan, plus Shantung, Shansi, and Honan.

19 Commissioners of Finance (2 for Kiangsu). Each reports directly to the board of revenue, for the emperor, as a check on the provincial governor.

18 Commissioners of Justice. Each reports directly to the board of punishments. With the above, one of the 2 chief commissioners in each province.
13 Salt Comptrollers
13 Commissioners of Grain
64 *Tao-t'ais* (intendants of circuits of prefectures or *fu*)
182 Magistrates of smaller prefectures or *t'ing* ⎫
198 Magistrates of large districts or *chou*   ⎪
139 Deputy magistrates of *chou*   ⎬ 1,892 magistrates
141 District or *hsien* magistrates of the fifth rank ⎪
1,232 *Hsien* magistrates of the seventh rank   ⎭
Total: 2,042 local officials

Apart from private secretaries, personal servants, and assistants brought with him, each official has in his orbit about sixty-five underlings drawn from the locality for a total throughout the empire of about 1.2 million clerks and about 500,000 runners—1.7 million understrappers in all. All are supported by their own venality. The official ordinarily does not leave his yamen. Communication with his superiors is by written dispatch. Runners go to the people or the people come to the yamen.

The man who does business over the counter with the mass of people is the district magistrate. A mere 1,892 of them deal with 400 million people. The magistrate is the "net and ropes" of provincial government, who hauls in a large share of its resources and who is bidden to do so without taxation causing disorder. To this end he sends out his tax collectors, keeps a population census and a land register, and acts as judge, jury, and prosecutor in all trouble cases brought before his law court. He punishes accused, accusers, and witnesses alike. That he punishes these in different degrees according to their social standing is the mark of his judicial benevolence and justifies the magistrate's name as one of the *fu mu kuan,* or father and mother officials, in the Confucian double-talk of government accountability. The fewer messages sent upward about his local troubles, the more the magistrate is credited by his superiors with a strong moral power to instruct the people by his filial example.

Local officials altogether number only 2,042. The majority of officialdom resides with central government in Peking, distributed throughout these main agencies:

CENTRAL GOVERNMENT

(Numbers refer to squares on the Promotion board)

Grand Secretariat or Inner Chancery (58). A sort of "cabinet" that confers with the emperor on matters of state and then publishes his decisions in the *Peking Gazette*. Seat of the highest officials in the imperial bureaucracy, the Grand Secretaries (four incumbents).

The Six Boards (36–41, under 44). Each board is headed by two presidents, one Manchu, one Chinese.

Imperial Academy of Learning (31)

Imperial Board of Astronomy (32)

Colonial Office (42)

The Censorate (43)

Office of Transmission (46). It opens memorials sent to the throne and forwards them to the Inner Chancery.

Supreme Court of Judicature and Review (47)

Hanlin Academy (61)

Various departments serving the imperial house, such as 33, 34, 48, 49, 50, 51, 57, and 64.

Officials at the metropolitan center outnumber provincial officials by ten to one. This is as it should be in a cosmological empire, where everything relating to the emperor's cause is most concentrated in and around the royal court.

Except for a few of the old patriarchs held as hostages at court for their followers, all officials return to their home communities after one or more triennial turns in office. Wearing their robes of office on ceremonial occasions at home, they carry on the imperial cause—a universal status system—in their informal capacity as elites of the realm.

The imperial statutes recognize that elites of the realm differ in power and influence. Sumptuary laws acknowledge an upper and a lower gentry, but both are accorded privileges over and above the peasantry. The levels recognized are:

P'in Kuan, "officials of various ranks." Officials, active and retired, from the first to the seventh rank, all holders of the *chin-shih* and *chu-jen* degrees, earned or purchased.

Shu-shih, "the mass of scholars." Officials of the eighth rank down to the unclassified *wei ju liu* rank and all licentiates, of regular or purchased status.

Shu-jen, "the mass of commoners."

Naturally, things are more ambiguous in reality. Elite status brings legal privileges. The district magistrate requires special permission from the emperor to enter any punishment against the *p'in kuan* for whatever crimes, and he may not physically punish the *shu-shih*. But the magistrate must be careful to know what connections make for de facto high status among people who do not have it de jure. In *Hung Lou Meng,* an eighteenth-century novel of manners, a new magistrate takes office in a district where he finds a murder case left dangling by his predecessor. He finds in the records the name of the murderer and proceeds to issue a warrant for his arrest. But one of the native office clerks advises him not to do so. The new magistrate, Yu-ts'un, is naïve and puzzled.

> "Your illustrious office," replied the Retainer, "has brought your worship here, and is it likely you have not transcribed some phylactery of your post in this province?"
>
> "What is an office-phylactery?" asked Yu-ts'un with alacrity.
>
> "Nowadays," explained the Retainer, "those who become local officers provide themselves invariably with a secret list, in which are entered the names and surnames of the most influential and affluent gentry of note in the province. This is in vogue in every province. Should inadvertently, at any moment, one give umbrage to persons of this status, why, not only office, but I fear even one's life, it would be difficult to preserve. That's why these lists are called office-phylacteries. This Hsueh family, just a while back spoken of, how could your worship presume to provoke? This case in question affords no difficulties whatever in the way of settlement; but the prefects, who have held office before you, have all, by doing violence to the feelings and good names of these people, come to the end they did."
>
> As he uttered these words, he produced from inside his purse which he had handy, a transcribed office-phylactery, which he handed over to Yu-ts'un; who upon perusal, found it full of trite and unpolished expressions of public opinion, with regard to the leading clans and notable official families in that particular district. They ran as follows:
>
> [Here follows a rundown on four powerful families.]
>
> "These four families," explained the Retainer, "are all interlaced by ties of relationship, so that if you offend one, you offend all; if you honour one, you honour all. For support and protection, they all have those to take care of their interest! Now this Hsueh, who is charged with homicide . . . , not only has he these three families to rely upon,

but his father's old friends, and his own relatives and friends are both to be found in the capital, as well as abroad in the provinces; and they are, what is more, not few in number. Who is it then that your worship purposes having arrested?"

The power base of the elite is the family and its home district. Out of this base, men reach for office and cultivate influential relationships. Office holding does not make for a bureaucratic career in partnership with the throne; it makes for political independence in quest of a territorial sphere of control in the home district.

But the local gentry keep sending sons up the Ladder to the Clouds or buy degrees for them. The emperor's counter-ploy is to admit enough commoners through the examination system, or to appoint men of commoner origin as superiors over officials of elite birth. The emperor thereby prevents officialdom from becoming so career oriented that it could become a homogeneous interest group poised against the throne. The ruling class bears more sons than its localities can carry in privilege; office is looked upon as a frontier on which to dispose of the surplus, an economic frontier that endangers the emperor's position if bureaucracy were to be taken as a professional career by all those ambitious young men. The emperor counters pressure from the elite and their reproductive surplus by filling the bureaucracy with a mixed group.

But on the whole, the emperor may look with satisfaction upon aspirants to office. They play Promotion, read the *Peking Gazette,* and long to climb that Ladder to the Clouds. By the time they have spent their youth digesting the Confucian classics, with its ideology of filial piety, ambition is returned to its source in the bosom of the ancestors.

CHAPTER 15

JACK-O'-BOTH-SIDES

It is the emperor's prerogative to distribute the advantages of office to Manchus, who have inherited the privilege by right of conquest. Chinese aspirants to office, who work for the prize through the examination system, are grieved to find nobility overrepresented in the system. They invade the royal prerogative with their insistence on merit as a basis for office holding, quoting Confucius to the effect that it is the ruler's duty to "employ the able, promote the worthy." This appeal is hard to deny, for the emperor himself is the patron and chief advocate of Confucian ideology.

Confucianism suits the emperor, in holding up his side of the struggle, because it glorifies the hereditary sovereignty of the ruler at the expense of his appointed officials, whose professional ethics are supposed to limit their ambitions just short of participation in court politics. Officials respect this limitation because what they want from office, and from the academic degrees that license them for consideration, is merely imperial recognition of their qualifications—literacy and managerial experience—to handle affairs in their own home districts.

Confucius is the jack-o'-both-sides who trims the balance between autocracy and feudalism. The balance may shift from one side to the other, but both sides appeal to the same doctrine.

The first emperor to patronize Confucian learning, starting with the Han dynasty, did so because it helped put an end to a birth elite not connected with the royal house—the condition of feudalism that prevailed in preimperial times. Feudal lords are rivals who combine to influence who will sit on the throne. And who sits on the throne influences who will preside as officers of state. The choosing of officials was a new kind of decision the rulers of Fusion China had to make when the size of their conquered territories exceeded their ability to administer them with kinsmen. The politics of empire succeeded the overloaded politics of feudalism after Ch'in Shih Hwang Ti conquered all the states and made administrative appointments to them.

A wooden statue of Confucius (1′5″ inches high) belonging to the K'ung family's ancestral temple in Ch'u hsien, Chekiang province. After a photograph courtesy of Dr. Chang Chi-yun, formerly minister of education, Republic of China. The accompanying text, written in a script current in the time of Confucius (Small Seal), is from the Lun Yu and reads: "Chi K'ang asked Master K'ung about government. The Master replied, 'To rule is to be correct. If you lead along a correct way, who will not dare follow in correctness?'" (XII:17).

Ch'in Shih Hwang Ti made his conquest in the name of the Legalist doctrine that exalts the supremacy of the ruler above the rights of anybody else to influence him in making appointments. This doctrine, and its practice, allows for no balance between the throne and the real pressures that exist to press against the emperor's sovereignty. As a result, the Ch'in dynasty fell in short order to a feudal reaction.

The Han emperors who followed that collapse were patrons of the Confucian scholars that Ch'in had repressed. It was the Han emperors who instituted the examination system, in which men are selected for office on the basis of their mastery of the Confucian classics. This system started on a modest basis, but in time, after the Sung dynasty, it came to play an important role in trimming the balance between the ambitious men of the realm and the emperor's creatures.

The examination system passes men on the basis of knowledge about a doctrine that emphasizes the duty of nonhereditary officers to serve their hereditary ruler with dispassionate loyalty. But men of merit so selected have this in common with the feudal lords of old—they raise their claim to serve as officers of state by virtue of a moral *right* to the position, a right based on learning if not on birth. Merit or birth, it is all the same when it comes to challenging the royal prerogative. And so it is that the old contest between the principles of autocracy and feudalism still continue to dominate imperial politics. And small wonder that Confucius came to stand as the jack-o'-both-sides in this contest. For it was he who first trained literate administrators to work for hereditary rulers whose affairs of state had gotten beyond the control of their kinsmen to handle. The pupils of Confucius met a real need to supply men who would do the job, yet kept their disinterest in the clan politics of the ducal court. All well and good. The Confucian stress on a detached job morality allowed the ruler to assign ambitious men outside the nobility to posts instead of fiefs. But tension with the emperor's hereditary favorites arises from the fact that the Confucian administrator lays claim to office by *reason* of that disinterested job morality. The Confucian official claims that his right as a gentleman by education has priority over that of a gentleman by birth.

The politics of empire, without surprise, is verbalized by all parties in the language of feudal politics as this resides in the Confucian canon. Ever since the Han dynasty, the lineal descendants of Confucius have gathered titles of nobility at the hands of various emperors. For example, the Sung dynasty emperor Jen Tsung conferred a ducal title that the K'ung family holds to this day. The seventy-seventh generation of the K'ung family is represented by a scholarly gentleman living in Taiwan in this year of the Master, 2521 A.K. (A.D. 1970). It is astonishing to find a genealogical record kept with unbroken attention from the fifth century B.C., an unbeatable record for genuine aristocracy anywhere in the world. But this record has been cultivated by the emperors themselves. The emperor gives this fine piece of hereditary recognition to the patron saint of ambitious men, who press against the sovereignty of the dynastic house, because it shows that he alone deals with titles of nobility. And who can doubt that these are the most valuable status markers to be had? The reply is: nobility doesn't count; "employ the able, promote the worthy."

The emperor, for his part, finds the feudalistic texts of Confucianism useful because they often talk about politics in terms of cosmological magic. Indeed, the emperor's title, the Son of Heaven, is taken from that of the Chou regent. In the *Shih Ching* it is said of King Wen, the greatest of all the Chou kings in the Confucian pantheon of political heroes:

> Brightness shines on earth below,
> An awful blaze from high up. ["Ta Ming"]

Magic is scarcely appropriate for a national leader but it is for a cultural leader, who deals with unsubstantial things.

Substantial control by the emperor recedes rapidly beyond the boundaries of his capital city. There he is supplied by the Grand Canal for the support of his court and of central government. As for local government, he is able to appoint the governors, but they in turn are masters of the influence peddling that gets the magistrates and other provincial officers appointed. And beyond that, the local gentry hold all affairs of the countryside in their hands. Local officials and local gentry—these are the Local Snakes that the Dragon brings into his realm only by virtue of the fact that he heads a series of ranks, rituals, titles, and degrees that these regional power persons find honorable. The collective goals of the Great Society are limited to the acceptance of a universal system of stratification that puts royalty and nobility ahead of the gentry. Royalty provides the ruling class with a model of ceremonial ranking to be applied at home or in office. The capital city is a concentrated center of cultural glory paradigmatic for the elite of the realm. In this universal status system (with peasants as nonpersons at the bottom) consists the idea of the Great Society. This is the essence of culturalism, the emperor's power to control symbolic goods, as contrasted with the truly administrative powers of nationalism to control the substantive distribution of men and materials.

Confucianism upholds the idea that culturalism consists in the enactment of right ritual on the part of the emperor for the good of his subjects. The elite imitate it. Commoners receive divine enlightenment from it without participation in it. Those who receive no enlightenment whatsoever from it are outside civilization, barbarians by definition.

Confucianism, then, is the center of a state cult around which the literati rally to their chief task of rationalizing the political order. They rationalize the class system, with its energy slaves at the bottom and the men of high culture in their graded ranks at the top.

Confucianists are the wise men of the Chinese Agrarian State who draw upon the prehistoric roots of their civilization for the job of cultural rationalization that is theirs to do. They incorporate magic and mimetic ritual from the time before the advent of civilization; they take cosmological thought about the hierarchical nature of the universe as this was carried forward to match with ceremonial gradations under the Chou regent. As it says in the *Li Chi:*

> Heaven is high, earth is low; all things are distributed between these two and differ in kind. [*Yo Chi,* I:28]

By making rational the magical thought of old, the Confucian literati are able to inform the liturgical leadership of the emperor with a practical sociology.

One of the most important rounds of ritual duties taken on by the Chou king is described in the *Yueh Ming,* or *Monthly Ordinances.* These duties officially aimed at regulating nature, but in effect they regulated the ceremonial life of the Chou feudatories under the cultural leadership of the king. The *Yueh Ming,* a book incorporated into the *Li Chi,* dates from the third century B.C. It gives astronomic characteristics of each month and its associated notes, numbers, tastes, sacrifices, and the like. The book further specifies what natural calamities will follow should the rituals not be carried out.

For example, the rite of meeting the spirits of spring is spoken of as the responsibility of the Chou king to observe as the representative of humankind working to release the energy of spring. These are magical rites in that they simulate what they aim to stimulate. The king wears green robes in spring, for example, and sacrifices on the eastern altar at that time. Each season has its arcane associations tied in by cosmological thinkers with the five elements and hundreds of other phenomena. A few sample correlations with the five elements are given in Figure 14.

In the spring, the king not only wears green robes, but he also eats wheat and mutton, plant and animal foods that go with wood, spring, east, and green, and he eats these foods in dishes carved with a sprout motif. In addition to eating out of the seasonably correct dish, the king in the first month of spring asks that his feudatories throughout the Chou domain remove fetters and manacles from prisoners, that no trees be cut down nor any heads be cut off. All this confinement and lopping is opposed to growth. If the rituals are not observed, the land will stay in the grip of winter and not let plants grow. The king gives out gifts to his feudal lords and urges them to do likewise to their vassals, thus inducing nature to be similarly generous with its gifts.

And so on. For each month the king presides as a priest over a seasonal parade of sacrifices that induce nature to do its work at the bidding of man. Man is represented by a priest-king, immured behind palace walls, in a sealed retreat from contagions that might spoil his worship of Heaven. Heaven worship regenerates the king's moral energies, which then emanate as spiritual radiations to all the people. His exclusive mastery of the calendar endows him with a regulating virtue by which he rules the course of time. By the same measure he is confined to ritual duties and removed from the exercise of authentic autocracy.

Chinese emperors have carried out some of the old monthly rites, such as unfettering prisoners during the first month of spring, down to the end of the monarchy. The calendar continues to represent imperial authority. A calendar, by definition, is a way of combining days into periods of civil, religious, and

FIG. 14   *Imperial arcana*

Elements	Seasons	Directions	Musical Notes	Colors	Grains	Domestic Animals	Tastes
wood	spring	east	*chio*	green	wheat	sheep	sour
fire	summer	south	*chih*	red	beans	fowl	bitter
earth	midseason	center	*kung*	yellow	panicled wheat	ox	sweet
metal	autumn	west	*shang*	white	hemp	dog	acrid
water	winter	north	*yu*	black	millet	pig	salt

cultural observances. Because imperial leadership is cultural leadership above all, use of the imperial calendar signifies recognition of that leadership in ceremonial matters pertaining to the Great Society.

Calendar making is the job of the royal astronomers. Only they may write about astronomical problems. The stars themselves are called "celestial officials." One of the chief duties of the censorate is to provide security for the imperial observatory, the Chinese equivalent of our Los Alamos. The emperor views with alarm the activities of independent astronomers, because they can have only one purpose in mind, and that is to make calculations and fix arcana for the use of a regional power setting out to rival the throne. This is what the T'aip'ing rebels did in preparation for their military move on Peking. They took on the Julian calendar for their own calendar, and invented their own numerology and a new etiquette for the placing of tea cups and chopsticks. All of this is treasonable behavior because it is associated with a rival cultural leadership. The royal calendar is a crucial test of loyalty.

The fact that the royal calendar evolved out of seasonal observances made by folk of the prehistoric Green Circle does not mean that the calendar is addressed to peasants for either agricultural or ritual guidance. It is rather the basis for a parade of sacrifices and rituals that bind officialdom to the imperial center in one ceremonial system. The emperor rules the course of time, and therefore a universal status system, out of a microcosmic version of the whole.

One of the awesome things about the imperial center as a place of concentrated cultural intensity is that people are awake there at night, while others go to bed at dusk and wake at dawn. But in Peking, astronomers are up, scanning the sky, and the emperor himself holds levees starting at 2 A.M. It is impressive for officials coming in from the provinces to have an audience at this hour, with gongs and drums banging away in the distance, the great silken mandarin squares on official robes shimmering in the luxurious illumination of blazing torches and lamps.

Actually, the leadership of the emperor, described in the Confucian language of mimetic harmony and contagious moral influence, is not magical at all. It is practical. The emperor, after all, is not the master of political substance but of political pageantry. This is the difference between nationalism and culturalism. The politics of the nation-state is nationalism, and the politics of the Agrarian State is culturalism. In culturalism the emperor's ceremonial duties are paradigmatic for a whole set of inflected forms of domestic and official ritual expressed in a cosmological idiom. He thereby provides the only kind of leadership the Chinese power elite will voluntarily follow.

Central to the cosmological idiom of imperial politics is dragon mythology. The dragon passes between Heaven and earth and is manifest in mist, clouds, and rain. Like a waterspout, the dragon has its head in the clouds, its tail in the water, and it belongs to all regions, celestial and terrestrial. So the emperor, the Mighty Dragon, is central to a cosmic scheme that links natural and social phenomena, and therefore that links every man in his place in the imperial hierarchy.

The political sociologists of the Confucian school, however, can read into cosmological thought the operating principles of cultural leadership. Take the following passage from the *Tso Chuan*. Any Confucian scholar, using it as a text, can deliver a homily on the mystification of social inequality.

> Heaven and Earth have their regular ways, and men take these for their pattern, imitating the brilliant bodies of Heaven, and according with the natural law of diversities of the earth . . . Heaven and Earth produce the six atmospheric conditions, and make use of the five material elements. These conditions become the five tastes, are manifested in the five colors, and displayed in the five notes. . . . There are nine emblematic ornaments of robes, with their six colors and five methods of display, to maintain the five colors. There are nine songs, the eight winds, the seven sounds, and the six pitch pipes, to maintain the five notes. There are ruler and minister, high and low, in imitation of the distinctive characteristics of the earth. There are husband and wife, with the home and the world abroad, the spheres of their respective duties. There are father and son, elder and younger brother, aunt and sister, maternal uncles and aunts, father-in-law and connections of one's children with other members of their mother's family, and brothers-in-law, to resemble the bright luminaries in Heaven. [X:xxv:1]

Elsewhere the *Tso Chuan* is more direct.

> The day has its ten divisions of time, and of men there are ten classes; and so it is that inferiors serve their superiors, and that superiors perform their duties to their ancestral spirits. Hence, the king makes his duke his servant; the duke the great

officer; the great officer the lesssser officer; the lesser officer, the lictor; the lictor, the crowd of underlings; the underling, the menial; the menial, the laborer; the laborer, the servant; the servant, the helper. There are also grooms for the horses, and shepherds for the cattle;—and there is provision for all things. [X:vii:3]

The king of Chou may be taken for the emperor, the duke for a provincial governor. The idea of a Great Society over which the emperor presides as a cultural arbiter of rank and status for all of China is based on a feudal model deriving from the Era of Fusion. The difference is that in feudal times, all the local states were headed by a hereditary nobility, whereas under empire, hereditary power is restricted to the imperial domain and the local states are made over into provinces to which officers are appointed by the throne.

Schoolboys learn about the inequalities of the imperial order in a beginner's reader that reports an imaginary dialogue between Confucius and Hsiang T'ou. Hsiang T'ou ("Fragrant Head") is a sweet and virtuous lad as well-known as George Washington in our school books. The boy is questioned by Confucius one day while the Master is out rambling the countryside with his disciples in a carriage.

"I wish to have you go with me, and fully equalize the empire; what do you think of that?"

The lad replied, "The empire cannot be equalized. Here are high hills, there lakes and rivers. Either there are princes and nobles, or there are slaves and servants. If the hills be leveled, the birds and beasts will have no resort; if the rivers and lakes be filled up, the fishes and turtles will have nowhere to go. Do away with kings and nobles, and the common people will have much dispute about right and wrong. Obliterate slaves and servants, and who will there be to serve the prince? If the empire be so vast and unsettled, how can it be equalized?"

Needless to say, the Master expresses delight with this answer. Nature itself provides a model for the power gap between peasants and elites.

Loyalty to the emperor's cultural leadership, celebrated in court rituals and court music, follows from the emperor's glamorization of privilege, not in his creating privilege in the first instance. Small wonder that Confucian scholastics rejoice in the language of the classics, such as the *Li Chi*, which say everything for the benefit of bureaucratic autonomy.

Nothing further in government is needed beyond the application of ritual and music. [*Yo Chi,* XXV:14]

The Confucian classics uphold the cosmic powers of the Mighty Dragon at the same time they justify earthly power and autonomy for the Local Snakes.

The Confucianists, however, were not the first political sociologists to work out a theory of empire. Confucius himself did so by way of his peculiar defense of Chou feudalism. He argued the case for a hereditary ruler over All-China who would be served by a nonhereditary bureaucracy.

But empire was first put into effect under the direction of a rival school of political sociology, the Legalist (*fa chia*).

The Legalists looked to empire as a way out of the internecine warfare between the feudal states during the Era of Fusion. One state would simply have to grow strong enough to defeat all the others and then impose its administration on the conquered territory. Legalist advisers to the state of Ch'in, which accomplished this, found a ready audience where military commanderies (*chün*) had proved their administrative capacity to win and hold control over the northern barbarian lands. The prince of Ch'in who made the initial conquest of empire, on Legalist advice, set himself up with a new title in recognition of his break with feudal tradition. As First August Sovereign of the Ch'in Empery, Ch'in Shih Hwang Ti bought out the surviving nobility, installed his personal representatives in the capitals of the conquered states, killed all other aspirants to office, and burned the literature of Confucianism, the chief ideological rival of Legalism. Within fifteen years the Ch'in empire was overthrown.

The Legalist thinkers had worked out an operational sociology of strong-arm government. They ridiculed the sociology of liturgical government advanced by the Confucian school.

Kids make up mud for rice, puddles for soup and wood shavings for meat. But when they go home for supper this play rice and fake soup cannot be eaten. So it is with all this nonsense about ancient kings and their filial piety. Ritual perfection cannot straighten out state affairs. The idea can be played with, but not used for running a government. [*Han Fei,* XXXII]

If ruler and minister act like father and son, does that mean that real fathers and sons never quarrel? Parents may love their children, yet children may talk back. So if ministers try to love their ruler, does that mean the state will have no disorder? The early kings loved the people, we are told. Parents love their children, we are told. But do children, much less the mass of people, keep order for all that? [*Han Fei*, XLIX]

The main Legalist objection to Confucianism is that it tries to identify state morality with private morality on the model of filial piety. This idea is dismissed by the Legalists with the sharp observation that such requires

. . . every lord of men to come up to the level of Confucius and all the common people to act like his disciples. It won't work. [*Han Fei*, XLIX]

Confucius objected to the Legalist theory that terror—harsh punishments for every infraction, great or small—would put an end to crime.

Try to keep order by means of legal regulations and people will evade punishments without conscience. Keep order by means of correct ritual and people will volunteer to follow the example of your moral power. [*Lun Yu*, II:3]

To which the Legalist reply is,

The most enlightened way of governing is to trust measures, not men. [*Han Fei*, LV]

The Legalist ruler keeps order by controlling a piece-rate system of direct rewards for obedience and cruel punishments for disobedience.

[He] does not count on people's doing him good. He makes sure they cannot do him wrong. [*Han Fei*, L]

The Chinese say that the triumph of Confucianism over Legalism is the triumph of human government over a Draconian one, of virtue over law, of benevolence over wickedness, of good over bad. Things are not that simple, but the belief that they are is very real. It expresses the strong feelings that go with the embracement of orthodoxy. Indeed, the emperor's patronage of a correct ideological line gives him the best advantage of all in acting as a cultural leader of the ruling class. To give currency to more than one theory of empire would destroy imperial politics. The writings of Han Fei and Lord Shang, the two most famous Legalist thinkers, are therefore pronounced heterodox. The definitive deprecation of Legalism is made by comparing its version of a story about a stolen sheep with the Confucian version.

THE STOLEN SHEEP

Confucian version

The Duke of Sheh informed Confucius to the effect that, "We have people around here who think a son is virtuous for stealing a sheep." Confucius replied that things were different where he came from. "The father conceals the crime of his son and the son conceals the crime of his father. There certainly is something upright in that." [*Lun Yu*, XIII:18]

Legalist version

In the state of Ch'u there was a man named Chi-kung. His father stole a sheep, so his son reported him to the magistrate. The magistrate ordered him tried and executed, for the son was loyal to the ruler even if unfilial to his father. The lesson is that an upright subject of the ruler can be an unfilial son. [*Han Fei*, XLIX]

The contrast between these stories is Exhibit A in the Confucian indictment of Legalism. Yet the two philosophies are not that far apart in many other respects. Both must agree to a large extent because both deal more or less with the same difficulties of managing state power in the Agrarian State. A few of those essential points of agreement are listed here in parallel columns. The Confucian side is represented by quotations from the *Lun Yu* on the left, and the Legalist side by quotations from *Han Fei Tzu*, except for the one from *Shang Yang*, on the right.

PRINCIPLES OF EMPIRE AGREED UPON BY CONFUCIUS AND HIS RIVAL, HAN FEI TZU

Confucius

Han Fei Tzu

1. Exalt the Hereditary Authority of the Sovereign

A ruler should attract his ministers by means of proper ritual. Ministers should serve him with devoted loyalty. [III:19]

Nothing is more valuable than the royal person, more honorable than the throne, more powerful than the authority of the sovereign, or more august than the position of the ruler. [IV]

Confucius   *Han Fei Tzu*

2. The Ruler Is in Charge of Orthodoxy

He who rules by ritual example is like the pole star, which keeps its place the while all the other stars turn around in homage to it. [II:1]

Law includes mandates and ordinances that are manifest in the official bureaus, penalties that are definite in the mind of the people, rewards that are due to careful observance of laws, punishments that are inflicted on the offenders against orders. It is what subjects and ministers take as a model. [XLIII]

3. Extend the Empire

If a sage king were to rise up, within a generation he could extend goodness to the whole world. [XIII: 12]

If the people attend to public duties and officials are in good order, then the state will become rich, then the army will be strong. In consequence, the hegemony of the world will be attained. To be a hegemonic ruler is the highest goal of the lord of men. [XLVI]

4. Systematize the Ideology

To rule is to be correct. If you lead along a correct way, who will not dare to follow in correctness? [XII:17] [This is the meaning of the ancient script accompanying the illustration at the head of this chapter.]

The law does not fawn on the noble; the string does not yield to the crooked. Whatever the law applies to, the wise cannot reject nor the brave defy. Punishment for fault never skips ministers, reward for good never misses commoners. [VI]

5. Foster a Nonhereditary Bureaucracy

Knowledge of office does not follow from hereditary rank. [XV:38]

Neither in high nor in low offices should there be an automatic hereditary suc-

Confucius   *Han Fei Tzu*

cession to the offices, ranks, lands, or emoluments of officials. [*Shang Yang,* IV:17:5a]

6. Accommodate Aspirants to Office through Merit

Am I worthy to be known? That is my aim in seeking office. [IV:14]

The reason why the intelligent ruler establishes posts, offices, ranks, and bounties is to promote the worthy and encourage men of merit. [IX]

7. Agriculture Is Basic

The ruling elite are given to moralization, the little people to the soil. [IV:11]

Public storehouses and granaries are full because of the people's devotion to the primary duties of tilling and farming. [XLV]

8. Peasants Are Directed Creatures Far Beneath the Ruler and His Agents

The ruling elite is like the wind, the little people like the grass. When the wind blows, the grass bends. [XII:19]

If someone wants to move a tree and pulls each leaf, he works hard but cannot shake the whole tree. If he holds the root from the right, and then from the left, then all the leaves will be shaken. Who is skillful in hauling in a net, draws in the rope and never pulls the knots, one after another, till he gets the whole net. For the same reason, magistrates are the roots and ropes of the people. [XXXV]

The real difference is that Legalism was ahead of its time. It set out operational plans for a totalitarian government that could not be realized until the development of the technical means of communication made use of by Hitler in mechanizing the lower leadership. Ch'in Shih Hwang Ti well understood that empire requires that a nonhereditary officialdom replace a feudal aristocracy; that officials must heed the ruler's arbitration of collective goals, but these goals must not be so close to his ruler as to allow officials to enter into partnership with the hereditary throne; and that if officials *must* be given some autonomy in the best interests of the royal house, they cannot be given so much that they will infeudate office. Such long tenure would give regional powers the force to decide occupancy of the throne. Ch'in Shih Hwang Ti, on Legalistic advice, tried to control his provincial governors as if they were administrative extensions of a central organ of government empowered to exercise substantive power over local manpower and resources.

The Confucian sociology of empire is concerned with the same problems. But it understands that tensions between officialdom and the throne cannot be abolished by imperial fiat. It accepts the substantive limits of the emperor's power and settles for the influence of cultural leadership. That is the lesson to be learned from the story about the stolen sheep. For Confucianists, the filial piety of the boy may be taken for the merging of office with family interests short of infeudation. The Legalist version of the story speaks for a policy of restricting autonomy altogether. After fifteen years, the Ch'in emperor was overthrown by a combination of military officers, civil officials, and estate owners who would not accept such controls. Actually, Legalism advocated a degree of despotic power no ruler until the twentieth century had the technical means to achieve. Still, there has always been a certain amount of seesaw movement between the hereditary and the nonhereditary elite to influence the composition of the ruling class. The figure of Confucius stands as the jack-o'-both-sides, keeping the balance. And the emperor, as the keeper of the orthodoxy, can have it both ways. He is accorded despotic majesty in his cosmic posture as a Mighty Dragon, while the Local Snakes go their own way except in their ritual subordination.

CHAPTER 16

GAMES CHINESE PLAY

PSYCHIATRIST Eric Berne wrote a best seller on the "psychology of human relationships" in a book called *Games People Play*. A more accurate title would be *Games Americans Play*. The games he describes are idioms of behavior his patients use as strategies to manipulate others. He spells out the underlying policy of those games with such apt formulas as: "See what you made me do," "If it weren't for you," and "Look how hard I've tried." Games are found out when the motive of the gamester is penetrated and revealed for the tool of manipulation that it is.

Such games as the good doctor has formulated for the insight of his patients he would not find among Chinese elite persons of traditional upbringing. Elite Chinese are not interested in motivation. They care for *what* people do, not *why* people do things.

In good games or bad, Americans inquire into the motives of others. This is noticeable in novel encounters, when people strike up a relationship for the first time. Each person must find his place in the group by the consensus of the others, depending on his interpersonal skills. The cocktail party is archetypical. People there are blanks at first, generalized others, who through jockey and banter, and other free-floating expressions of sentiment, finally acquire personality and place for a fleeting moment of encounter. The game of one-upmanship is played here in the polite boasting that goes with elevating oneself as a means of putting down others. Stephan Potter's description of one-upmanship is a comic treatment of the way in which westerners feel each other out in novel and impromptu situations. They joke about this and that, jostling for position while gradually revealing something of their personality and feelings.

In the game of one-upmanship, polite lies about oneself are paired with the need to sound out the personality of others. The truth about self is possible to conceal because the whole

The Tso-i, *second position. After one of a series of staged photographs illustrating Chinese body ritual, in W. Gilbert Walshe,* Ways that are Dark: Some Chapters on Chinese Etiquette and Social Procedure, *Shanghai, 1906.*

personality is not necessary to expose in any one setting among a series of partial situations and brief encounters. Americans switch from one setting to another—from family to job to school to church to bowling team to club to cocktail party —as easily as they switch television channels. But if one is *sincere,* he will display his true self honestly, and not leave the other guessing about his feelings, motives, or intentions.

Lies about self can be effective only if surrounded by uncertainties. The uncertainties of fluid interactional settings make of each encounter a puzzle box that must be unlocked if any order of procedure and deference is to come about. The key is penetration into motives. How sincere is the other guy? That is, does he display his feelings honestly?

The probing of motives is repugnant to Chinese sensibilities. The Chinese want to know *what* the other person is going to do (as a matter of predictability), not *why* he does it (the unpredictable element). Inquiry into the inner lives of others is regarded as dirty. One need not look into these matters in any case. The Chinese make it a conscious policy to keep action apart from feelings. The Chinese see two things, and keep them apart, where the Americans see only one thing.

Compare the American cocktail party with the archetypical Chinese situation, the dinner party. Nobody will be invited who does not know his standing relative to everybody else. Rank is fixed in the seating plan. Everybody is expected to do all the right things with the right people in bowing and gesturing and in verbal ritual. Uncertainties are ruled out by the rules of politeness.

All in all, there are some basic differences between American games and Chinese games. Some of these may be tabulated as follows:

AMERICAN GAMES	CHINESE GAMES
Situations are the same for all men; the limits of the game are set by ability and ambition.	Situations depend on who is playing the game, and mobility (change of status) is disallowed.
One has a free choice in the use of language and status symbols.	One speaks in the language appropriate to one's station and displays accurate status symbols.
While people in general may come by the above honestly, once mastered, they may be doffed or donned at will, given a choice of situation.	There is no uncertainty about the above, and therefore no need to inquire into the "real" person behind the image because the situation is fixed by the part one has to play in it.
Nobody believes that the image of self presented to others has a lasting effect, how else change it?	The image of self presented

AMERICAN GAMES

It is believed that one's image is not one's inner self; the self is to be discovered and admired for one's choice of image.

CHINESE GAMES

to others is a permanent attribute fixed by age, sex, and social status.

It is believed that one's image of self is congruent with the person, that there is a one-to-one correspondence between what a person is and what he projects.

Small wonder that westerners, especially Americans, find duplicity in the Oriental concept of sincerity. What is it the Chinese hide behind the mask of politeness?

Westerners regard politeness as empty formality. Samuel Johnson defines politeness as a "fictitious benevolence." Rousseau speaks of politeness as a dishonest irony that enables men "to assume the appearance of every virtue without the reality of one." And E. E. Cummings complains of a lack of spontaneity when he says, "Politeness is dead but not yet buried imagination." Westerners mistrust polite formality because it is said to mask sincerity, sincerity conceived as a virtue bred in the honest display of personal feelings.

Thus the American enlisted man who personally dislikes his commanding officer will deliver the required body ritual—a salute—but he will do so too slowly or from too great a distance, i.e., with just enough imperfection to get the message of feeling across without getting gigged for omitting the ritual altogether. The soldier, if he lacks respect for his officer, feels bound to display that disrespect and yet get away with it. Sly ritual insubordination is the measure of sincerity; it reveals feelings within the technicalities of the body ritual.

What the Americans think of as sincerity, the Chinese look upon as rudeness. The Chinese have their own concept of sincerity, *hsin,* but westerners view *hsin* as a license to lie and give fictitious benevolences. *Hsin* is one of the Five Virtues. Sincerity is thus bound up with the formalities of right conduct, ceremony, ritual, politeness—in a word, with *li. Li* is fundamentally inequalitarian and undemocratic. As the *Tso Chuan* says, "*Li* arranges people in their ranks." Sincerity means doing the right thing for the right person in the right rank, including kinsmen. Sincerity, or *hsin,* is the fifth—but not the least—of the Five Virtues, which are:

1. *Li*—politesse. Right conduct in maintaining one's place in a hierarchical order; correct ritual or accepted procedure.
2. *Jen*—humanity or benevolence. Delivering the right ritual to the person whose rank deserves it.
3. *I*—justice or righteousness. The self-satisfaction that one has done the right thing in the performance of *li.*
4. *Chih*—wisdom. The knowledge of correct behavior and of when to apply it.
5. *Hsin*—sincerity. The honesty and genuineness of any transaction in which one has performed *li* correctly without the mistake of leaking out inappropriate feelings.

A daughter-in-law has to kowtow to her mother-in-law every morning whether or not the girl likes or respects the woman. The girl may hate her mother-in-law's guts. But sincerity calls for her to deliver the kowtow with no revealing imperfection. If she let her true feelings leak out, as does the soldier with his slipshod salute, her position in the family would be destroyed. She could be beaten to death or ignominiously returned to her family of origin.

For the Chinese, to be insincere means to deny another the *li* due him by his position in a series of high and low positions. Anything less than ritual perfection to a superior communicates rejection of authority. One's private feelings belong to a different world, at least among inferiors. Superiors give a show of feeling in their satisfaction with proper ritual from below by relieving the inferior from going through the whole routine. A pleased mother-in-law may let the daughter-in-law off with three knockings out of the total requirement in kowtowing of three bows and nine knockings.

The difference between western and Chinese concepts of sincerity is that western sincerity is aimed at gratifying the personal feelings of others. Chinese sincerity is aimed at harmony (*ho*). Harmony means that high and low keep their place in the structure. Chinese sincerity is respect for status, not a kindness to the person occupying it. Westerners in China at first are flattered by the courtesies given them as visiting dignitaries. These same dignitaries are hurt when they discover the honor is not given to their ego but to their position. Hence the western opinion that Chinese are masters of deceit: inscrutable, sinister, *insincere.* One nineteenth-century handbook on Chinese etiquette and social procedure is entitled *Ways that Are Dark,* after a line in Bret Harte's poem, "The Heathen Chinee." The painting at the head of this chapter is made after a photograph in that book.

The western view that Chinese politeness is a game of deceit is summed up in the figurative vocabulary of "face." Everything is just a shallow matter of keeping, getting, or losing face. Face is the English translation of *mien-tze,* which literally means the same thing, physiognomy. The translation has been borrowed from the Chinese and applied in Anglo-American usage to mean superficial prestige or unearned esteem in the eyes of others. The *Random House Dictionary* gives this gloss under definition 7:

> **face.** Outward show or pretense, esp. as a means of preserving one's dignity when under stress or of concealing a detrimental fact, condition, etc.

In Chinese usage, "face" is a figure of speech for a power-oriented quality of interaction connected with a position of authority in some kind of enduring group structure. It is a name for the dynamic action of power persons and the real basis for their power. There is nothing superficial about *mien-tze.* It is the name for everything elites of the realm hold to their advantage.

Face is not a quality of behavior commoners can have, by definition, any more than *li* is something peasant "ignoramuses" can learn. Of gentlemen, the peasant says they have "land and face," i.e., power and property. Face behavior embodies the Five Virtues entire, whose object is to maintain system stability in power relationships. As the *Li Chi* says:

> *Li* does not apply below among the common people, *fa* does not apply above. [*Chu Li,* I:iv:10]

Li, the code of gentlemanly conduct, is voluntarily observed by elites because they are responsible for conserving the structure of the Great Society. Penal law, or *fa,* is reserved for peasants; they have no stake in the imperial cause.

Face is no mere cosmetic feature of poise or self-expression. Face stands for what is most important in the only human

relationships that really count, those between persons of unequal status—and *everyone* is unequal. Everybody is indi-
viduated by status relative to others in one nexus of power
relationships or another, in family and clan, between teacher
and pupil, patron and client. Even the emperor bows to his
teacher, for a teacher is superior to a student by definition,
and to be superior is to be like a father, which is as permanent
a status as being a son. Power distinctions, once entered into
by birth or contract, endure forever, as implied in the proverbial saying, *yi erh wei shih, chung shen wei fu:* one day a
teacher, a father for life. Or at least the formalities endure.
What content goes into the relationship, of course, depends on
sentiment. To lose face in an important relationship is to lose
everything. When suicide is accepted as an honorable response
to loss of face, face is not trivial. Face involves the most profound ideas of right and wrong in handling human relations.
What is right and good is what upholds the graded ranks of
status differences. What is wrong and bad is what confuses
status identity. Face is the name for one's conduct in office,
for the acting out of one's status duties.

What is ethical in human relationships, then, rests with
proprieties rather than with personal feelings; with performance, not motives. Face is how one looks doing what one has
to do. What one has to do is give ritual obedience to superiors.
This is not at all a fictitious benevolence but a show of sincerity—a genuine concern for system stability, a contribution
to harmony.

Loss of face is the consequence of making a mistake in
one's interpersonal behavior. One becomes a nonperson in a
set of relationships that has no substitute. Chinese therefore
pay close attention to what they are doing in their communications with others. There is a high degree of sociological
awareness involved, one reason why they find relevance in the
feudal dictates of ritual found in the *Li Chi.*

> The *chun-tze* watches over the manner in which he maintains
> his intercourse with other men. [*Li Chi,* II:14]

> *Li* prevents the rise of disorder and confusion, and is like a
> dike which prevents the overflow of water. [*Ching Chieh,* 7]

> If the outward demeanor be for a moment without gravity and
> respectfulness, indifference and rudeness will show themselves.
> [*Yo Chi,* III:24]

In western transactions, the show of indiscriminate, spontaneous affect is treasured as the hallmark of sincerity. For the Chinese, it is the worst kind of human ugliness. The best thing a person can do for himself, and the most sincere thing he can do for others, is to pay attention to the niceties of politesse whether he feels like it or not.

Li places a limitation on the freedom to experiment with a free display of feelings. Behavioral freedom, the key to the spontaneity of fluid action situations in the West, is disallowed as an instrument for testing novel avenues of mutual adjustment or for affirming degrees of personal intimacy. This does not mean that behavioral reserve comes out of smothered emotions. There is actually no reason why the Chinese have to control their feelings more than other people. They are free to express themselves outside their ritual duties. An inferior is obliged to say "yes" to his superiors, but he can do "no" and send around a third party to explain. And there is emotional satisfaction in performing the right ritual.

What looks like repression to westerners is an indifference by Chinese to an exposure of personal motives. There is nothing to hide. Everything depends on definitions of fixed status positions, as in the joint family. Nearness to or remoteness from the family head is decisive. All obligations and rights follow from that. No cheating about one's status is possible because everybody's position is known to everybody else. The element of uncertainty, which in the West makes for lies about self and for guessing into the motives of others in telling *their* lies, is missing from Chinese face-oriented relationships. The game of one-upmanship is impossible to play. A man who can be lied to is not involved enough to know the difference. Chinese roles have an either/or quality. One plays one's part or he does not. One can have this or that relationship with another or he cannot have any at all. This makes for legalized, not personalized, relationships.

Blunders of propriety, then, are criminal acts. People are easy to insult. The Confucian rules of propriety are dikes against that crime. Confucius dramatizes the lesson in a story told to his disciple Wan Chang. Confucius means to explain that a person should always make the right signals according to his status. He tells the story about Duke Ching of Ch'i who mistakenly summoned his huntsman with a plumed flag. The huntsman did not answer and the duke got mad enough to kill him. But this huntsman stood his ground on probity at the risk of his neck; he would not answer a summons improperly given. Wan Chang asked Confucius what summons *would* be proper for a huntsman, and the Master replied:

> With the wave of a coon-skin hat. A commoner should be summoned with a plain flag, a knight with a flag embroidered with dragons, and a nobleman with a flag topped with a feather plume. When the forester was summoned with a nobleman's flag, he rather wanted to die than go. Neither could he have gone if signaled by a knight's flag. [*Meng Tzu*, V:ii:8]

The business about who gets called with what flag is meaningful among Chinese elite persons of traditional upbringing who are still living today. Relationships are regulated by careful boundary controls whose limits are set by *li*. No boundary controls, no relationship. In other words, no call to action without the correct signal as governed by the formalities appropriate to a person's standing relative to another.

This generalization about Chinese behavior I observed for myself some years ago when I lived with an upper-class family in New York City. The woman of the household was Mary Yang, who finally adopted me as her "dry son," I stayed so long. But at first, Mary had some little difficulty understanding what I was up to. Doing fieldwork for a doctoral dissertation, yes. This did not explain everything, however. One day at teatime, she came up with the answer.

> "Smokey [a nickname her teen-age daughters applied to me as their 'Uncle Smokey,' after the comic strip Smokey Stover], I think you must have been a Chinese in your former life. You speak Chinese, you like Chinese food, and you know Chinese face. But you must have been a very bad Chinese, because in this life you are a white man."

If I were Chinese in my former life, then I must be attempting to recover memory of it by studying Chinese ways. But the Buddhist theory of reincarnation is no article of profound faith for Mary, so I concluded that she used the idea only as a superficial explanation in the more serious matter of exercising control over my behavior in her house, such as keeping beer out of the refrigerator—or did I not really want to recover the lost life I was looking for?

In any case, Chinese face behavior is still very much like

that business about the flags. Face relations are power oriented. They are legalized for the upholding of a person's social status as if it were an office of public responsibility; such relationships are unlike the friendly interpersonal relationships of the West, which are given to the free exchange of sentiment and feelings between people.

One Sunday afternoon, three of Mary's crowd of callers that day decided to play bridge, while the others continued their conversation in another room. I was designated to take the fourth hand, but not until one of the other three asked if I could play well enough to sit with them. This gentleman had never met me before and did not know my status in the household as an adopted son. I answered "yes" to his question, but he asked further, "Are you sure?" before accepting me as his partner. He was a serious bridge player and I was not. My partner was a very good player, and it was not long before he discovered that I had vastly overrated my own ability to play the game. He openly spoke contempt for a serious mistake I made in the opening round. Mary overheard the cursing I took from my unhappy partner, who occupied North, and without saying a word she entered our room, motioned West aside and occupied the position herself. She played West's hand just long enough to make a stupefying blunder herself, and then exclaimed, "Ai-ya! I can make a mistake, too." She then returned the seat to West and went back to her conversation. Thereafter, North spoke not a single word of criticism, whatever his private thoughts.

Mary's action had "saved face" for me, she explained later. She did this by rectifying the miscalculation of my partner that he had the right to swear at me because he and I were strangers. She acted out a routine that communicated to him that he owed me deference as a privileged person in her household. He was not to swear at my bad card playing even if I had exaggerated my ability. But in reality, it was I, not my partner, who made the unsettling miscalculation. My partner justifiably replied to an unaccomplished boast. The boast was no mere travesty of self-possession in Chinese eyes, however. It was more than an embarrassing impropriety. It was a crime. A crime because what I had done was an *unpredictable* act of impropriety. I had acted out of character. Mary knew this but not North. She then entered the game so that she herself could mishandle the cards by way of redefining my blunder as one that anyone could make. Even *she* could make similar mistakes, she made it known, thereby redefining my mistake as a *predictable* error of judgment. She saved my face by demonstrating that she, too, could do an unpredictable thing. My error was excusable now that it was defined as never having been an accident to begin with. Mary simply imposed this definition on reality as a signal to North that he owed me deference as an adopted son in her household. I had made the mistake of not looking *my* part. But never mind. North still owed the deference he ought to owe me even if I *had* acted out of character. The whole thing was rectified by a redefinition of my behavior.

To western sensibilities, this kind of face-saving exercise is the height of hypocrisy and insincerity. Saving face is a lie because what is saved is appearances: how one looks in a role, not how one actually behaves. But the Chinese are quite conscious of the distinction between form and content, and they place a high value on correct forms. A concern for protocol and form is the height of sincerity because it means that the minimal conditions of maintaining a relationship are in operation at all times, no matter how one feels about it; form is a contribution to the relationship, not to the other person. Westerners find Chinese hypocritical because they say one thing and do another. Westerners require that the action correspond to the actor. But Chinese give precedence to the actor over the action. A fixed status system must be upheld at all costs. A person's conformity to the part he is supposed to play means loyalty to the relationship or group he interacts in. To not play the part, or not to know it well enough to play it without an accidental blunder, is a criminal act against that relationship or group organization. Put the other way around, attention to form over content is the test of sincerity.

Saying one thing and doing another is not hypocritical to Chinese because they are prepared to pay attention to both levels of communication and westerners are not. Chinese communication is high-context communication. Westerners believe that a sincere communication ought not conceal another level of meaning. Chinese are viewed as insincere because it is not realized that for them there *is* no hidden message. It comes through, loud and clear.

Consider the following letter written by Mary to an official of the Hanching Alumni Association. On the surface, everything is polite, and no aggressive improprieties are exposed. Yet the desired result of the letter, mimeographed for circulation among those other members joined in a project to perform Chinese operas, was to remove the official from his post. The Chinese style of aggression is sanctimonious. The message is: "You can't say I've hurt you because even though I *did* hurt you in fact, I said nothing at all improper, impolite, or unexpected." Mary's letter is a masterpiece of sanctimonious aggression. And it worked.

Except for using initials in place of real names, I reprint the letter exactly as Mary typed it on a ditto master sheet, in English. Her thoughts are Chinese, however. How could it be otherwise? She and her colleagues belong to an internationalized elite—people with a traditional upbringing and a western education. When they came to America they did not read Eric Berne's book, or any sociology book about America, in order to learn how to play American games. They came to America with Chinese games in their head.

Here is the letter (used with her permission), followed by an explication of the message.

[home address]
New York City
December 25, 195—

Mr. X.L.Y.
[home address]

Dear Mr. X.L.Y.:
Merry Christmas. A couple of invitations were turned down because I felt it is very important to write you a good long letter.

Your special delivery of December 21st reached me on December 23rd (Monday) when I got home from the office. I have been waiting for a chance to have a lengthy talk with you hoping to clear up many recent confusions. Since such a chance is lacking and the receipt of your letter of the 21st, I will try my best to write you what I intended to talk with you. May I start from the beginning to review somewhat the history of our Alumni Association which may not be too familiar with you for your short acquaintance with the organization.

Way back in the year 1942 long before your graduation, the Alumni Association started to be very active in Chungking, the Chinese War Capital then. A big financial campaign was held there in 1944 to help out our refugee camps in Chengtu and our Hanching spirit of unity and harmony was very well demonstrated among the alumni members. Ever since, members all over the world have been in very close contact with here and there and each year we must meet at least two times for close ties. I, myself, have followed our activities without interruption since 1942 and many shared the same viewpoint as mine that we are very short of manpower volunteering service to the association. In the year 195_ we were very delighted that you volunteered your service as the National Chairman when it was first declined by Mrs. K.Y.C.M., then by Mrs. Y.M.W.C. To me, you really worked very hard for the interest of Hanching after you took over the Chairmanship, so when I worked on nominating names for our Incorporation Committee, I strongly recommended you.

After the association was incorporated in New York, whenever meetings were called, it was very often only attended by you, S.Y. and myself. It was in one of these early meetings we felt we must work out something to raise some funds for our newborn organization to function. Because S.Y. is at the same time the chairman of the New York Opera Club, we decided to utilize his influence to request the members of that club to give a free performance for us for our money raising purpose. We started our preparation half a year ago planning to make a success next February.

Since your enthusiasm and energy was recognized, I recommended you to be the chairman of the Fund Raising Committee and S.Y. supported me. There was never any election for the post and according to our Hanching tradition it is not necessary to have one. Hanching is well known and proud of a special quality, that is, there is never any difference of opinion after any meeting.

It seems to me recently our usual qualities are fading away which symptom has never occurred once before the year 195_. Take for instance, you asked me to give you an opera production budget, and I gave you one. I am responsible for every figure I put down and every figure I put down is a necessity. Whether we can afford all the figures are our problems to be discussed in a meeting, and definitely any one's approval or disapproval does not solve the problem. Furthermore, it is never a Hanching style to disapprove another member's suggestion just based upon personal decision.

My answer to your writing is that you are very unfamiliar with true Hanchingism and I don't blame you because of your short acquaintance. I dare say that our Hanching people hate nothing more than bureaucracy. We are a bunch of simple people from the same institution never with any private ambition to make use of any public organization and we want to maintain it to be so. There has been and is always unity and harmony with us, so let us all try to preserve it.

May I appeal to you as an older sister that let us forget our own likes, dislikes, authorities and red tapes, but do our utmost best to put work into action for the improvement and good of our Association as a whole. Whosoever is willing to render service and help in a down to the earth hard working manner, he or she is welcome. We cannot afford wall decoration for standstills. We can only go forward as we all promised.

I write this letter to you purely for the good of our organization because we need straightforwardness to start our sound buildup, so that more members will be interested in rendering services without restrictions.

One of our loyal members, Y.M.Y.L. offered his office at the UN and called an intercommittee meeting on January 3, 195_, one copy of which notice was sent to you. Please attend the meeting and put all necessary things into action, because we cannot afford to lose any more time.

Your cooperation is very much needed by the new organization of ours.

Yours sincerely,
Mary Yang

Circulated among members
concerned with the opera
project.

Mary's strategy was to make this man lose face, i.e., to make him withdraw his presence from the Hanching Alumni Association.

No open charges were made against his misdeeds—which were of some moment on an international scale. The aggressive intent against him was sanctified by Mary's colophonic note of the letter's circular distribution.

Mary addresses the chairman of the fund raising committee from the metaphorical vantage point of an elder sister. From this high ground she entreats his cooperation and hard work so that the alumni association can "go forward." She bids him attend the next meeting with expeditious attention to his duties. The vocabulary of kinship does not, however, communicate sisterly advice, but rather, announces that Mary is the chairman's senior by virtue of her prior graduation from Hanching University, and that she is his senior forever more.

Mary alludes to her seniority in a brief historical recital, beginning with the sentence, "Way back in the year 1942, long before your graduation, the Alumni Association started to be very active. . . ." The hidden predicate, so to speak, contains reference to her own charter membership in the organization. The chairman is made to understand the weight of Mary's authoritative position rather than to receive her counsel. She outwardly expresses the need of the association for his cooperation, but in actuality, she harbors no expectations that he even continue his membership, much less redouble his efforts to fulfill the requirements of office.

Mary does not accuse the official of wrongdoing. She rather commends him for his dedication, which led the association membership to recognize him as their chairman—but not without adding that this recognition might have been due only to a shortage of "manpower volunteering service." Again observing proper formalities, she voices concern that "our usual qualities are fading away" ever since he secured his important position. In this way, she levels the subtle moral charge that he worked hard only until he got the position he wanted, then subverted it for the sake of purposes outside the organization. But Mary calls attention to this treason only discreetly. She retains her comforting, didactic tone of sisterly advice in her very disclosure of treason, when she explains, in effect, that we old-timers from Hanching University never would behave that way. Establishing that the chairman, as a newcomer to the ranks of the Hanching alumni, had fallen short of the highest ideals of the Hanching spirit—sheerly as a result of his junior status—affords Mary the perfectly legitimate opportunity to express solicitude for him, and for the fate of the alumni association as well. But her solicitude deepens into outrage. Pointed as her disguised charges of ethical laxity may be, yet they alone do not serve to wholly disqualify the chairman, for the actual content of the letter so far reveals only a dissatisfaction regarding his unfamiliarity with Hanchingism.

The proprieties employed by Mary outwardly display a remedial intent. She offers sisterly advice for the improvement of the chairman's inexperienced leadership, in keeping with the moral qualities of solidarity that bind all members of the Hanching alumni together in their pursuit of common objectives. Mary does not even hint at the chairman's international activity. She does not so much as intimate that he failed his office. She rather commends him for his dedicated exertions, which led the association to appoint him as its national chairman—but not without adding that this appointment was due only to a shortage of "manpower volunteering service."

Mary politely accords the chairman the right to benefit from the wisdom of her seniority, insofar as his office might better be occupied. But she effectively shuts off any avenue of moral rectification by denying that the alumni association possesses sufficient power differences to admit authority of whatever ethical complexion. In a word, Mary defines his office out of existence by defining the group as an organized structure out of existence.

Mary paints a picture of amorphous, egalitarian sentimentality by saying, "We are a bunch of simple people from the same institution" who "hate nothing more than bureaucracy." The sodality of the membership is just a "simple bunch of people." It is maintained by nothing more than a "down to earth hard working manner" on the part of each individual, everyone independently contributing his share of work "for the improvement and good of our Association as a whole." For Chinese, this is a picture of no organization at all.

The decisive move in Mary's strategy of sanctimonious aggression was to bring the whole organizational weight of the Hanching Alumni Association to bear on a denial of its structure, in which the repudiated chairman might assume power. She backed up her definition of the alumni association as an organization with no power structure with every possible reference to its actual power structure. In her phrase, "We are a bunch of simple people from the same institution never with any private ambition to make use of any public organization," Mary mobilizes the power of "public organization" to back up her definition of its membership as merely a "bunch of simple people." This picture of no organization is aimed at eliminating "private ambition" on the part of the target, who planned to use the organization as a source of collecting funds and illegally moving them abroad. Mary empowers the Hanching Alumni Association to sanction her definition of its formlessness by referring to what are in fact its undying organizational qualities, which she variously names "Hanching tradition," "Hanching style," "Hanching spirit," and still more doctrinally, "Hanchingism."

Concluding the letter, Mary ostensibly submits a piece of routine business information as a reminder that the chairman should attend a forthcoming meeting, "and put all necessary things into action, because we cannot afford to lose any more time." Here the association's formal existence is underlined by open reference to its bureaucratic committee structure. Altogether, Mary rallies Hanchingism and the device of a circular letter—which in itself reflects formal channels of communication—to the enforcement of her definition of the Hanching Alumni Association as an organization lacking sufficient structure to permit its chairman continued exercise of his discredited brand of authority. Mary directs the organizational momentum of the association toward a denial of its power positions by way of undercutting the chairman's position in it, no matter how politely she behooves him attend his official duties. He found there was nothing to attend to, given Mary's redefinition of the situation, and he promptly resigned.

Mary kept the legal formalities of harmony, yet delivered the aggressive goods. Such are the usages of politeness, in fair weather and foul. It is these legal norms that Chinese try to maintain, rather than trying to be a "good guy" to each other with open-ended relations. And this avoids being a "bad guy" when the excuse for the relationship comes to an end.

The Chinese are conscious of the fact that they work with form to a good end, apart from feelings. As Mary says, "Better to have superficial tranquility even if you're a volcano inside." This is the viewpoint of people who need a relationship even though they do not like it, the very situation in which members of the joint family often are put in maintaining a defensive kinship organization against the outside world.

Chinese brought up in such a traditional situation need a fantasy outlet for their feelings to be expressed pure and simple. The outlet is imagined to be friendship. There are many degrees of friendship recognized by the Chinese, but one degree above all—that of the "intimate friendship"—is prized as an opportunity to spill out all the spontaneity and expressiveness that is missing in all other relationships of formal obligation.

Friendship is made all the more attractive because—it is thought—it is the one relationship that is not governed by the proprieties. In the native view, friends may share feelings openly, and need not concern themselves with strategies of social distance keeping. But Chinese friendship does not in fact offer a retreat from the norms of predictability. Friendship is not, in the end, a careless, open-ended relationship any more than any other. To be true, friendship is everything that everything else is not. But the alternative itself is highly defined. It is circumscribed by default.

I found this out one day to my surprise when I returned to visit an intimate Chinese friend of mine after several years absence from the city. When I returned, my friend made no mention of the gap in time since our last encounter. He immediately picked up the sticky thread of our previous discussions as if no interval had occurred. He related his new hardships and the effort he was putting into overcoming them: his changing his career from the social sciences to the physical sciences under changed political conditions. He showed me a letter and some photographs he had just received from his wife, and a parcel of clothes he had purchased for his children and was about to send to Formosa. In turn, I lay bare my woman troubles. He expressed his sympathy, and then delivered his unabashed opinion—a proper thing between friends who exchange the intimacies of their personal lives. My friend explained that with a higher degree from Columbia University I could make a professional career in Formosa if I wanted to.

"I think we will then be able to go to Formosa together. I will get recommendations for you from so-and-so in the government. You will be holding American professional status, yet you are not like an American, and this will make you acceptable in Formosa. I myself could return home right now, have *amah,* servants, live with my wife, drink, but I have to deny it all. I had four years with my wife, and six years away from her in study. Now I have to shift my field of study to meet a political problem. . . .

"One must work hard, must work *completely* hard for the future. Do not be a dreamer. I am sorry, but I want to say that you have been naïve and stupid. Naïve and stupid. When you are a professor, what will the faculty think of such a woman if you marry her? They will embarrass you and make you look naïve. You must have a warm, comforting wife, not a romantic actor or artist or intellectual wife—not very pretty, perhaps. No wonder there is trouble already. I will introduce you to a good Chinese wife in Formosa."

At this point my irreducible American soul came to the surface. This resumption of our friendly intimacies without any preliminary banter about "how have you been all this time" as a means of exploring any needed adjustments in the relationship aroused some anxiety. And I blurted out:

"Why do you want to do all this for me, going to Formosa together, advising me how to get a Chinese wife and a job there?"

My friend knew where the relationship stood if I didn't, and he came back with loud, even angry, tones:

"What? Are you suspicious or something? It is *friendship!* I want to be an elder brother to you. We can cook Chinese dinner together and take walks along Riverside Drive and talk about our problems."

There is no question that he used the prerogatives of close friendship to advise and criticize me. He cast the relationship in kinship terms, a standard procedure, and as the elder party assumed responsibilities for me belonging to the role of an elder brother. Indeed, his seniority gave him the power to define the content of the friendship in which I was assigned the role of a younger brother. He was forced to spell out these roles in so many words out of exasperation for my misunderstanding or "suspiciousness." But he could easily accommodate my misperception of the situation as just one of those vagaries that younger siblings always are getting away with because of the favoritism shown them.

To rectify my careless inattention, my friend was prompted to state the rules. This is doubly significant.

In the first place, my friend showed some anxiety in his loudness of tone when he discovered that I might possibly have been playing the wrong part. I was supposed to have known all along that I was playing the younger to his elder brother. He was alarmed at the prospect that his role might appear ambiguous to me, because I seemed not to be reading his signals correctly. Of course I did not because I am not Chinese, and at that time I did not yet understand Chinese behavioral cues. Chinese do not habitually interact with persons outside of a graded system of roles, so that even in friendships if the one partner unwittingly acts improperly, the other will be left to cope with an ill-defined, ambiguous situation. For Americans, fluid relationships are normal, but for Chinese it is a discomforting case of social Brownian movement. They lose their point of reference. *Deliberate* impropriety is preferred to inadvertent error. In the former at least *some* standard of deviation may be measured against desirable performance. To that extent my friend was allowed to understand that my slipshod performance was the advantage I had taken of the leeway given a younger brother in the kinship model of friendship. But that I might be *unaware* of what I had done—my suspiciousness indicated that—raised the specter of unregulated encounter. As the senior partner he set about to resolve the ambiguity by spelling out the parts for both of us to acknowledge, then and there.

Without hesitation he specified the behavior that would be contained by the friendship. We would "cook Chinese dinner together and take walks along Riverside Drive and talk about our problems," i.e., that we would enjoy mutuality in action and emotional expression. In short, he declared that friendship consisted of equality and informality.

But friendship is really a case of formalized informality. It is not in fact an area of behavioral freedom exempt from ranked status duties that govern family or public life. In order to sustain the role equality that Chinese value in friendship for the emotional involvement it allows, my friend had to apply power differences belonging to the kinship model of voluntary brotherhood in his definition of friendship. He was called upon to enforce predictability in that very relationship he valued for its equities and exchange of affect. In Chinese friendship, the senior partner is obliged to police the relationship for its social content, making sure that it shall in fact contain role equality. The norm of reciprocity reserved for friendship is ratified by a nonreciprocal obligation on the part of the person in charge of the definition, even though the definition repudiates unequal responsibility.

Friendship, then, is only symbolically a relationship of equality and informality. One party is dependent on the definition of informality and the other is obliged to defend and enforce it. The Chinese say that, if a person is polite, it is not friendship. But the very unambiguousness of informality as the defining characteristic nonetheless is maintained by formal controls. Friendship is a case of formalized informality.

In these examples of good Chinese games—face saving, sanctimonious aggression, and formalized informality—there is one guiding strategy of communication: to give or withhold status. Even in friendships there is no getting around what essentially are power distinctions, narrowly defined by *li*, which can be manipulated as a resource to give or take away. Hence, Chinese society is a face society—the currency of interpersonal exchange is not feelings of personal regard, as in American games, but salutations of role in a system of unequal statuses. Americans give and take away love; Chinese give and take away face, but not for trivial reasons. Whereas the Americans rarely distinguish between affection for the person and respect for his status, the Chinese always do. The Chinese idea of sincerity is bound up with making this distinction, the American in not making it. Chinese perceive and act upon two realities, form (status) and content (feelings). The formalities are obligatory if there is to be any relationship at all; the feeling content is optional. But Americans perceive only one combined reality and act upon it by way of expressing self, and by doing this without responsibility for system stability or harmony. Westerners view the habit of distinguishing between form and content as the element of duplicity that lies at the bottom of Oriental inscrutability; but it is a habit the Chinese themselves take as a virtue that makes for superiority, because they are able to see *two* things where westerners see only one—the superiority of the intricate over the simple.

The rules of behavior among the Chinese elite that make for harmony are epitomized as the *chi chiao* or Seven Obligations, those between emperor and officialdom, father and son, husband and wife, brother and brother, friend and friend, elder and junior, and host and guest.

The high culture of traditional Chinese society that once upheld the Seven Obligations and Five Virtues is no longer in existence. But the values of interpersonal behavior are conservative. They have been carried by Mary Yang in her head outside the old supportive social structure. So long as persons of her generation are alive—elite persons of traditional up-bringing under the empire and a modern education under the Republic—the anthropologist still has a chance to participate in some aspect of that old structure. Some little sociological aspect of the Chinese Agrarian State, now defunct in its home-land, lives on in my relationship with my Chinese mother.

Epilogue

End of the
Agrarian State

CHAPTER 17

FROM FOLK SOCIETY
TO MASS SOCIETY

On 24 July 1901, the Ch'ing house created the *Wai-wu-pu*, or board of foreign affairs. With that move, China admitted her vulnerability to the steamboat powers of the West. On that date China officially stopped drawing on her own past exclusively and merged her civilization, a closed sequence of development from the advent of the political state there in 1700 B.C., with a global *oikoumenê*.

But China's new foreign outlook followed upon a turnabout in attitude toward her by the very western nations that had forced her to deal with them. Before the industrial revolution westerners came to China seeking trade, not markets. As a source of exotic trade goods, such as tea, and silk, China was an exotic place. Marco Polo told the wonders of thirteenth-century Oriental splendor; sixteenth-century Jesuit missionaries praised Confucianism as the highest and most natural form of human morals; the Physiocrats of the Enlightenment in the eighteenth century urged the reform of European governments on the model of the Chinese civil service and its marvelous system for the selection of merit through examination. As a market for the manufactures of coke-and-iron technology, however, China was viewed as contemptible, deserving of economic exploitation, even by force.

British gunboats in the Opium War alerted China to the dangers of isolation. The Opium War ended in a no-contest victory for England with the Treaty of Nanking in 1842, the first of a succession of like protocols that signed away China's tariff autonomy and territorial rights to western nations and westernized Japan. The English fought for open markets and the end of the Co-hong monopoly. The Co-hong was a guild of Canton merchants licensed by the throne from about 1720 to trade with westerners. The foreign trade monopoly and its great wealth was allotted to a privileged circle of merchants in return for their being responsible for the behavior of the foreigners. The Co-hong accordingly did not allow foreigners to reside where they traded. The English waxed indignant over being treated like so many tribal barbarians, forced to keep their distance, just at the same time the Chinese throne waxed indignant over the importation of opium at the expense of a great outgo of silver. The emperor deputed one of his viceroys to stop the traffic. Tongue in cheek, the English readily signed an agreement to the effect. They very well understood the nature of imperial government and knew that it could not possibly begin to enforce any laws whatsoever for the regulation of opium traffic. Their realistic view educated the unrealistic Chinese view. The commissioner seized a batch of opium, burned it, and the war was on, a pushover engagement between British gunboats against Chinese forts and junks in the waters around Canton. The humiliation of defeat written into the Treaty of Nanking was in great part the outcome of Chinese failure to realize that imperial culturalism was no match for western nationalism. Unequal treaties signed from that time on remained in force until 1942.

Flying over the British gunboats were flags. The flag is an emblem of genuine national sovereignty, underwritten by a constitution, a document spelling out the organic laws of nationhood. The politics of culturalism in the Chinese Agrarian State flew no flag and possessed no written constitution. The little provincial armies and navies of imperial China flew banners inscribed with the names and titles of their officers. The titles were of imperial issue but substantive loyalties were strictly local. The political history of China following those first cannonading days at Canton has been the history of attaining a flag and a constitution in the name of a Chinese nation-state.

Nationalism requires an industrialized military technology, a plurality of economic landscapes to pay for it, and centralized government to manage these resources for the good of military supply. China learned from the T'aip'ing rebellion that she could not have the guns alone without confronting these other features that allow provincial government to become stronger than central government.

The T'aip'ing rebellion was the effort of a rival dynasty centered in south China to move its armed forces northward between 1850 and 1864 for the capture of Peking. A decisive blow against the rebel forces was dealt by the provincial army of Kiangsu under the leadership of its governor, Li Hung-chang. Li supplied his troops, drilled by western instructors, with modern rifles manufactured in arsenals of his own construction. The wealth to build these arsenals came out of Li's control over the maritime customs of Shanghai, China's most important port of trade at that time, and taxation of commerce in the whole Shanghai area. This gave to Li Hung-chang economic resources greater than any commanded by central government in Peking. While Li Hung-chang himself was personally loyal to the imperial cause, the example of provincial power based on a modern army set the pattern for other governors as well. They equipped their own armies by exploiting the growing commercial resources of internal trade, coming out of the port cities, by applying a transit tax on it in their regions. Such regional machines infringed on imperial sovereignty because they were based on real armies supplied from real economic resources alternative to the grain tribute. The fall of the monarchy in 1911 simply verified the triumph of regionalism over empire.

The Agrarian State had the life crushed out of it between the jaws of a giant vise, between the pressures of foreign power from the outside and from regionalism on the inside. Any new leadership group seeking political power over all of China would have to challenge both those threats to unity with the centralized unity of nationhood.

The transformation from an Agrarian State to a nation-state in China took place in two steps because there were really two Chinas responding to the impact of the West: the China of high culture and the China of folk culture. The elite first absorbed the impact and then impressed change on the nonelite. The intellectual basis for a nation was worked out in experiments with flags, constitutions, and law codes by the culture-contacted leadership groups of transitional China, the period from (say) the Opium War to the end of the Republic in 1949. After 1949, with the installation of a totalitarian government under a Communist flag, change was visited from above on the peasant masses.

First the elite lost its insulation from the outside world; the traditional literati of high culture became a modern intelligentsia. This transformed elite then lost its insulation from the masses under it by persuading them that they, too, were somebody else—no longer a *non*privileged folk retreating from privilege into their village society, but an *under*privileged people deprived of citizenship within a national whole. With this persuasion completed by terror and propaganda, the Agrarian State in China has come to an end.

A centralized despotism in theory has become one in fact, with the power to destroy folk culture, and with the mind to do so, owing to ideas of progress, modernization, and economic development imported from the industrialized western nation-states. The cities of China today are centers of transformation, impressing change on the countryside. The cities of traditional China were centers of culture change, too, but in the reverse direction. They rather carried forward into orthodoxy, at the hands of the literati, a body of sociological observations in literature and laws that was continuous with the native folk culture. By contrast, the articles of planning, even the ethics of planning to be found in the urban headquarters of Communist directed change, are not indigenous and therefore are inconsistent with the values and experience of folk culture. And deliberately so, because the aim is to overcome and remake the Green Circle.

Control over folk culture takes the form of three levels of formal organization where three levels of nonorganized social structure existed before. At the highest level is the commune, an administrative unit corresponding to the maximal unit of traditional community culture, the marketing community, an area of from eighteen to twenty villages centered on its market town. The minimal unit of traditional community culture, the village, corresponds to the production brigade. But routine work is carried out on a daily basis by the production team, which is a village neighborhood of from twenty to thirty households. It would show an extreme lack of knowledge about their own country if the Chinese Communists did not attempt to graft their systems of control onto the traditional roots of rural life.

The real social unit of agricultural labor is no longer the family, but the production team. Family life among the peasantry—now converted into farmers—has reduced to keeping a household budget, which involves a cost-accounting of work points earned, and of rearing children. Much of the life space of husband and wife is occupied in service with a militarized group that works land collectivized on a village-wide basis. Inasmuch as collectivization under conditions of intensive farming must be a substitute for mechanization, the purpose of team organization cannot be to raise agricultural productivity. Rather, it is an instrument of mobilization, a way of organizing people for doing other tasks, during the traditional slack season, at government bidding.

The People's Republic of China is a totalitarian society. The leadership refers to it as a species of democracy, the New Democracy. That follows. Democracy in this usage is equated with participation. Peking says that it has brought peasants and workers into the political process. It has indeed. That does not mean these people share in the decision making but that they participate in knowledge about, and contribute to the goals of, the national society.

Under dynastic rule it was said:

> The people can be made to follow government policy; but they cannot be made to understand it. [*Lun Yu,* VIII:9]

But under party rule the people *are* made to understand government policy. In traditional society, when it was said, "Heaven is high and the emperor is far away," the little people of the Green Circle were excluded from audience to political communications of any kind. The government of the emperors was authoritarian. It restricted political messages to the small minority that participated in the imperial cause—messages about the justification for power, the ethics of ruling, and theories of society and history.

> He who holds no political office does not discuss matters of state. [*Lun Yu,* VIII:14]

The emperor did not tell commoners who to hate, what to cheer, or why they must work hard. But the new totalitarian state agitates, propagandizes. It must engage the participation of the folk so they may be mobilized for national goals by the new ruling elite.

But if 640 million peasant farmers are to be trumpeted out of their Neolithic fastness they must first be trained to hear the note. The peasant is not attuned to advertising messages, commercial or political. The party theoreticians sitting in Peking find that communism is the foreign doctrine most suitable to elicit national patriotism because it is more Chinese than Confucianism. Confucius is said not to be Chinese enough because his doctrines upheld power on the part of a minority. But communism is everybody's ideology, irrespective of class.

The new doctrine pictures the triumph of the regime as the outcome of outraged peasants and workers who whistled themselves up like a hurricane and swept out the old order and installed a new one in their own interests. It is bootless to argue that the picture is false. The Communist revolution was led from above, and its leaders, mostly elite persons of the Republican regime, were moved by imported ideas of interclass struggle and of poverty as a curable social ill. The injection of these ideas into a nonprivileged folk culture is one way of arousing it to a newly discovered sense of underprivilege. The myth of a self-transforming people is itself an agency of change. So too is participation in mass organizations. Mass organizations are levers of action. The peasant, in the very process of being manipulated, ceases to be a peasant. He is made over into a rural proletarian.

Slogans that enjoin the peasant to work productively under Chairman Mao so as to make China a rich and strong socialist country penetrate the isolation of community culture in a way the lofty paternalism of the emperors never did, nor intended to. The emperors, lacking the communications technology to mechanize a lower echelon of command, satisfied themselves with a strictly liturgical sway over their passive subjects. But the operational sway of the Communist party, empowered by electric channels of feedback communication, places agents of change in the very midst of the rural community, in the communes and in the brigades and villages.

Communist party members and their trained activists, the *kan pu* or cadres, are the agents of change. Their numbers, for their role in merging state and society, contrast with the smaller percentage of the population represented by the gentry, of which they are the successors.

	c. 1840	*1957*
Population	400,000,000	600,000,000
Elite	1,100,000	20,000,000
	(gentry de jure)	(party members)
Civil Officials	25,000	1,500,000

The changes worked by a huge expansion of the government sector are reflected in the increased number of man-days absorbed by rural labor, which in pre-Communist times were limited by seasons of enforced idleness in the agricultural cycle. Planned interference in the village round of life takes up this slack.

	1920s	1957
Number of man-days per year	172	250

Organization gets results.

But to get organization, the leadership must set up its agents of change as models to imitate, reversing the traditional peasant attitude toward his betters as models to avoid.

The present regime is conscious of promoting a new style of peasant life designed to remake peasants into farmers. This new style is given its idealized version in the outlook and action of the *kan-pu*. The *kan-pu* have their origin in the combat leaders of guerrilla warfare against the Japanese in Occupied China during World War II. Now, after twenty years as masters of China, the ranks of the *kan-pu* have swollen to the size of an enormous bureaucracy. Not surprisingly, this bureaucracy has tended to settle down into a series of nicely defined hierachical ranks, each with its own prerogatives in food, goods, and housing. But Mao is not yet ready to allow the inevitable to happen.

One of the targets of the cultural revolution, actually a party purge, is this very status consciousness. An editorial in the *Jen-Min Jih-Pao* for 21 July 1966 stressed:

> It is absolutely impermissible for Communist Party members to take the attitude of bourgeoise overlords toward the masses. The great proletarian revolution is precisely a revolution against bourgeoise overlords. If a Communist does not learn modestly from the masses, but adopts the attitude of a bureaucrat towards them, in what sense is he a Communist? This is absolutely contrary to the Communist Party style of work. . . . Our Communist Party style is to have close links with the masses, learn from them and wholeheartedly serve the people.

The complaint here is that the old egalitarian spirit of the early revolutionary comrades is fading away in a bureaucratic setting. One object of the cultural revolution, therefore, has been to revolutionize the bureaucracy. But this involves cultivating opposites of habit and attitude. On the one hand the *kan-pu* is asked to keep alive the "Red" spirit of the old-time revolutionary, and on the other he is asked to achieve "expert" competence in handling an administrative position in a two-way chain of command.

The model of virtue to be imitated, then, is the *kan-pu,* a person who is both Red and expert. One of the sayings in *Quotations from Chairman Mao,* a new *Sacred Edict* that really means to reach a wide audience, gives the definitive style:

> It is necessary to maintain the system of cadre participation in collective productive labor. The cadres of our Party and state are ordinary workers and not overlords on the backs of the people. By taking part in collective productive labor, the cadres maintain extensive, constant and close ties with the working people. This is a major measure of fundamental importance for a socialist system. [XXIX]

The *kan-pu* is somehow expected to be one with the masses at the same time he moves them to action as a middleman for directives from above. This extreme combination of leadership qualities is unfamiliar in the West and at first glance it may appear suitably mysterious for an East that has not yet lost its enigma.

Yet the conception of the cadre who is at once Red and expert is a practical one in the light of the problems faced by the government in breaking down the traditional boundary controls of the Green Circle. The cadre embodies the necessary qualities for imitation by a peasantry that before took elite persons as a model of stellar remoteness to avoid.

The cadre is held up as a model of high involvement with the regime's national policies and with its means of carrying them out.

So endeth the last of the Agrarian States.

Bibliography
and Notes

THIS appendix is divided into three parts, Chapter References, Classical Sources, and Suggestions for Further Reading.

The Chapter References contain the reading assignments in English, Chinese, and Japanese that I gave to my Tokyo University students on each lecture topic. Some of these materials I donated to the departmental library. The Chinese novels and short stories listed here in English translation my students were able to find in Japanese.

The Classical Sources are listed alphabetically by their romanized titles. They are the ancient Chinese writings most frequently cited in this book. Quotations are identified by chapter and verse as numbered in the translations listed here. Specialists will note that I have retranslated most of the quotations to fit the bias of my argument.

The Suggestions for Further Reading are compiled from books in my own library. Those dated after 1968, when the manuscript was completed, have not gone into the actual making of this book, but they are relevant.

CHAPTER REFERENCES

1

Hatada Takashi, "Chūgoku ni okeru senseishugi to 'Sonraku kyōdōtai riron'" ("Absolutism and the Theory of the Chinese Village Community"), in *Chūgoku Kenkyū,* vol. 13, 1950, pp. 2–13.

Fukutake Tadashi, *Chūgoku nōson shakai no kōzō (The Structure of Chinese Village Society),* 2nd edition, Yūhikaku, Tokyo, 1951.

Liao T'ai-chu, *I ko Ch'eng-chiao ti Ts'un-lo She-ch'u (Sociological Aspects of a Rural Community),* Yenching University Monographs, Peiping, 1941.

Leon E. Stover, "Complementary Boundary Controls in Chinese Subcultures," paper read before the Fourth Conference of the Society of Japanese Ethnology, Tokyo, May 1965. Mimeo.

Note: For the marketing area, see G. William Skinner, "Marketing and Social Structure in Rural China," parts I, II, and III, *Journal of Asian Studies,* XXIV, nos. 1–3, 1964–65.

2

Chang, Kwang-chih, *The Archaeology of Ancient China,* Yale University Press, New Haven, 1963.

Miyazaki Ichisada, *Chūgoku Kodaishi Gairon (A Summary of Ancient Chinese History),* Harvard-Yenching-Dōshisha Eastern Cultural Lectures Committee, monograph no. 8, Kyoto, 1955.

Julian H. Steward, *Theory of Culture Change,* University of Illinois Press, Urbana, 1955, chaps. 3, 4, and 11.

Note: For the pattern of Bronze Age and Iron Age cultures, see Carleton S. Coon, *The Story of Man,* Alfred A. Knopf, New York, 1962, chaps. 7 and 8. For the developmental sequence among the archaic civilizations, see chap. 11 in Steward; my Figure 1 is modified after tables 4 and 5 there. For Indo-European charioteers, see William H. McNeill, *The Rise of the West,* University of Chicago Press, Chicago, 1963, pp. 106 and 218. For events in the state of Lu, see Hsu Cho-yun, *Ancient China in Transition,* Stanford University Press, Stanford, 1965. For feudalism as a type under culture change, see Stanislav Andreski, *The Uses of Comparative Sociology,* University of California Press, Berkeley and Los Angeles, 1964, p. 161.

3

Ch'en Tsu-ying, *The Miao Frontier in Hunan,* unpublished M.A. thesis, the University of Washington, Seattle, 1947. Microfilm.

Robert Redfield, *The Primitive World and Its Transformations,* Cornell University Press, Ithaca, 1956.

Paul A. V. Spencer, "Impressions of Chinese Agriculture," *Royal Central Asian Journal,* vol. 44, part 1, 1957.

Glen T. Trewartha, "New Maps of China's Population," *Geographical Review,* vol. XLVII, no. 2, 1957.

Wu Ching-tzu (1701–1754), *The Scholars,* a translation by Yang Hsien-yi and Gladys Yang of *Ju Lin Wai Shih,* Foreign Languages Press, Peking, chap. 43.

4

J. H. Boeke, *Economics and Economic Policy of Dual Societies,* Institute of Pacific Relations, New York, 1955.

Ch'en Han-sheng, *Industrial Capital and Chinese Peasants,* Kelly and Walsh, Shanghai, 1939.

Fei Hsiao-t'ung, "Problems of Rural Industrialization," *China Economist,* vol. I, no. 4, 1948, pp. 102–109.

Mao Tun (1896–   ) *Spring Silkworms and Other Stories,* tr. by Sidney Shapiro, Foreign Languages Press, Peking. All quotations from the title story, pp. 35, 36, 37–38.

NOTE: The quotation from *Rickshaw Boy* by Lao She (1898–1966) is from p. 21 in a translation by Evan King, published by Reynal and Hitchcock of New York in 1945. For beggars as a class of expendables, see Gerhard Lenski, *Power and Privilege,* McGraw-Hill, New York, 1968, pp. 280–83.

5

Lu Hsun (1881–1936), "The Divorce," tr. in *Selected Works of Lu Hsun,* vol. I, Foreign Languages Press, Peking.

Saeki Tomi, "Shindai no kyōyaku, chihō ni tsuite—Shindai chihō gyōsei no isshaku," ("On the Hsiang-yao and Tipao in Ch'ing Times—Local Government under the Ch'ing"), *Tōhōgaku,* no. 28, 1964, pp. 91–100.

Toyoshima Seiei, "Chūgoku seihokubu ni okeru suiri kyōdōtai ni tsuite," ("Community Water Facilities in Northwest China"), *Rekishigaku Kenkyū,* no. 201, 1956, pp. 24–35.

NOTE: The joke about the gentleman in hell comes from p. 193 of *A Nun of Taishan and Other Translations,* tr. by Lin Yu-tang, Commercial Press, Shanghai, 1936.

6

Fei Hsiao-t'ung, "P'ing Yen Yang-ch'u 'Kai-fa Min-li Chien-she Hsiang-ts'un' " ("A Criticism of Yen Yang-ch'u's 'Rouse the People's Power and Reconstruct the Villages' "), *Kuan Ch'a* vol. I, no. 1, 1948.

Lao Hsiang, "Ah Chuan Goes to School," in *A Nun of Taishan and Other Translations.* All quotations are from pp. 123, 125, 127–8, and 133–4.

Oyama Hikoichi, *Chūgoku-jin no Kazoku-seido no Kenkyū (Studies in the Chinese Family System),* Seki-shoin, Tokyo, 1952.

Eric Wolf, "Types of Latin American Peasantry," *American Anthropologist,* vol. 57, no. 3, 1955, pp. 452–471. The phrase "cult of poverty" is Wolf's.

NOTE: A. L. Kroeber coined the term "homoyogeniture" for use by Norman Jacobs in *The Origin of Modern Capitalism and Eastern Asia,* Hong Kong University Press, 1958, p. 149. The phrase "mutual suspicion" is from the title of chapter XXIV of A. H. Smith's *Chinese Characteristics,* F. H. Revell Co., New York, 1894. Selected translations from the *Ta Ch'ing Lu Li* may be found in G. Jamieson's *Chinese Family and Commercial*

Law, Kelly & Walsh, Shanghai, 1921. On average family size, see F. L. K. Hsu, "The Myth of Chinese Family Size," *American Journal of Sociology,* vol. XLVII, no. 5, 1943, pp. 555–562.

7

Fei Hsiao-t'ung, "Peasantry and Gentry: An Interpretation of Chinese Social Structure and Its Changes," *American Journal of Sociology,* vol. LII, no. 1, 1946, pp. 1–17.

————, China's Gentry: *Essays in Rural-Urban Relations,* University of Chicago Press, 1953.

Wu Ching-tzu, *The Scholars,* chap. 3, from which all the quotations are taken.

8

J. J. M. DeGroot, *The Religion of the Chinese,* The Macmillan Co., New York, 1910.

Bronislaw Malinowski, *Myth in Primitive Psychology,* W. W. Norton Co., New York, 1926.

Robert Redfield, "The Folk Society," *American Journal of Sociology,* vol. LII, pp. 292–308.

NOTE: The Evan King novel mentioned in this chapter was published in 1955 by Rinehart and Co. of New York. A translation of *Strange Stories from a Chinese Studio* is available by Herbert A. Giles from an American edition published in 1925 by Boni and Liveright, New York. The P'u Sung-ling novel, *A Marriage to Awaken the World,* has never been translated into English. It was first published in 1870 and is available in a recent (1957) Chinese printing of two volumes from the Chung-hwa Book Company in Hong Kong.

9

Fei Hsiao-t'ung, *Peasant Life in China,* Kegan Paul, Trench, Trubner and Co., London, 1939. The quotations used are from pp. 119, 182, and 181.

Robert Redfield, *Peasant Society and Culture,* University of Chicago Press, 1956. The quotation is from p. 123.

A. H. Smith, *Village Life in China,* Fleming H. Revell Co., New York, 1899, chap. XX. Quotations are from pp. 213, 214, 216, 218, and 327–8.

10

Chi Ch'ao-ting, *Key Economic Areas in Chinese History,* George Allen and Unwin, London, 1936.

Owen Lattimore, *Inner Asian Frontiers of China,* American Geographical Society, New York, 1940.

11

Chen Shao-kwan, *The System of Taxation in China in the Tsing Dynasty, 1644–1911,* Columbia University Studies in History, Economics and Public Law, no. 143, 1914. My Figure 8 is adapted from tables and figures on pp. 31 and 33.

Li Pao-chia, *Reminiscences of a Chinese Official: Revelations of Official Life under the Manchus,* Tientsin Press, 1922. This is an anonymous translation of forty-seven chapters of *Kuan Ch'ang Hsien Hsing Yi,* 1903, 1904–5. The long quotation is from pp. 21–22.

Robert M. Marsh, "The Venality of Provincial Office in China and in Comparative Perspective," *Comparative Studies in Society and History,* vol. IV, no. 4, 1962, pp. 452–466.

NOTE: My table of remissions is drawn from statistics supplied by Hosea Ballou Morse, *The Trade and Administration of the Chinese Empire,* Longmans, Green and Co., London, 1908, pp. 82–3. On the size of the gentry, see Figure 4 in Chang Chung-li, *The Chinese Gentry,* University of Washington Press, Seattle, 1955, p. 138. On the size of the gentry's Gross National Product, see Supplement 2 in Chang Chung-li, *The Income of the Chinese Gentry,* University of Washington Press, Seattle, 1962.

12

Aisin-Gioro Pu Yi, *From Emperor to Citizen,* vol. 1, Foreign Languages Press, Peking, 1964. Quotations are from pp. 62–3, 125, 127, 41, 42, 44, and 45.

John C. Pelzel, "Notes on the Chinese Bureaucracy," *Systems of Political Control and Bureaucracy in Human Societies,* American Ethnological Society, 1958, pp. 50–57.

Wu Han, Fei Hsiao-t'ung, *et al., Huang Chuan Yu Shen Chuan (The Emperor's Power and the Gentry's Power),* Kwanch'a Press, Shanghai, 1949.

13

Hu Hsien-chin, *The Common Descent Group in China and Its Functions,* Viking Fund Publications in Anthropology, no. 10, New York, 1948.

Uchida Chiyū, "Kahoku nōson ni okeru dōzoku no saishi gyōji ni tsuite" ("Ancestral Worship in Agricultural Communities in North China"), *Tōhō Gakuhō Kyōto,* vol. 22, 1953, pp. 59–94.

NOTE: The title of Morrison's article is "Worship at the Tombs."

14

Miyazaki Ichisada, *Kakyo* (*The Examination System*), Chūō-kōron-sha, Tokyo, 1963.

P'an Kuang-tan and Fei Hsiao-t'ung, "K'e-chu yu she-hui liu-tung" ("The Examination System and Social Mobility"), *She-hui K'e-hseuh*, Vol. IV, 1947, pp. 1–21.

NOTE: The passage from *Hung Lou Meng* is in a translation by H. Bencroft Joly, *The Dream of the Red Chamber,* Book I, Kelly and Walsh, Shanghai, 1892, pp. 58–9.

15

W. H. Newell, "The Sociology of Ritual in Early China," *Sociological Bulletin,* vol. V, no. 6, 1957, pp. 1–13.

Kojima Yūma, *Chūgoku no seijishisō,* (*Political Thought in China*), Harvard-Yenching-Dōshisha Eastern Lectures Committee, monograph no. 1, Kyoto, 1956.

NOTE: For a comparison of Confucian and Legalistic thinking, see Miner S. Bates, *The Establishment of the Chinese Empire,* Ph.D. dissertation, Yale University, New Haven, 1935.

16

Leon E. Stover, *"Face" and Verbal Analogues of Interaction in Chinese Culture: A Theory of Formalized Social Behavior Based Upon Participant-Observation of an Upper-Class Chinese Household, Together with a Biographical Study of the Primary Informant,* Ph.D. dissertation, Columbia University, New York, 1962.

————, "*Li* and *Mien-tzu* in Upper Class Chinese Culture," paper read before the Third Conference of the Society of Japanese Ethnology, Tokyo, May 1964. Mimeo.

17

Robert Redfield and Milton Singer, "The Cultural Role of Cities," *Economic Development and Cultural Change,* vol. III, no. 1, 1954, pp. 53–73.

Leon E. Stover, "Communism in the Historical-developmental Sequence in China," paper read before the 58th Annual Meeting of the American Anthropological Association, Mexico City, December, 1959. Mimeo.

NOTE: The comparative figures on man-days of work per year are taken from Chao Kuo-chun, *Agricultural Development and Problems in China Today,* Indian Council of World Affairs, Sapru House, New Delhi, 1958, p. 4.

CLASSICAL SOURCES

Ch'un Ch'iu: In James Legge, *The Chinese Classics,* vol. V, Oxford University Press, 1872.

Han Fei Tzu: W. K. Liao, *The Complete Works of Han Fei Tzu,* 2 vols., Arthur Probsthain, London, 1939 and 1959.

Hsiao Ching: James Legge, *The Hsiao King,* 2nd edition, Oxford University Press, 1899.

Kuan Tzu: Lewis Maverick, *Economic Dialogues in Ancient China: Selections from the Kuan-tzu,* Southern Illinois Press, Carbondale, 1954.

Li Chi: James Legge, *Sacred Books of the East,* vols. XXVII and XXVIII, Oxford University Press, 1885.

Lun Yu: In James Legge, *The Chinese Classics,* vol. I, Oxford University Press, 1893.

Meng Tzu: In James Legge, *The Chinese Classics,* vol. II, Oxford University Press, 1895.

Shang Yang: J. J. Dyvendak, *The Book of Lord Shang,* University of Chicago Press, 1928.

Sheng Yu: F. W. Baller, *The Sacred Edict, with a Translation of the Colloquial Rendering,* 2nd edition, American Presbyterian Mission Press, Shanghai, 1907.

Shih Ching: In James Legge, *The Chinese Classics,* vol. IV, Oxford University Press, 1871.

Shu Ching: In James Legge, *The Chinese Classics,* vol. III, Oxford University Press, 1865.

Sun Tzu: Samuel B. Griffith, *Sun Tzu, the Art of War,* Oxford University Press, 1963.

Tso Chuan: In James Legge, *The Chinese Classics,* vol. V, Oxford University Press, 1872.

SUGGESTIONS FOR FURTHER READING

THE AGRARIAN STATE (Comparative)

Robert J. Braidwood, *The Near East and the Foundations for Civilization,* The Condon Lectures, Oregon State System of Education, Eugene, Oregon, 1952.

Robert J. Braidwood and Gordon R. Willey, *Courses Toward Urban Life,* Aldine, Chicago, 1962.

Rushton Coulborn, *The Origin of Civilized Societies,* Princeton University Press, 1959.

Milton Covensky, *The Ancient Near Eastern Tradition,* Harper and Row, New York, 1966.

Glyn Daniel, *The First Civilizations,* Thomas Y. Crowell, New York, 1968.

William Theodore deBary and Ainslie T. Embree (eds.), *Approaches to Asian Civilization,* Columbia University Press, New York, 1964.

E. N. Eisenstadt, *The Political Systems of Empires,* Free Press, Glencoe, 1963.

Frederic K. Lehman, *Anthropological Parameters of a Civilization: the Ecology, Evolution and Typology of India's High Culture,* Ph.D. dissertation, Columbia University, New York, 1959. Carbon copy courtesy of the author.

John Meskill (ed.), *The Pattern of Chinese History,* D. C. Heath, Boston, 1965.

Sally Falk Moore, *Power and Property in Inca Peru,* Columbia University Press, New York, 1958.

M. Frederick Nelson, *Korea and the Old Orders in Eastern Asia,* Louisiana State University Press, Baton Rouge, 1945.

Denis Sinor (ed.), *Orientalism and History,* W. Heffer, Cambridge, 1954.

Julian H. Steward, *et al., Irrigation Civilizations: A Comparative Study,* Social Science Monographs I, Pan American Union, Washington, D.C., 1955.

Bruce G. Trigger, *Beyond History,* Holt, Rinehart and Winston, New York, 1968.

Karl A. Wittfogel, *Oriental Despotism,* Yale University Press, New Haven, 1957.

PREHISTORY AND EARLY CIVILIZATION

Davidson Black, *et. al., Fossil Man in China,* Geological Memoirs, Series A, No. 11, The Geological Survey of China, Peiping, 1933.

Cheng Te-K'un, *Archaeology in China: Prehistoric China,* W. Heffer, Cambridge, 1959.

———, *Archaeology in China: New Light on Prehistoric China,* W. Heffer, Cambridge, 1966.

———, *Archaeology in China: Shang China,* University of Toronto Press, 1960.

———, *Archaeology in China: Chou China,* W. Heffer, Cambridge, 1963.

Pierre Teilhard de Chardin, *Early Man in China*, Institute de Géo-Biologie, Pékin, 1941.

Pierre Teilhard de Chardin and Pei Wen-chung, *Le Néolithique de la Chine*, Institute de Géo-Biologie, Pékin, 1944.

Judith M. Treistman, *The Prehistory of China*, Doubleday, New York, 1972.

Li Chi, *et al.*, *Ch'eng Tzu-yai: The Black Pottery Culture Site at Lung-shan-chen in Li-ch'eng-hsien, Shantung Province*, Yale University Publications in Anthropology No. 52, Yale University Press, New Haven, 1956.

William Watson, *China Before the Han Dynasty*, Thames and Hudson, London, 1961.

————, *Cultural Frontiers in Ancient East Asia*, Edinburgh University Press, 1971.

Paul Wheatley, *The Pivot of Four Quarters: A Preliminary Inquiry into the Origins and Character of the Ancient Chinese City*, Aldine, Chicago, 1971.

FEUDALISM

Rushton Coulborn (ed.), *Feudalism in History*, Princeton University Press, 1956.

Wolfram Eberhard, *Conquest and Rulers: Social Forces in Medieval China*, E. J. Brill, Leiden, 1952.

Marcel Granet, *Chinese Civilization* (tr. Kathleen E. Innes and Mabel R. Brailsford), Routledge and Kegan Paul, London, 1930.

Friedrich Hirth, *The Ancient History of China to the End of the Chou Dynasty*, Columbia University Press, New York, 1908.

Kaizuka Shigeki, *Confucius* (tr. Geoffrey Bownas), George Allen and Unwin, London, 1956.

Liu Wu-chi, *Confucius: His Life and Times*, Philosophical Library, New York, 1955.

Herbert F. Rudd, *Chinese Social Origins*, University of Chicago Press, 1928.

Richard L. Walker, *The Multi-State System of Ancient China*, Shoe String Press, Hamden, Conn., 1953.

EMPIRE

Derk Bodde, *China's First Unifier*, E. J. Brill, Leiden, 1938.

John A. Harrison, *The Chinese Empire*, Harcourt Brace Jovanovich, New York, 1972.

Michael Loewe, *Imperial China*, Frederick A. Praeger, New York, 1965.

Franz Schurmann and Orville Schell (eds.), *Imperial China*, Vintage Books, 1967.

HISTORY

O. Edmund Clubb, *Twentieth Century China*, Columbia University Press, 1964.

Wolfram Eberhard, *A History of China*, University of California, Berkeley, 1969.

C. P. Fitzgerald, *China: A Short Cultural History*, Cresset Press, London, 1950.

Immanuel C. Y. Hsu, *The Rise of Modern China*, Oxford University Press, New York, 1970.

―――― (ed.), *Readings in Modern Chinese History*, Oxford University Press, New York, 1971.

Pierre Huard and Ming Wong, *Chine D'hier et D'aujourd'hui*, Horizons de France, Paris, 1950.

Kenneth Scott Latourette, *The Chinese: Their History and Culture*, 4th edition, Macmillan, 1964.

Henry McAleavy, *The Modern History of China*, Frederick A. Praeger, New York, 1967.

C. H. Philips (ed.), *Handbook of Oriental History*, The Royal Historical Society, London, 1951.

Edwin O. Reishauer and John K. Fairbank, *East Asia: The Great Tradition*, Houghton Mifflin, Boston, 1960.

David Nelson Rowe, *Modern China: A Brief History*, D. van Nostrand, Princeton, 1959.

Zen E-tu (E-tu Zen Sun) and John de Francis (eds.), *Chinese Social History*, American Council of Learned Societies, Washington, D.C., 1956.

ECONOMIC HISTORY

Chen Huan-chang, *The Economic Principles of Confucius and His School*, Faculty of Political Science at Columbia University, New York, 1911.

E. Stuart Kirby, *Introduction to the Economic History of China*, George Allen and Unwin, London, 1954.

Mabel Ping-hua Lee, *The Economic History of China*, The Faculty of Political Science at Columbia University, New York, 1921.

Nancy Lee Swann, *Food and Money in Ancient China*, Princeton University Press, 1950.

Yang Lien-sheng, *Money and Credit in China: A Short History*, Harvard University Press, Cambridge, 1952.

GEOGRAPHY

L. H. Dudley Buxton, *China: The Land and the People*, Oxford University Press, 1929.

George B. Cressey, *China's Geographical Foundations*, McGraw-Hill, New York, 1934.

Albert Herrman, *An Historical Atlas of China*, new edition, edited by Norton Ginsburg, Aldine, Chicago, 1966.

J. E. Spencer and William L. Thomas, *Asia, East by South: A Cultural Geography*, John Wiley, New York, 1971.

T. R. Tregear, *A Geography of China*, Aldine, Chicago, 1965.

Tuan Yi-fu, *Landscapes of the World: China*, Aldine, Chicago, 1969.

DEMOGRAPHY

S. Chandrasekhar, *China's Population: Census and Vital Statistics*, 2nd edition, Hong Kong University Press, 1960.

Chen Ta, *Population in Modern China*, University of California Press, Berkeley, 1946.

Ho Ping-ti, *Studies on the Population of China*, Harvard University Press, Cambridge, 1959.

Leo A. Orleans, *Every Fifth Child: The Population of China*, Eyre Methuen, London, 1972.

AGRICULTURE

John Lossing Buck, *Chinese Farm Economy*, Commercial Press, Shanghai, 1930.

F. H. King, *Farmers of Forty Centuries*, privately printed, Madison, 1911.

Walter H. Mallory, *China: Land of Famine*, American Geographical Society, New York, 1928.

Ramon H. Myers, *The Chinese Peasant Economy: Agricultural Development in Hopei and Shantung 1890–1949*, Harvard University Press, Cambridge, 1970.

Dwight H. Perkins, *Agricultural Development in China 1368–1968*, Aldine, Chicago, 1969.

T. H. Shen, *Agricultural Resources of China*, Cornell University Press, Ithaca, 1951.

V. D. Wickizer and M. K. Bennett, *The Rice Economy of Monsoon Asia*, Food Research Institute, Stanford University, 1941.

LAW AND GOVERNMENT

Derk Bodde and Clarence Morris, *Law in Imperial China*, Harvard University Press, Cambridge, 1967.

H. S. Brunnert and V. V. Hagelstrom, *Present Day Political Organization of China*, Shanghai, 1912. Pirated edition by the Book World Co. of Taipei, undated.

Ch'ien Tuang-sheng, *The Government and Politics of China,* Harvard University Press, Cambridge, 1950.

Ch'u T'ung-tsu, *Law and Society in Traditional China,* Mouton, The Hague, 1961.

John K. Fairbank and Teng Ssu-yu, *Ch'ing Administration: Three Studies,* Harvard Yenching Institute Studies XIX, Harvard University Press, Cambridge, 1961.

Hsieh Pao-chao, *The Government of China 1644–1911,* Johns Hopkins University Press, Baltimore, 1925.

Charles O. Hucker, *The Traditional Chinese State in Ming Times,* University of Arizona Press, Tucson, 1961.

Paul M. A. Linebarger, *Government in Republican China,* McGraw-Hill, New York, 1938.

Franz Michael, *The Origin of Manchu Rule in China,* Johns Hopkins University Press, Baltimore, 1942.

Sybille van der Sprenkel, *Legal Institutions in Manchu China,* Athlone Press, London, 1962.

THE CIVIL SERVICE

Wolfgang Franke, *The Reform and Abolition of the Traditional Chinese Examination System,* Center for East Asian Studies, Harvard University, 1960. Mimeo.

Ho Ping-ti, *The Ladder of Success in Imperial China,* Columbia University Press, New York, 1962.

E. A. Kracke, *Civil Service in Early Sung China,* Harvard University Press, Cambridge, 1953.

Johanna M. Menzel (ed.), *The Chinese Civil Service,* D. C. Heath, Boston, 1963.

Étienne Zi, *Pratique des Examines Littéraires en Chine,* Variétés Sinologiques no. 5, Shanghai, 1894.

LOCAL GOVERNMENT

Chu T'ung-tsu, *Local Government in China under the Ch'ing,* Harvard University Press, Cambridge, 1962.

Hsiao Kung-chuan, *Rural China: Imperial Control in the 19th Century,* University of Washington Press, Seattle, 1960.

Y. K. Leong and L. K. Tao, *Village and Town Life in China,* George Allen and Unwin, London, 1915.

ROYALTY AND NOBILITY

E. Backhouse and J. O. P. Bland, *Annals and Memoirs of the Court of Peking,* William Heinemann, London, 1914.

Harold L. Kahn, *Monarchy in the Emperor's Eyes,* Harvard University Press, Cambridge, 1971.

J. Bouvet, *Histoire L'Empereur de la Chine*, Meyndert Uytwerf, Paris, 1699. Reprinted in Tientsin, 1940.

Isaac Taylor Headland, *Court Life in China*, Fleming H. Revell, New York, 1909.

Reginald F. Johnson, *Twilight in the Forbidden City*, D. Appleton-Century, New York, 1934.

Princess Der Ling, *Kow Tow*, Dodd Mead, New York, 1929.

William Edward Soothill, *The Hall of Light: A Study in Early Chinese Kingship*, Philosophical Library, New York, 1952.

GENTRY AND OFFICIALS

Chow Yung-teh, *Social Mobility in China: Status Careers among the Gentry in a Chinese Community*, Atherton Press, New York, 1966. See my review, *American Anthropologist*, 69:6 (December 1967).

André Duboscq, *L'Élite Chinoise, Ses Origines, Sa Transformation après L'Empire*, Nouvelles Editions Latines, Paris, 1945.

Wolfram Eberhard, *Social Mobility in Traditional China*, E. J. Brill, Leiden, 1962.

Lady Hosie, *Two Gentlemen of China*, J. B. Lippincott, Philadelphia, 1924.

Robert M. Marsh, *The Mandarins: the Circulation of Elites in China*, Free Press, Glencoe, 1961.

Robert C. North, *Kuomintang and Chinese Communist Elites*, Stanford University Press, 1952.

PEASANTRY (Comparative)

Jack Potter, May N. Diaz, and George M. Foster (eds.), *Peasant Society: A Reader*, Little, Brown, Boston, 1967.

Eric R. Wolf, *Peasants*, Prentice-Hall, Englewood Cliffs, 1966.

——, *Peasant Wars of the Twentieth Century*, Harper and Row, New York, 1969.

PEASANTRY

Chen Han-sheng, *The Chinese Peasant*, Oxford Pamphlets on Indian Affairs, Bombay, 1945.

Fei Hsiao-t'ung and Chang Chih-i, *Earthbound China*, University of Chicago Press, 1945.

Sidney D. Gamble, *Ting Hsien: A North China Rural Community*, Institute of Pacific Relations, New York, 1954.

W. R. Geddes, *Peasant Life in Communist China*, The Society for Applied Anthropology, Monograph no. 6, 1963.

Cornelius Osgood, *Village Life in Old China*, Ronald Press, New

York, 1963. See my review, *American Anthropologist*, 67:4 (1963).

C. K. Yang, *A Chinese Village in Early Communist Transition*, The Technology Press, Cambridge, 1959.

Martin C. Yang, *A Chinese Village*, Columbia University Press, New York, 1945.

COMMERCE

John Stewart Burgess, *The Guilds of Peking*, Columbia University Press, New York, 1928.

Chen Ta, *Emigrant Communities of South China*, Institute of Pacific Relations, New York, 1940.

Chow Kwong-shu, *A Handbook of Chinese Trade Customs*, Far Eastern Press, Shanghai, 1933.

Maurice Collis, *Wayfoong: The Hongkong and Shanghai Banking Corporation*, Faber and Faber, London, 1967.

Esson M. Gale, *Salt for the Dragon*, Michigan State College Press, Lansing, 1953.

Albert Feuerwerker, *China's Early Industrialization*, Harvard University Press, Cambridge, 1958.

D. K. Lieu, *The Silk Industry of China*, Kelly and Walsh, Shanghai, 1941.

Frank M. Tamagna, *Banking and Finance in China*, Institute of Pacific Relations, New York, 1942.

Osmond Tiffany, Jr., *The American's Sojourn in the Celestial Empire*, James Munroe, Boston, 1849.

Edith E. Ware, *Business and Politics in the Far East*, Yale University Press, New Haven, 1932.

DUAL ECONOMY

Agrarian China: Selected Source Materials, compiled and translated by The Institute of Pacific Relations, Kelly and Walsh, Shanghai, 1938.

G. C. Allen and Audrey G. Donnithorne, *Western Enterprise in Far Eastern Economic Development*, George Allen and Unwin, London, 1954.

J. H. Boeke, *The Interests of the Voiceless East: Introduction to Oriental Economics*, University Pers, Leiden, 1948.

Chang Pei-kang, *Agriculture and Industrialization*, Harvard University Press, Cambridge, 1949.

Chen Han-seng, *Agrarian Problems in Southernmost China*, Kelly and Walsh, Shanghai, 1936.

T. S. Chu and T. Chin, *Marketing of Cotton in Hopei Province*, Institute of Social Research, Bulletin III, Peiping, 1929.

J. B. Condliffe, *China Today: Economic,* World Peace Foundation, Boston, 1932.

Marion J. Levy and Shih Kuo-heng, *The Rise of the Modern Chinese Business Class,* Institute of Pacific Relations, New York, 1949. Mimeo.

D. K. Lieu (Director), *A Study of the Rural Economy of Wuhing, Chekiang,* The China Institute of Economic and Statistical Research, Shanghai, 1939.

Shih Kuo-heng, *China Enters the Machine Age,* Harvard University Press, Cambridge, 1944.

R. H. Tawney, *Land and Labor in China,* George Allen and Unwin, London, 1932.

TECHNOLOGY

Rudolf P. Hommel, *China at Work,* John Day, New York, 1937.

Joseph Needham, *Science and Civilization in China,* Vol. IV, part 3 (Civil Engineering and Nautics), Cambridge University Press, 1971.

———, *The Grand Titration,* George Allen and Unwin, London, 1969.

William Willetts, *Chinese Art,* 2 vols., Penguin Books, Harmondsworth, 1958.

INTERNAL MARGINALS

Chen Han-seng, *Frontier Land Systems in Southernmost China,* Institute of Pacific Relations, New York, 1938. Mimeo.

Wolfram Eberhard, *The Local Cultures of South and East China,* E. J. Brill, Leiden, 1968.

John F. Embree and William L. Thomas, *Ethnic Groups of Northern Southeast Asia,* Yale University Asian Studies, New Haven, 1950.

C. P. Fitzgerald, *The Southern Expansion of the Chinese People,* Barrie and Jenkins, London, 1972.

David Crockett Graham, *Songs and Stories of the Ch'uan Miao,* Smithsonian Miscellaneous Collections, Vol. 123, no. 1, Washington, D.C., 1954.

———, *The Customs and Religion of the Ch'iang,* Smithsonian Miscellaneous Collections, Vol. 135, no. 1, Washington, D.C., 1958.

A. F. Legendre, *Kientchang et Lolotie,* Librairie Plon, Paris, 1910.

F. K. Lehman, *The Structure of Chin Society: A Tribal People of Burma Adapted to a Non-Western Civilization,* University of Illinois Press, Urbana, 1963.

Man Shu: Book of the Southern Barbarians (tr. Gordon H. Luce),

Southeast Asia Program, Data Paper no. 44, Cornell University Press, Ithaca, 1961. Mimeo.

S. Pollard, *In Unknown China,* Seely, Service, London, 1921.

Archibald Rose and J. Coggin Brown, *Lisu (Yawyin) Tribes of the Burma-China Frontier,* Baptist Mission Press, Calcutta, 1910.

Herold J. Wiens, *China's March Toward the Tropics,* The Shoe String Press, Hamden, Conn., 1954.

FROM TRIBE TO PEASANT (The Min Chia Case)

C. P. Fitzgerald, *The Tower of Five Glories,* Cresset Press, London, 1941.

Francis L. K. Hsu, *Under the Ancestors' Shadow,* Routledge and Kegan Paul, London, 1949.

Joseph F. Rock, *The Ancient Na-Khi Kingdon of Southwest China,* 2 vols., Harvard University Press, Cambridge, 1947.

EXTERNAL MARGINALS

Charles Bell, *Tibet Past and Present,* Oxford University Press, 1924.

Isabella Bird Bishop, *Among the Tibetans,* Fleming H. Revell, New York, 1894.

Vicomte D'Ollone, *In Forbidden China* (tr. Bernard Miall), Small, Maynard, Boston, n.d.

Robert B. Ekvall, *Fields on the Hoof: Nexus of Tibetan Nomadic Pastoralism,* Holt, Rinehart & Winston, New York, 1968.

Rene Grousset, *The Empire of the Steppes: A History of Central Asia* (tr. Naomi Walford), Rutgers University Press, New Brunswick, 1970.

Owen Lattimore, *The Mongols of Manchuria,* George Allen and Unwin, London, 1934.

——, *Mongol Journeys,* Jonathan Cape, London, 1941.

——, *Studies in Frontier History,* Mouton, La Haye, 1962.

H. Desmond Martin, *The Rise of Chingis Khan and His Conquest of North China,* The Johns Hopkins Press, Baltimore, 1950.

Hans Stubel, *The Mewu Fantzu: A Tibetan Tribe of Kansu,* Human Relations Area Files, New Haven, 1958.

Karl A. Wittfogel and Feng Chia-sheng, *History of Chinese Society: Liao (907–1125),* The American Philosophical Society, Philadelphia, 1949.

PHILOSOPHY AND WORLD VIEW

W. G. Beasley and E. G. Pullyblank (eds.), *Historians of China and Japan,* Oxford University Press, London, 1961.

H. G. Creel, *Sinism: A Study of the Evolution of the Chinese World View*, Open Court Press, Chicago, 1929.

William Theodore de Bary (ed.), *Sources of Chinese Tradition*, Columbia University Press, New York, 1960.

C. P. Fitzgerald, *The Chinese View of Their Place in the World*, Oxford University Press, London, 1964.

Fung Yu-lan, *A History of Chinese Philosophy*, 2 vols. (tr. Derk Bodde), Princeton University Press, 1952.

Charles S. Gardener, *Chinese Traditional Historiography*, Harvard University Press, Cambridge, 1961.

Edward Herbert, *A Confucian Notebook*, John Murray, London, 1950.

E. R. Hughes, *Chinese Philosophy in Classical Times*, J. M. Dent & Sons, London, 1942.

Liu Wu-chi, *A Short History of Confucian Philosophy*, Penguin Books, Harmondsworth, 1955.

W. A. P. Martin, *The Lore of Cathay*, Fleming H. Revell, New York, 1912.

Joseph Needham, *Science and Civilization in China*, vol. 2 (History of Scientific Thought), Cambridge University Press, 1956.

Elbert Duncan Thomas and Edward Thomas Williams, *Chinese Political Thought*, Prentice-Hall, New York, 1927.

Arthur Waley, *Three Ways of Thought in Ancient China*, George Allen and Unwin, London, 1939. Available as a Doubleday Anchor Book, New York, 1956.

Arthur F. Wright (ed.), *Studies in Chinese Thought*, The American Anthropological Association, Memoir no. 75, 1953.

RELIGION

Chan Wing-tsit, *Religious Trends in Modern China*, Columbia University Press, New York, 1953.

Clarence Burton Day, *Chinese Peasant Cults*, Kelly and Walsh, Shanghai, 1940.

Wolfram Eberhard, *Chinese Festivals*, Henry Schuman, New York, 1952.

David Crockett Graham, *Folk Religion in Southwest China*, Smithsonian Miscellaneous Collections, vol. 142, no. 2, Washington, D.C., 1961.

Marcel Granet, *Fetes et chansons Anciennes de la Chine*, Leroux, Paris, 1919.

Edwin D. Harvey, *The Mind of China*, Yale University Press, New Haven, 1933.

Lewis Hodus, *Folkways in China*, Arthur Probsthain, London, 1929.

Francis L. K. Hsu, *Religion, Science and Human Crisis: A Study of China in Transition,* Routledge and Kegan Paul, London, 1952.

Karl Ludwig Reichelt, *Religion in Chinese Garment,* Lutterworth Press, London, 1951.

John K. Shryock, *The Temples of Anking and Their Cults: A Study of Modern Chinese Religion,* Librairie Orientaliste Paul Geuthner, Paris, 1931.

———, *The Origin and Development of the State Cult of Confucius,* Paragon Book Reprint Corp., New York, 1966. Orig. pub. 1932.

Laurence G. Thompson, *Chinese Religion: An Introduction,* Dickenson Publishing Co., Belmont, 1969.

Holmes Welch, *The Parting of the Way: Laotzu and the Taoist Movement,* Methuen, London, 1958.

E. T. C. Werner, *A Dictionary of Chinese Mythology,* Kelly and Walsh, Shanghai, 1932. Reprinted by the Julian Press, New York, 1961.

———, *The Origin of the Chinese Priesthood,* The Shanghai Times, Shanghai, 1941.

G. Willoughby-Meade, *Chinese Ghouls and Goblins,* Constable, London, 1928.

Arthur F. Wright, *Buddhism in Chinese History,* Stanford University Press, 1959.

C. K. Yang, *Religion in Chinese Society,* University of California Press, Berkeley, 1961.

KINSHIP AND MARRIAGE

Feng Han-yi, *The Chinese Kinship System,* Harvard University Press, Cambridge, 1948.

Maurice Freedman, *Chinese Lineage and Society: Fukien and Kwangtung,* Athlone Press, London, 1966.

Morton H. Fried, *Fabric of Chinese Society,* Frederick A. Praeger, New York, 1953.

Daniel H. Kulp, *Country Life in South China: The Sociology of Familism,* Bureau of Publications, Teachers College, Columbia University, New York, 1925.

Olga Lang, *Chinese Family and Society,* Yale University Press, New Haven, 1946.

Marion J. Levy, Jr., *The Family Revolution in Modern China,* Harvard University Press, Cambridge, 1949.

Lin Yueh-hwa, *The Golden Wing: A Sociological Study of Chinese Familism,* Oxford University Press, New York, 1947.

Liu Hui-chen Wang, *The Traditional Chinese Clan Rules,* J. J. Augustin, Locust Valley, New York, 1959.

M. H. van der Valk, *Conservatism in Modern Chinese Family Law,* E. J. Brill, Leiden, 1956.

H. P. Wilkinson, *The Family in Classical China,* Macmillan, London, 1926.

C. K. Yang, *The Chinese Family in the Communist Revolution,* Technology Press, Cambridge, 1959.

CULTURE AND SOCIETY

Etienne Balazs, *Chinese Civilization and Bureaucracy,* (tr. H. M. Wright), Yale University Press, New Haven, 1964.

John Barrow, *Travels in China,* W. F. M'Laughlin, Philadelphia, 1804.

Derk Bodde, *China's Cultural Tradition,* Holt, Rinehart and Winston, New York, 1965.

H. de Chavannes de la Girandiere, *Le Chinois,* Alfred Mame et Fils, Tours, 1870.

Raymond Dawson (ed.), *The Legacy of China,* Oxford University Press, London, 1964.

Justice Doolittle, *Social Life of the Chinese,* 2 vols., Harper and Bros., New York, 1865.

Robert K. Douglass, *Society in China,* A. D. Innes, London, 1894.

John K. Fairbank (ed.), *Chinese Thought and Institutions,* University of Chicago Press, 1957.

Adele M. Fielde, *A Corner of Cathay,* Macmillan, New York, 1894.

Louis J. Gallagher (tr), *China in the 16th Century: The Journals of Matthew Ricci,* Random House, New York, 1953.

Chester Holcombe, *The Real Chinaman,* Dodd, Mead, New York, 1895.

M. Huc, *A Journey Through the Chinese Empire,* 2 vols., Harper and Bros., New York, 1855.

Simon Kiong, *Quelques Mots sur la Politesse Chinoise,* Variétés Sinologiques, no. 25, Shanghai, 1906.

J. Macgowan, *Men and Manners of Modern China,* T. Fisher Unwin, London, 1912.

Harley Farnsworth MacNair (ed.), *China,* University of California Press, Berkeley, 1946.

W. A. P. Martin, *The Chinese,* Harper and Bros., New York, 1881.

W. H. Medhurst, *The Foreigner in Cathay,* Scribner's, Armstrong, New York, 1873.

Francis H. Nichols, *Through Hidden Shensi,* Scribner's, New York, 1902.

[John R. Peters, Jr.], *Miscellaneous Remarks upon the Government, History, Religions, Literature, Agriculture, Arts, Trades, Manners, and Customs of the Chinese, as suggested by an Examination of the Articles in the Chinese Museum,* John F. Trow, New York, 1849.

A. H. Smith, *The Natural History of the Chinese Boy and the*

Chinese Girl, Printed at the North China Herald Office, Shanghai, 1890.

S. Wells Williams, *The Middle Kingdom,* 2 vols., Scribner's, New York, 1883.

CULTURE AND PERSONALITY

Ruth Bunzel, *Explorations in Chinese Culture,* Columbia University Research in Contemporary Cultures, New York, 1950. Ditto.

George H. Danton, *The Chinese People,* Marshall Jones, Boston, 1938.

Wolfram Eberhard, *Guilt and Sin in Traditional China,* University of California Press, Berkeley, 1967.

Francis L. K. Hsu, *Americans and Chinese,* Henry Schuman, New York, 1953.

———, *Clan, Caste and Club: A Comparative Study of Chinese, Hindu and American Ways of Life,* D. Van Nostrand, Princeton, 1961.

Harold R. Isaacs, *Scratches on Our Minds,* John Day, New York, 1958.

Robert J. Lifton, *Thought Reform and the Psychology of Totalism,* W. W. Norton, New York, 1961.

H. Nakamura, *The Ways of Thinking of Eastern Peoples,* Japanese Government Printing Bureau, Tokyo, 1960.

Richard Wilhelm, *Chinese Economic Psychology,* Institute of Pacific Relations, New York, 1947. Mimeo.

AUTOBIOGRAPHY

Chao Buwei Yang, *Autobiography of a Chinese Woman* (tr. Chao Yuenren), John Day, New York, 1947.

Chiang Monlin, *Tides from the West,* Yale University Press, New Haven, 1947.

Chiang Yee, *A Chinese Childhood,* John Day, New York, 1952.

Chow Chung-cheng, *The Lotus Pool,* Appleton-Century-Crofts, New York, 1961.

Han Suyin, *Destination Chungking: An Autobiography,* Little, Brown, Boston, 1956.

Hsieh Ping-ying, *The Autobiography of a Chinese Girl* (tr. Tsui Chi), George Allen and Unwin, London, 1943.

Koo Hui-lan, *Hui-lan Koo: A Autobiography of Madam Wellington Koo,* Dial Press, New York, 1943.

Helena Kuo, *I've Come a Long Way,* D. Appleton-Century, New York, 1942.

Lee Yan-phou, *When I Was a Boy in China,* Lothrop, Lee and Shepard, Boston, 1887.

Liang Yen, *Daughter of the Khans,* W. W. Norton, New York, 1955.

Pardee Lowe, *Father and Glorious Son,* Little, Brown, Boston, 1943.

Park No-yong, *Chinaman's Chance: An Autobiography,* Meador, Boston, 1943.

Ida Pruitt, *A Daughter of Han: The Autobiography of a Chinese Working Woman, from the Story told her by Ning Lao T'ai T'ai,* Yale University Press, New Haven, 1945.

Sheng-cheng, *A Son of China* (tr. Marvin Mclord Lowes), W. W. Norton, New York, 1930.

Siao-yu, *Mao Tse-tung and I were Beggars,* Hutchinson, London, 1961.

Tcheng Souman, *My Revolutionary Years: The Autobiography of Madame Wei Tao-ming,* Scribner's, New York, 1943.

S. Tretiakov, *A Chinese Testament: The Autobiography of Tan Shih-hua,* Simon and Schuster, New York, 1934.

Christiana Tsai, *Queen of the Dark Chamber,* Moody Press, Chicago, 1953.

B. van Vorst, *A Girl from China (Soomay Tcheng),* Frederick A. Stokes, New York, 1926.

Yung Wing, *My Life in China and America,* Henry Holt, New York, 1909.

LITERATURE

Ch'en Shou-yi, *Chinese Literature: A Historical Introduction,* Ronald Press, New York, 1961.

C. T. Hsia, *A History of Modern Chinese Fiction,* Yale University Press, New Haven, 1961.

Huang Sung-k'ang, *Lu Hsun and the New Culture Movement of Modern China,* Djambatan, Amsterdam, 1957.

Odile Kaltenmark, *Chinese Literature,* Walker and Company, New York, 1964.

Lin Yutang, *A History of the Press and Public Opinion in China,* Kelly and Walsh, Shanghai, 1936.

Burton Watson, *Early Chinese Literature,* Columbia University Press, New York, 1962.

MODERN FICTION

Eileen Chang, *The Rice Sprout Song,* Scribner's, New York, 1955.

Chao Shu-li, *Changes in Li Village* (tr. Gladys Yang), Foreign Languages Press, Peking, 1953.

C. T. Hsia, *Twentieth Century Chinese Stories,* Columbia University Press, New York, 1972.

Liu T'ieh-yun, *The Travels of Lao Ts'an* (tr. Harold Shadick), Cornell University Press, Ithaca, 1952.

Mao Tun, *Midnight* (tr. A. C. Barnes), Foreign Languages Press, Peking, 1957.

Pa Chin, *The Family* (tr. Sidney Shapiro), Foreign Languages Press, Peking, 1958.

Selected Works of Lu Hsun (tr. Yang Hsien-yi and Gladys Yang), Foreign Languages Press, Peking, 1960.

Edgar Snow (ed.), *Living China: Modern Chinese Short Stories*, George G. Harrap, London, 1936.

Wang Chi-chen (tr.), *Contemporary Chinese Stories*, Columbia University Press, New York, 1944.

Yeh Chun-chan, *Mountain Village*, G. P. Putnam's Sons, New York, 1947.

Yeh Sheng-tao, *Schoolmaster Ni Huan-chih* (tr. A. C. Barnes), Foreign Languages Press, Peking, 1958.

Yuan Chia-hua and Robert Payne, *Contemporary Chinese Short Stories*, Transatlantic Arts, London, 1946.

CHINA AND THE WORLD *OIKOUMENÊ*

Foster Rhea Dulles, *China and America*, Princeton University Press, 1946.

John K. Fairbank, *The United States and China*, 2nd edition, Harvard University Press, Cambridge, 1958.

John K. Fairbank, Edwin O. Reischauer, and Albert M. Craig (eds.), *East Asia: The Modern Transformation*, Houghton Mifflin, Boston, 1965.

Albert Feuerwerker (ed.), *Modern China*, Prentice-Hall, Englewood Cliffs, 1964.

Wesley R. Fishel, *The End of Extraterritoriality in China*, The University of California Press, Berkeley, 1952.

Michael Greenberg, *British Trade and the Opening of China 1800–42*, Cambridge University Press, 1951.

John A. Harrison, *China Since 1800*, Harcourt, Brace and World, New York, 1967.

Joseph R. Levenson, *Confucian China and Its Modern Fate: The Problem of Intellectual Continuity*, University of California Press, Berkeley, 1958.

——— (ed.), *Modern China: An Interpretive Anthology*, Macmillan, London, 1971.

Herrymon Maurer, *Collision of East and West*, Henry Regnery, Chicago, 1951.

S. M. Meng, *The Tsungli Yamen*, East Asian Research Center, Harvard University, 1962. Mimeo.

Franz H. Michael and George E. Taylor, *The Far East in the*

Modern World, revised edition, Holt, Rinehart and Winston, New York, 1964.

C. Northcote Parkinson, *East and West,* Houghton Mifflin, Boston, 1963.

Victor Purcell, *The Boxer Uprising: A Background Study,* Cambridge University Press, 1963.

Franz Schurmann and Orville Schell (eds.), *Republican China,* Vintage Books, New York, 1967.

Stanley Spector, *Li Hung-chang and the Huai Army: A Study in Nineteenth Century Chinese Regionalism,* University of Washington Press, Seattle, 1964.

Jonathan Spence, *To Change China: Western Advisors in China 1620–1960,* Little, Brown, Boston, 1969.

Sir George Staunton, *An Authentic Account of An Embassy from the King of Great Britain to the Emperor of China,* 2 vols., Wogan, Cross, Byrne, Rice, Halpin and Kelly, Dublin, 1798.

Teng Ssu-yu and John K. Fairbank (eds.), *China's Response to the West,* Harvard University Press, Cambridge, 1954.

Arthur Waley, *The Opium War Through Chinese Eyes,* Macmillan, New York, 1958.

Mary C. Wright, *The Last Stand of Chinese Conservatism,* Stanford University Press, 1957.

COMMUNIST CHINA

A. Doak Barnett, *Communist China and Asia: Challenge to American Policy,* Vintage Books, New York, 1960.

————, *Cadres, Bureaucracy, and Political Power in Communist China,* Columbia University Press, New York, 1967.

Frederic H. Chaffe, *et al., The United States Army Area Handbook on Communist China,* U.S. Government Printing Office, Washington, D.C., 1967. I wrote chapters 4, 5, 6, and 11.

C. P. Fitzgerald, *The Birth of Communist China,* Penguin Books, Harmondsworth, 1964.

Hsu Kai-yu, *Chou En-lai,* Doubleday, New York, 1968.

Chalmers A. Johnson, *Peasant Nationalism and Communist Power,* Stanford University Press, 1962.

John Wilson Lewis, *Leadership in Communist China,* Cornell University Press, Ithaca, 1963.

William T. Liu (ed.), *Chinese Society under Communism: A Reader,* John Wiley, New York, 1967.

Joan Robinson, *The Cultural Revolution in China,* Penguin Books, Harmondsworth, 1969.

Stuart Schram, *Mao Tse-tung,* Penguin Books, Harmondsworth, 1967.

Franz Schurmann, *Ideology and Organization in Communist China,* University of California Press, Berkeley, 1966.

Franz Schurmann and Orville Schell (eds.), *Communist China*, Vintage Books, 1967.

James R. Townsend, *Political Participation in China*, University of California Press, Berkeley, 1968.

Kenneth R. Walker, *Planning in Chinese Agriculture*, Aldine, Chicago, 1965.

Richard L. Walker, *China under Communism: The First Five Years*, Yale University Press, New Haven, 1955.

Index

"Advancing in Officialdom," gaming board of, 215, 216–17 (figs.), 218, 219 (fig.)

Agrarian State, 1, 3, 4, 5, 7, 8, 15, 16, 18–19, 20, 24, 30, 38, 67–68, 70, 77, 79–80, 81, 90, 101, 127, 143, 166, 183, 215, 234; bureaucracy in, 205; end of, 267–74

Agriculture: Neolithic, 38; Yang-shao, 39–40, 41; swidden, 40, 66, 71; Lung-shan, 41–42; Miao, 66; Commercial, 84–85

All-China, 153, 236; All-China budget, 192

Altar of Heaven, 185, 204

Analects of Confucius, 17

Ancestor worship, 57, 124, 206, 207, 211

An-Yang, 47, 48, 49; royal tombs at, 45, 46

Ape-men (*Australopithecus*), 30–31

Arcane associations with each season, 231, 232 (fig.)

Aristocracy: military, of the Local Kingdoms, 179, 180; fall from power of, 179, 180

Bandit gangs, 192

Barbarians and barbarian conquests, 65, 67, 70, 71, 72, 74, 75, 152, 153, 154, 156, 157, 160, 163

Behavior among Chinese elite, 261–62

Berne, Eric, 242, 253

Body ritual, Chinese, 243 (*illustr.*)

Book of Odes (Shih Ching), 201, 229

Bronze Age: origins of Chinese Agrarian State, 5; once and always Bronze Age, 24–61; civilization and warfare, 43, 45, 48, 49, 55

Buddhism, 124, 126, 131, 250

Budget: imperial, 170–71 (fig.), All-China, 192; ritual, 192, 195 (fig.)

Bullies, village, 134–36, 138

Bureaucracy in Agrarian State, 205

Bureaucratic rank, insignia of, in game of "Promotion," 219 (fig.)

Calendar, representing imperial authority, 231–32 (fig.), 233

Canal systems, short, 151, 154

Canals, transport, 148 (fig.), 154

Cemeteries, 40, 41, 42

Central government, 170–71 (fig.), 170–73, 187; three obligations owed to, 190–91

Central or provincial civil services, appointments made to, 221–23 (figs.)

Ceremonial spending and extravagance, 130–31

Ceremonial status system, 190

Chan Kuo period, 55, 70; troops of, 60

Chang Chung-li, 182

Chapple, Eliot, 3

Chi Ch'ao-ting, 143, 144

Chi family, 54, 58, 153

Chi chiao (Seven Obligations), 262

Ch'i-tan ruler, 162

Chia Taotai and flood relief, story of, 174–75

Children of the Black-Haired Peoples (King), 126

Ch'in: state of, conqueror of all others, 60–61; dynasty, 146 (fig.), 148 (fig.), 149, 151, 153, 158, 161 (fig.), 163

Ch'in Shih Hwang Ti, 61, 62, 149, 150, 226, 228, 236, 241

China Proper, 35, 68–69 (map), 162, 163; peasantry of, 72; eighteen provinces of, 187–88

China Repository for 1832 (Morrison), 207–9

Chinese Dragon Throne, 164, 165

Chinese familism, 101, 102 (*illustr.*), 103–6, 122, 210

Chinese historical-developmental sequence, 28, 29 (fig.)

Chinese nation-state, 166

Chinese National Association of the Mass Education Movement, 107

Ch'ing government and dynasty, 67, 143, 146 (fig.), 148 (fig.), 161 (fig.), 163, 164, 166, 203, 204, 267

Chinghis, 162, 163

Ch'ing Ming (spring festival), 207, 209, 210

Chou dynasty, 48, 49, 51, 54, 58–59, 61, 160, 161 (fig.), 201, 205, 229, 230, 235

Ch'un-ch'iu period, 50, 52 (fig.), 53

Chung Kuo "Central State", 50
City-state, description of, 42, 45, 48
Civil services, appointments made to, 221–23 (*figs.*)
Clan: and Chinese kinship, 209, 210–11; politics, 209, 210; temple and ancestral tombs, ceremonies at, 210–11
Clansmen, royal and powerful, 190, 193, 207
Clique and petitioning activities, 190, 194, 195
Co-hong monopoly, 267–68
Commentaries of Tso, The (Tso Chuan), 50, 51
Communist China, 9, 269, 270
Communist–party members, 272–74
Communists, Chinese, 9, 269, 270, 272–74
Concubines and wives, 195–96, 211
Confucian: ideology, 177, 201, 202, 211–12, 249; vs. Legalist ideology, 237–40; learning and tradition, 201, 202, 225
Confucianism, 8–9, 62, 124, 151, 153, 159, 163, 230, 267, 271–72
Confucius: quoted, 14–15, 17, 47, 54, 90, 185, 187, 219; sacred carp associated with, 41; death of, 50, 55; the age of, 51; power and kinship in the age of, 52 (*fig.*), 53; as masterless *shih*, 55; impoverished condition of Confucius's father, 56; state cult of, 57, 125; promotion of new brand of political loyalty by, 58; birthday of, 212; as jack-o'-both-sides, 226–41; statue of, 227; doctrines of, 269–70
Coon, Carleton S., 3
Corvée labor, 157–58, 159, 172
"Country Boy Withdraws from School, A" (Lao Hsiang), 107–12
Cult of ancestors, 139
Cult of the dead, 40, 41, 43, 124
Cult of Poverty, 6, 7, 101–12, 115, 130, 134, 135, 139
Cults of worship, 128
Culturalism, 189–90, 230, 233–34
Culture eras, Chinese, 28, 29 (*fig.*)
Currency: manipulation, 168; printed, evolvement of, 180
Customs duty, as general excise tax, 173

Dead, Cult of the, 40, 41, 43, 124
Degrees and degree holders, how awarded, 220–21, 225
DeGroot, J. J. M., 125
Democracy, New, 271

Demons or specters, 125, 127, 128, 129
"Divorce, The" (Lu Hsun), 98–99, 114 (*illustr.*)
Dragon, bronze, from late Chou period, 186 (*illustr.*)
Dragon, imperial, symbolical of the emperor, 185–200
Dragon, Mighty, the, and the Local Snakes, 8, 149, 177, 185–200, 204
Dragon mythology, 234
Dragon Throne of the emperor, 187, 189
Dynastic: code, 101–2, 103; government, 143; history, 144, 146 (*fig.*); partitions of, 146 (*fig.*), 153–54, 156, 158–63, 161 (*fig.*); succession, 158–59, 161 (*fig.*), 163
Dynasties, conquering, 48, 49

Eastern Tsin empire, 156, 161 (*fig.*)
Eiichiro, Prof. Ishida, 2
Elite and elite status, 115–16, 119, 125, 129, 131, 156, 163, 211, 225, 250, 261–62, 269
Emperor: power, duties, and symbolism of, 185–200; local officials, relationship of, to the emperor, 190–200; wives, concubines, and eunuchs of the emperor, 195–97
Empire: politics of, 193; flow charts of, 193, 194 (*fig.*), 195 (*fig.*)
England, in the Opium War, 267, 268
Era of Cultural Fusion, 49–61
Era of Cyclical Imperial Conquests, 28, 29, 30, 61–62, 146 (*fig.*), 179
Era of Fusion, 28, 29, (*fig.*), 235, 236
Era of Regional and Florescent States, 27, 28, 29, 42–49
Eunuchs of imperial palace, 195–97
Examination system, 219–25, 226, 228

"Face" and face behavior, 119, 120, 121, 247, 248, 250–52, 255, 262
Farming, 26–27, 36, 42, 151, 152; Yang-shao farming, 39–40, 41; Lung-shan agriculture, 41–42; Miao agriculture, 66
Fei Hsiao-t'ung, 134, 139
Feudal lords and warrior overlords, 43, 49, 50, 54, 55, 151
Feudal system, titles, and states, 193, 205, 226
Feudalism, destruction of, 50, 55, 58
Filial piety, 201–2, 204, 211, 212, 214, 225
Fishing and hunting, by ancient men, 32, 36, 39, 66, 71

Five Dynasties, 146 (*fig.*), 155, 158, 160, 161
Five Dynasties and Ten kingdoms, period of, 20
Five Virtues, 245, 246, 247, 262
Flood control and irrigation systems, 144, 146, 154, 155, 157, 164–65
Flood relief, 174–75
Folk community, 5, 13–23, 24, 26, 27
Folk culture of the Chinese peasantry, 2, 6–7, 9, 13, 19, 21, 65, 89, 101, 104, 127, 129, 270
Food-gathering, 27, 28, 29 (*fig.*), 36, 37, 38, 39, 66
Formative Era: of food-gathering background, 27, 28, 29 (*fig.*), 36; of basic technologies and folk culture, 38–42
Fox Woman, The (P'u Sung-Ling), 126, 127
Friendship, Chinese concept of, 258–62
Funerals: ceremonial spending on, 130–31; and ancestors, 201–14
Fusion China, 150, 179, 226

Games Chinese play, 242–63
Games People Play (Berne), 242
Gardening, hand, 68, 70, 157
General Code of Laws of the Ch'ing Empire, 102–3
Gentry: managerial role of, 94–97; Republican, 82; culture, 104; families, 119; local, 179–84, 189, 225
Geological periods, 33 (*fig.*)
Geopolitical: basis of imperial unity, 20–21, 28, 143, 144; history of empire, 150–66
Grain: cultivation of, 38, 39, 66, 70, 152; transportation of, 165
Grain Transport Service, 165
Grand Canal, 146, 148, 154, 157, 159, 187; second Grand Canal, 164
Great Khan, 163
Great Society (*ta t'ung*), 14–15, 17, 19, 21, 22, 24, 25, 26, 28, 77, 101, 188, 189, 214, 229
Great Wall of China, 35, 70, 71, 74, 149, 151, 152, 157
Green Circle (folk community), 5, 13–23, 24, 26, 27, 62, 65, 77, 78, 80–81, 82, 84, 87, 89, 90, 92, 93, 94, 101, 105, 106, 107, 126, 127, 128, 129, 144, 167, 183, 188, 270, 271, 274

Han dynasties, 72, 146 (*fig.*), 148 (*fig.*), 151, 153, 154, 155, 156, 161, (*fig.*), 226, 228

Han Fei, 236, 237, 238
Han Fei Tzu, 238–40
Hanching Alumni Association, letter written to, 252–58
Hierarchical order, 205
High culture of the Chinese elite, 2, 3–4, 7–8, 9, 21, 25, 65, 89, 101, 113, 115–16, 126, 127, 129, 144, 262
Hill tribes and peasants, 65–78; comparison between, 77–78
Homoiogeniture, 101–4, 180
Hsia dynasty, 161 (*fig.*), 162
Hsiang T'ou, 235
Hsiao Ching, 202
Hsien (unit of empire), 149, 150, 175
Hsuan T'ung, 196
Hung Lou Meng (a novel), 224–25
Husbandry, sanctimonious, 133–40
Hu Shih, 197–98

I Ching, 185
Ice Age, 30, 34, 35
Imperial authority, calendar representing, 231–32 (*fig.*), 233
Imperial budget, 170–71, 192
Imperial Clan Court, 203
Imperial unity, 20–21, 28, 143, 151
Income: three sources of, 181; derived from government service, 180–82
Industry in China, 81–83
Iron Age development and technology, 24, 25, 26, 28
Irrigation systems and flood control, 144, 146, 154, 155, 157, 164–65

Jack-o'-both-sides, Confucius as, 226–41
Jade Emperor, 124, 125
Java Man, 31, 33 (*fig.*)
Jen Tsung, 229
Jesuit missionaries, 267
Johnston, Reginald F., 197, 198

Kan-pu, 272–74
K'ang-Hsi emperor, 89, 212
Kara-Khitai state, 162
Key Economic Areas (KEA), 143, 144, 145 (*map*), 146, 153, 154, 155, 157, 158, 165
Key Economic Areas in Chinese History (Chi Ch'ao-ting), 143
Key Strategic Area (KSA), 153, 155, 158, 162, 163
Khubilai, 162, 163
King, Evan, 126
Kinship and power in the age of Confucius, 49, 52 (*fig.*), 53
Kitchen God, The, 122–32

Kung-Yang commentary on *Ch'un Ch'ui*, 53

Ladder to the clouds, 215–25
Land: prestigiousness of, 181; rents from, 182
Lao Hsiang, 107, 108
Laws, and the Sacred Edict, 90–94
Legalism and Legalist doctrine, 228, 236, 237, 240, 241; vs. Confucian version, 237–40
Li Chi, 204, 230, 235, 247, 248
Li Hung-chang, 269
Liang dynasty, 161 (*fig.*)
Liang Kwang, vice-royalty of, 159
Li Yun, 204
Lin Kung, 208, 209
Lin Yu-tang, and humorous story about the gentry, 94
Literacy, and men of high culture, 25, 44, 101, 104, 183
Liu Sung dynasty, 161 (*fig.*)
Local gentry of the Establishment, 179–84, 189, 225
Local government, 173–77
Local officials, relationship of, to the emperor, 190–91, 192–200
Local Snakes vs. Mighty Dragon, 8, 149, 177, 185–200, 204
Longhouses, 40, 41, 43, 45
Lords of the Soil, 167–84
Lu, 50, 51, 153; dukes and rulers of, 53–54, 58
Lu Hsun, stories of, 98–100, 114
Lun Yu, 17, 54, 56, 57, 185, 187, 188, 204, 227, 237, 238, 271
Lung-shan: pottery, 37, 38, 42; agriculture, 41–42; people, 43, 65; cult of the dead, 40, 41, 43; shamans, 43–44, 46–47

"Madman's Diary" (Lu Hsun), 99
Magistrate, district, 173–74, 175, 177, 222
Magistrates, and the Sacred Edict, 90–97
Manchuria, 161, 164, 192
Manchu aristocracy, 203, 204
Manchus, 152, 162, 163, 164, 192, 202–3, 226
"Mandate of Heaven," 163–64, 188
Mao, Chairman, 272, 273, 274
Mao Tun, 85
Marriage, ceremonial spending on, 130
Mass society, from Folk society to, 267–74
Merchant class in traditional China, 177–78
Mesolithic period, 33 (*fig.*), 36, 37, 39, 41

Miao: hill tribes, 65–66 (*illustr.*), 67; agriculture, 66; frontier, historic battles on, 72–73; people, 74, 75, 76, 77–78
Military aristocracy of the Local Kingdoms, 179–80
Military commanderies, 149, 150, 153, 236
Military machine of the emperor, 192
Mill, John Stuart, 167, 183
Min Chia language, costumes, holidays and gods, 72
Ming dynasty, 74, 146 (*fig.*), 148 (*fig.*), 161 (*fig.*), 163
Money, in China's agrarian economy, 167–68
Mongolia, 161
Mongols, 72, 152, 163, 165
Monopoly, Co-hong, 267–68
"Monopoly," game board of, 215
Morrison, Robert, 207

Nan Chao, barbarian kingdom, 72
Nan Man (Southern Barbarians), 65, 67, 70, 71, 72, 74, 75
Nan Pei Ch'ao, southern dynasties of, 157
Nation-state, Chinese, 166
Nationalism and culturalism, difference between, 233–34, 268
Neolithic period, 33 (*fig.*), 35, 36, 37, 38, 39–40, 41, 42
Northern and Southern Dynasties, 156
Northern Sung period, 162
Nurhachi, 203

Obligations owed to central government, 190–91
Occupations, fundamental and accessory, 113–21
Officials: Chinese, 173–74, 194; local, relationship of, to the emperor, 190–91, 192–200
Opium War, 165, 267, 269
Oracle bones, 43–44
Overlords, warrior, and feudal lords, 43, 49, 50, 54, 55

Pa and Shu cultures, 61
Pa-ku (eight-legged essays), 219–20
Paleolithic period, 30, 32, 33, (*fig.*), 34, 36, 39
Parade of sacrifices, seasonal, 231
Partitions, two, of dynastic history, 144, 146 (*fig.*); first partition, 146 (*fig.*), 153–54, 156, 161 (*fig.*); second partition, 146 (*fig.*), 153, 155, 158–63, 161 (*fig.*)

Peasant Life in China (Fei Hsiao-t'ung), 134
Peasant religion, 122–32
Peasant Society and Culture (Redfield), 133
Peasantry, status differences of, wealth as determining, 119
Peasants and hill tribes, 65–78; comparison between, 77–78
Peking Gazette, 179, 180, 225
Peking man (*Sinanthropus*), 31, 33 (*fig.*), 34
People's Republic of China, 82, 85, 271
P'ing-tze, Chi, 54, 57, 58
Pit house, 40, 42
Pleistocene epoch (Ice Age), 30, 32, 33 (*fig.*), 34, 35, 36
Political activism, 190
Political power, and wealth, 181, 215, 219
Pottery, Chinese, 36–38, 41, 42, 45
Poverty, Cult of, 6, 7, 101–12, 130, 134, 135, 139
Power: and kinship, in the age of Confucius, 49, 52 (*fig.*), 53; wealth and prestige, as origin of, 215, 219; power distinctions, 248
Preagricultural culture period, 28, 29, 37
Principles of Anthropology (Chapple & Coon), 3
Principles of Political Economy (Mill), 167
Privileged and non-privileged persons in Chinese Agrarian State, 168–69
"Promotion" game, 215, 216–17 (*figs.*), 218, 219 (*fig.*) 225
Provinces: as unit of empire, 149; troops for defense of, 192
Provincial or central civil services, appointments made to, 221–23 (*figs.*)
Pu Yi, Aisin-Gioro: autobiography of, 196–97; telephone installation for, 197–98; pomp in life of, 198–200

Quotations of Confucius, 14–15, 17, 47, 54, 90, 185, 187, 219
Quotations from Chairman Mao, 274

Rank: as measure of elite status, 119, 213, 244; and ritual system, 212–14, 244; bureaucratic, insignia of, in game of "Promotion," 219 (*fig.*)
Ranking, ceremonial, 229–30

Recent Geological Epoch, 33 (*fig.*), 34, 35
Redfield, Robert, 133, 136, 140
Regionalism, defeat of, 160
Religion, peasant, 122–32
Reminiscences of a Chinese Official, The, 174
Rents derived from land, 182
Republic of China, 82, 85, 271
Republican: gentry, 82, 94–97; regime and government, 128, 171–72, 197, 272
Revenues, government, 170, 172
Rites, monthly, 231
Ritual (*in alphabetical order*): budget, 192, 195 (*fig.*); Chinese body, 243 (*illustr.*); court, 205; deference, 191; domestic, 205; rank and ritual system, 212–14, 244; statistics, 195 (*fig.*)
Rivers to Glory, 143–66, 147 (*illustr.*)
Romance of the Three Kingdoms (Lo Kuan-chung), 154
Royalties for salt, as government income, 173, 178, 179

Sacred Book of the Original Vows of the Kitchen God, 122
Sacred Edict (Sheng Yu), 89, 90–94, 96–97, 104, 106, 128, 130–31, 135, 137, 138, 183–84; and the four-part stratification of class differences, 113, 115, 121
Sacrificial ceremony, 207–9
Salt (*in alphabetical order*): monopoly, 172, 178; production of, 169 (*illustr.*), 173, 178, 179; royalties, 172, 173, 178, 179; smugglers, 179
San Kuo Chih Yen I (Lo Kuan-chung), 154
San Kuo period, 154–55
Scholar-statesmen, 182
Scholars, The (Wu Ching-tzu), 75, 116–18, 120–21, 174
Seiichi, Prof. Izumi, 2
Seven Obligations, 262
Shamans, 43–44, 46–47
Shang kings and dynasty, 43, 44, 49, 61, 161 (*fig.*); burial of, 46
Shang: meaning of, 46, 47; royal government in Shang times, 79
Shang priests, 43, 44
Shang Ti, 44, 45, 46, 47, 204
Shang Yang, 238, 240
Shen-nung, legendary emperor, 79, 80 (*illustr.*)
Shih, of feudal hierarchy, 55, 56, 57, 58
Shu Ching, 44, 187

Shu, kingdom of, 154, 155
Shu-Han dynasty, 161 (fig.)
Shun, 185, 206
Sincerity, Chinese concept of, 245–46
Sink of Death, 6, 79–88, 106, 115, 181
Sino-Japanese War, 155
Six Dynasties, 156
Sixteen Kingdoms, 156
Smith, A. H., 134, 135, 136–37
Social inequality, 113–21
Soil, Lords of the, 167–84
Son of Heaven, title adopted by
  emperors, 46, 47, 124
Southern Barbarians (Nan Man),
  65, 67, 70, 71, 72, 74, 75
Southern and Northern Dynasties, 156
Southern Ch'en dynasty, 161 (fig.)
Southern Ch'i dynasty, 161 (fig.)
Southern Liang dynasty, 161 (fig.)
Southern Sung, 162
*Spring and Autumn Annals (Ch'un
  Ch'tu)*, 50, 51, 55
Spring, rite of meeting of spirits of,
  231
"Spring Silkworms," 85–87
Squeeze economy and system, by
  government officials, 174, 175–76,
  192
Stars in heaven, 113–21
Status differences of peasants, wealth
  as determining, 119
Status system, emperor's, 185–200,
  212–13
Steppe and steppelanders, 151, 152;
  steppe horseman, 152
Steward, Julian H., 23, 28
Stock breeding, 71, 151, 152
"Stove men," producers of salt, 178
Strange Tales from a Chinese Studio
  (P'u Sung-Ling), 126
Subjects of the realm, 89–100
Sui dynasty, 146 (fig.), 148 (fig.),
  157, 158, 161 (fig.)
Sui Grand Canal, 154, 157, 158,
  164, 179
Sun Tsu, 60
Sung dynasty, 48, 152, 156, 158, 159,
  160, 161, (fig.), 162, 180, 229
Superstitions and spirit world, 125–26
Swidden agriculture, 40, 42, 66, 71,72

Tael, Chinese ounce, 168
Tai peoples, 153–54
T'aip'ing rebellion, 155, 268–69
*Tale of a Conjugal Union to Arouse
  the World, The*, 126
Tang dynasty, 72, 146 (fig.), 148
  (fig.), 158, 159, 161 (fig.), 203
Tao and Taoist conception, 124, 125,
  127, 131

Tartar tribes, 149, 151, 153, 158, 161,
  162
Taxes and taxation, 157, 170, 171,
  172, 173, 182, 192, 194 (fig.)
Temples: official, 127–28; village,
  129, 130
Ten Kingdoms, 158, 159, 160 (fig.);
  and Five Dynasties, period of, 20
"Three Huan," 54, 55, 58
Three Kingdoms, 146 (fig.), 154
Toba Wei dynasty, 156
Tombs: ancestral, 207–11; ceremonies
  at, 210–11; royal tombs at An-
  Yang, 45–46
Tools and implements, use of, 32, 35,
  38, 39, 66–67
Toynbee, Arnold, 38, 39
Transport canals, 148 (fig.)
Transport River (Yun Ho), 146
Transporting fund, 172
Treaty of Nanking, 267, 268
Tribal culture, 65
Tribute grain, 159, 165, 172
Tsin empire, Eastern, 156, 161 (fig.)
Tso Chuan, 234–35
Tsao-shen, the kitchen god, 122, 123
  (*illustr.*), 129 *see also* Kitchen
  God
Tsin empire, 154, 155–56

Unities, three, of dynastic history,
  144, 146 (fig.), 152; first unity,
  146 (fig.), 151–53, 158, 161 (fig.);
  second unity, 146 (fig.), 157–58,
  161 (fig.); third unity, 146 (fig.),
  160, 161 (fig.), 163–66

Village Life in China (Smith), 134
Village scene, stylized, 14 (*illustr.*)
Village temples, 129, 130

Walshe, W. Gilbert, 243
Warring States period, 149, 151, 152
Warrior overlords and feudal lords,
  43, 49, 50, 54, 55, 151; destruction
  of feudalism, 50, 55, 58
Ways that are Dark, 243 (*illustr.*),
  247
Wealth: landed, 105; as determining
  status of peasantry, 119; following
  political power, 181, 215, 219
Wei, house of, 154, 155
Western Chou feudalism, compared to
  changes in the Era of Cultural
  Fusion, 58–59
Western Tsin dynasty, 155–56
Worship, cults of, 128
Wu, Ching-tzu, 75, 116, 120, 174
Wu, house of, 154, 155
Wu-tai, 158, 159

Yamen, 92, 135
Yang-shao culture, 37–38, 39–40, 41
43, 65, 66, 72
Yellow Emperor, myth of the, 79
Yellow River Conservancy, 165, 174

Yin and Yang, 122, 124
Yuan dynasty, 48, 72, 146 (fig.), 148
(fig.), 161 (fig.), 163
Yuan Grand Canal, 164
Yueh Ming, 230